BE THE PERSON YOU WANT TO BE

Harness the Power of
Neuro-Linguistic Programming
to Reach Your Potential

John J. Emerick, Jr.

PRIMA PUBLISHING

*To the many people in the world who struggle to make their lives fulfilling
and satisfying. May you find your dreams fulfilled with an ease and joy
that you had never expected possible.*

© 1997 by John J. Emerick, Jr.

All rights reserved. No part of this book may be reproduced or transmitted in
any form or by any means, electronic or mechanical, including photocopying,
recording, or by any information storage or retrieval system, without written
permission from Prima Publishing, except for the inclusion of quotations in
a review.

PRIMA PUBLISHING and colophon are registered trademarks of Prima
Communications, Inc.

Illustrations by Esther Szegedy

Library of Congress Cataloging-in-Publication Data

Emerick, John J.
Be the person you want to be: harness the power of neuro-linguistic
programming to reach your potential / John J. Emerick, Jr.

    p.   cm.
    Includes index.
    ISBN 0-7615-0806-6
    1. Self-actualization (Psychology)   2. Neuro-linguistic programming.
    I. Title.
    BF637.S4E45 1996
    158'.1—dc20   96-35451
                                                      CIP

    98 99 00 01 HH 10 9 8 7 6 5 4 3 2
Printed in the United States of America

HOW TO ORDER:

Single copies may be ordered from Prima Publishing, P.O. Box 1260BK,
Rocklin, CA 95677; telephone (916) 632-4400. Quantity discounts are also
available. On your letterhead, include information concerning the intended
use of the books and the number of books you wish to purchase.

Visit us online at http://www.primapublishing.com

CONTENTS

ACKNOWLEDGMENTS

MY HEARTFELT APPRECIATION goes out to the many special people who have helped bring this book into being. While I take full responsibility for any of its imperfections, I recognize that its merits have been based in large part on the contributions and inspirations of those around me.

In alphabetical order (more or less):

Special thanks to Richard Bandler. Your trainings, publications, and dedication to NLP have helped inspire me to further explore the field. Your creativity has been a long-standing source of inspiration for me. Thanks also to John Grinder and the many others who played a role in the creation of NLP.

Special thanks to Sally Bronner for your encouragement and support. It was your unquestioning belief in my abilities that helped inspire me through times of doubt.

Special thanks to Mahni Dugan for your helpful insights, assistance, and unselfish dedication to helping this book serve those for whom it is intended. I cherish the contributions you made in this endeavor.

Special thanks to Myra Becnel, Wiltz Goutierrez, and Dee and Omer Kursat. Your friendship and support provided the perfect environment for me in striving to make this book a reality.

Special thanks to Suzette Haden Elgin for your book *The Gentle Art of Verbal Self-Defense,* which first inspired me to study NLP.

Special thanks to Dolores Emerick and Ann Guffey for your continued faith and confidence in the directions I have taken.

Special thanks to Georgia Hughes, Debra Venzke, and the others at Prima Publishing for your confidence, support, and meaningful contributions. You have made the process of publishing this book an absolute joy. I feel honored to have had such a talented group of professionals to work with.

Special thanks to Jan and John Marszalek. It was your guidance and training that helped me not only to learn the majority of this information, but also to make my life vastly more fulfilling.

Special thanks to Charles Posey. You not only showed me how to apply these skills to everyday life, but you also continue to show me how important a deep and lasting friendship can be.

Special thanks to Julie Silverthorn and John Overdurf for the kind support you gave me with such open hearts.

Special thanks to Jeff Sullivan for your attentive and supportive feedback. Your clarity of thought and keen insights—and your generosity in sharing both—filled a very important role in shaping this book.

Special thanks to Esther Szegedy. Your generous efforts have become as much a part of this book as any of its text.

Special thanks to Wendy Zhorne. You are a true partner in bringing this book to others.

Special thanks to Desi Danielson, Yazmina Lakshanni, Sue Sowders, and Kari Zabinski for your helpful and supportive feedback in the early stages of this book.

Special thanks to Connie Rae Andreas, Steve Andreas, Robert Dilts, the late Todd Epstein, Christina Hall, and Tad James. Through training with each of you I have been motivated to continue my exploration of NLP.

And special thanks to those whom I have not mentioned or might have forgotten. Thank you for your understanding.

To each and all of you, I offer my warmest appreciation.

CHAPTER 1

ARE YOU THE PERSON YOU WANT TO BE?

W*HAT KIND OF PERSON* do you want to be? Do you want to be a happy person? Someone who brightens up a room just by walking into it, spreading good spirits and charm to all who are fortunate enough to be around? Do you want to be a capable person, someone who succeeds in any endeavor? Someone who can handle a crisis without getting ruffled and who is a source of strength for those who fear and worry? How about a person whom people love to spend time with? Someone who develops deep relationships through being a loyal and supportive friend? Do you want to be a dependable person whom people can place their trust in, who always delivers, whose word can be trusted? How about a caring, nurturing, passionate lover, always with the right thing to say, always knowing the perfect way to transform any situation into a romantic interlude? For a moment, consider the kind of person you want to be.

Keeping this ideal in mind, imagine yourself at work some afternoon. It's 3:00 p.m., and your two-week vacation, the one you've been working toward for the past six months, is just two hours away. You really need the rest this vacation will bring, and you're looking forward to unwinding on the plane. But these last two hours are quickly turning into chaos. You've worked all week to get things organized so you can

1

leave without worrying about the job, but you still have several important things left to do. As soon as you start to get any of them done, the phone rings, someone bursts in, or things outside start going wrong.

After an agonizingly long phone call, two more people sneak into your office with questions. Earlier in the week, nobody had any concerns about your leaving, but today everybody has questions, and no one remembers a thing you've said all week.

Another emergency arises—a bad one. If you don't handle it, things will just get worse. It's really important that you get things calmed down—people are depending on you—and it's your job. But why now, when you're about to leave?

And now you remember that you still need to confirm your airline reservations and order your special meal for the plane ride. The people you're supposed to visit don't even know which flight you're arriving on.

Your spouse is home getting ready for the trip. You had planned to be home early to shoulder some of the load. But you won't even have time to pack all your own stuff.

There's no time to think of that now. The office is in chaos, and Lloyd and Sue are going to have a field day with this one! Every time you leave for more than a few days, Lloyd stirs up a big problem in your department and makes sure everybody knows about it. He always makes it look as if you dropped the ball, and he jabs away at your reputation and your department. When you finally straighten things out, nobody cares about the truth; your colleagues just hold on to the lasting impression that you're lousy at your job.

Sue thinks your vacation is the perfect time to take over your department. She changes everything she possibly can and makes doubly sure she gets the changes cemented in as fast as possible. By the time you get back, everyone's already accustomed to the new policies and procedures.

The most important thing you need to do is to write your monthly report. Your boss is counting on you, and you promised to deliver, but the report is a lot more work than you realized. You can't work late, because you'll miss your plane. But you can't leave your boss hanging either.

No sooner do you start writing than Mary Jo comes into your office, in tears. She knows you're rushed, but she also knows that she needs the support of her best friend right now. She's never asked much of you, but today's the day. You've got to help her.

Just as Mary Jo begins her story, your spouse calls after having spent the whole day doing your errands. Now some other things are out of hand, and your help is needed. More than that, this call is about a need to know that you love and support this beautiful person in your life. But time is running out; two more people line up outside your office and your worried boss is calling on another line to make sure you've finished the report.

With the crisis outside, Lloyd and Sue plotting away to discredit you, thirty people coming to you for help, Mary Jo having a life crisis, your spouse reaching out to you, and your boss frantically trying to get his hands on that report you haven't written yet—and the fact that your whole vacation will crumble if you don't make some phone calls quickly—what can you do? It's 3:45 p.m. already, and that plane isn't going to wait!

Now, in this new context, consider again the kind of person you want to be. Do you want to be a happy person? A capable person? A person always there for a friend in need? A dependable person? A positive, caring, nurturing, passionate lover? What kind of person will you be this afternoon as you speed out of the office toward your ever elusive vacation?

Fast forward for a moment to your exit from the office. You managed to complete most of your tasks, even scraping out a shoddy report to your boss. But it was a beehive of activity, and there's going to be some fallout. As you get on the freeway, you feel yourself breathe a sigh of relief. All the office problems are at least two weeks away.

You have to rush home, of course, because you're running very late. Traffic is awful this time of day, so you try a shortcut, but it's a bad one, and you're locked in. You think about stopping to call home but realize that you still haven't called the airline! And of course you still haven't called the people you're visiting.

After the longest commute home of the year, you barely get the car in Park as you lunge out the door. You burst into your home to see the love of your life frantically trying to fit three suitcases of stuff into a garment bag and a carry-on. Your welcome home turns into a rapid-fire series of frantic cries ranging from "What the hell are you doing? We're going to miss our plane!" to "Did you remember to call ahead and give our arrival time?"

So consider again the kind of person you want to be. Do you want to be a happy person? A capable person? A person always there for a friend in need? A dependable person? A positive, caring, nurturing, passionate lover? What kind of person will you be as the two of you try to do four hours' worth of tasks in the next sixty minutes?

You've probably played out a similar scenario. We live busy lives in a busy society, and we just don't have time to think about how to bring out the best in ourselves.

Given the afternoon you just imagined, consider again how happy and cheerful you would be. Would you be that source of strength for your coworkers? How about for your spouse? Or would you be a frantic mess yourself, angered and stressed about the craziness of it all? Would you take the time Mary Jo needed to help her get through her situation, or would you give her a few kind, shallow words and send her on her way? Would you live up to your word, and deliver on that report, or would you let your boss down? Would you do it right, or would you just slap it together? Would you be a supportive, patient, and loving spouse, or would you make it all worse by losing control yourself? Would you set the tone of your vacation with a bit of romance, or would you begin it with worry and irritation?

And how would you feel about yourself when you realized three days later that you didn't even come close to being the person you wanted to be on that stressful afternoon?

Good News

If you've ever discovered that you are not being the person you would like to be because of the circumstances you find yourself in, then I have some good news and some bad news for you.

The bad news is that you don't have time to read this book. You've got a million things to do, you can never find the quiet, uninterrupted time you need, and you might not even like reading very much anyway. Besides, you're so tired that you'd rather just vegetate in front of the television and try to escape from the world.

The good news is that you probably have far more time available to you than you realize, and reading this book can help you learn how to make the time. This book is an easy read, a fast read, and you can get through most of it in the time you'd spend watching one or two basketball games or reading a few magazines.

The better news is that reading this book also may help you gain more time than you've ever had before—for the rest of your life! Take a few hours now, up front, and consider this time an investment. It's like putting money into a great stock, getting a great return on your investment, and using the interest to supplement your income for the rest of your life. I guarantee that if you use just some of the information in this book, you will find yourself with more time on your hands, perhaps more than you've ever had before. You'll even be able to enjoy it more. The best news is that you've already started!

The Rewards of Making It Happen

Not too many years ago, I was always finding myself in situations like the one I just described. I felt as if I had no control over my life. Work was a frustrating nightmare, and despite getting good measurable results (like solving difficult technical problems, saving the company large amounts of money, and so on), I found that I was having real problems. People were sabotaging my efforts; it was hard to get things done; and I just couldn't get projects moving the way I wanted. I wasn't getting raises, and I wasn't getting promoted. Even worse, I felt lousy about the whole process. Each day seemed like an endless series of difficult, frustrating, and disheartening events, one after the other. Although I considered myself an emotionally strong person, the situation was starting to overwhelm me.

My personal life wasn't much better. I had a series of relationships that I knew weren't right for me, but I went through them anyway. These took a toll on me emotionally, and my preoccupation with work made it difficult for me to cultivate friendships. The few people I spent time with were only acquaintances. My old friends were drifting further and further away as my time for them was reduced to almost nothing. I spent virtually none of my time looking at personal growth, nor did I have any hobbies to speak of, outside of playing some tennis here and there. I spent my days off either going to bars or resting, because I was mentally exhausted. My spiritual life was virtually nonexistent; in fact, I never even gave that aspect of my life a moment's notice. My life seemed so busy, but I never had time for anything fulfilling.

As life seemed to be getting more and more difficult, I responded by working harder and trying more. I had difficulty getting things done with others, so I just did more by myself. Yet even that didn't work, and I felt very lonely and burdened. Life got harder, and I felt worse. I had no idea what the problem was, nor how to resolve it. I was a smart guy with a good heart who tried very hard, yet things just weren't working for me. I was not the person I wanted to be, nor was my life the life I wanted to have.

My overall emotional health was battered, and for the first time in my life, my physical health deteriorated. This became my wake-up call, and I finally heard it. So I started looking seriously for answers.

In my search, I found Neuro-Linguistic Programming (NLP). It seemed like a chance occurrence, but I realize now that it wasn't. It never is. My true desire to change my life was the impetus that allowed me to take what the world was offering me. In this case, the world offered me NLP.

Today, my life is vastly different. It isn't the kind of flamboyant life that you see on *Lifestyles of the Rich and Famous,* but it is absolutely perfect for me. Each day, I wake up and look around with an overwhelming appreciation for being alive and having a wonderful life. I spend most of my time happy, energized, motivated, friendly, and appreciative. The kinds of difficulties I used to have in the workplace have been replaced with feelings of ease and surety. I've taken what was once a weakness, my level of communication skills, and transformed it into my most precious strength. This strength has helped me transform all parts of my life.

I've restored balance to my life. My health is good again, and I feel better than I've felt in my entire life. I've drawn beautiful people into my life, and the quality and depth of my friendships are better now than ever before. I'm more connected spiritually than at any other time in my life, and I've incorporated that connection into every aspect of living. I have more money than I've ever had, and it came to me as I pursued the things that I enjoy. Emotionally, I spend my time feeling resourceful and positive. In many ways, I know that my life is better than it's ever been, and it's getting even better. Every day, I continue down the fulfilling path of being the person I want to be.

I *learned* the process of transforming myself, and in this book I share a good part of that transformation process with you. Perhaps, like me, all you've been needing is to know how.

A Snapshot of Your Own Life

It took me years of anguish to finally realize that things weren't working very well for me. As I look back on it, I wish someone would have called my attention to what was going on and would have let me know there was a better way.

The actual process of change was easy. However the process of realizing that I wanted to change, of waking up and paying attention to my problems, was more difficult. I didn't have a snapshot of my life, but it sure would have helped. So let's call your attention to some aspects of your life and give you the opportunity to take your own snapshot.

I've listed some questions you may wish to consider. I've given point values for corresponding answers, and you can add up the points to see how you rank on the evaluation that follows the questions. Be objective, and don't be too hard on yourself. Keep in mind that all these items will be addressed in this book.

1.   Do you feel that much of your life and what happens during your day is out of your control?
Seldom (3); Occasionally (2); Often (1)

2.   Do you seem to have to work harder and longer just to keep up with the expectations placed upon you?
Seldom (3); Occasionally (2); Often (1)

3.   Do people criticize your good ideas?
Seldom (3); Occasionally (2); Often (1)

4.   Do conversations sometimes leave you feeling worse than you did before they started?
Seldom (3); Occasionally (2); Often (1)

5.   Do you get interrupted when you would like to keep speaking?
Seldom (3); Occasionally (2); Often (1)

6.   Do you routinely feel anger or frustration when you're relating to others?
Seldom (3); Occasionally (2); Often (1)

7.   Do you know how to really know what a person wants?
Often (3); Occasionally (2); Not Sure (1)

8.   Do you notice when people give you mixed messages, and do you know how to deal with them?
Often (3); Occasionally (2); Not Sure (1)

9.   Do you feel unappreciated by important people in your life?
Seldom (3); Occasionally (2); Often (1)

10.   How often do you feel as if you're on the defensive in groups or in meetings?
Seldom (3); Occasionally (2); Often (1)

11.   Does it seem as if people get the best of you in conversation?
Seldom (3); Occasionally (2); Often (1)

12. *How would others rate your interpersonal skills?*
Excellent (3); Average (2); Poor (1)

13. *Do you have relatively similar success in each of the following areas: career, finances, family, health, romantic relationships, friendships, personal growth, and spirituality?*
Balanced(3); Mostly balanced (2); Out of balance (1)

14. *When you enter into a conversation, do you generally have an idea of what you would like to accomplish with that conversation, or do you just take what you get?*
Know what you want (3); Some of both (2);
Take what you get (1)

15. *When you negotiate or make agreements with others, is your focus more on satisfying your outcomes or satisfying their outcomes?*
Equally yours and theirs (3); Predominantly yours (2);
Predominantly theirs (2)

16. *When you disagree with someone, are you able to persuade them to see your view?*
Often (3); Occasionally (2); Seldom (1)

17. *Do people feel motivated after speaking with you?*
Often (3); Occasionally (2); Seldom (1)

18. *Do you know when you're subjected to verbal abuse?*
Yes (3); Sort of (2); Not really (1)

19. *Do you feel change and improvement has to take a long time?*
In some situations (3); In many situations (2); In most situations (1)

20. *Do you work with people to synergistically get more things accomplished, or do you primarily work alone?*
Mostly working synergistically with people (3); Some of both (2); Mostly alone (1)

21. *Do you feel that your emotions are something beyond your control?*
Seldom (3); Occasionally (2); Often (1)

22.   *Why are you reading this book?*
For your own reasons (3); It seems like a good thing
to do (2); For someone else's reasons (1)

**23.   *Do you know what you're doing when you try to
communicate and persuade?***
Often (3); Occasionally (2); Seldom (1)

Triple Bonus Questions

24.   *Are you succeeding in your life?*
Definitely (9); Not as much as you should be (6);
Not at all (3)

25.   *How do you feel about yourself?*
Wonderful and proud (9); Pretty good (6);
Discouraged (3)

Quadruple Bonus Question

**26.   *Do you feel that you have the ability to make your life be
the way you want it to be?***
Completely (12); Mostly (8); Partially (4)

If you decided to assign point value to your answers, add
up your points, and determine where you are on the following scale:

Over 92:   *Extremely Effective.* You are probably successful and
fulfilled in your life. You have plenty of emotional freedom
and discretionary time, and you are already well along your
way to being the person you want to be. You certainly don't
need any help with what you're doing, but you probably realize that you're the type of person who often gets the most
out of books like this. This book can help you expand your
understanding and increase your awareness of your skills.
This added understanding and awareness may help you on
those rare occasions when you find yourself uncertain about
how to handle a situation. In addition, you will probably
appreciate the discussions of the special aspects of NLP the
most, since they are likely to be new material for you. Great
job and enjoy!

76–92: *Effective.* You are probably successful, but you could benefit from learning other skills. You are likely to be using and relying upon your "natural" skills, which have served you well, but you're finding they're not quite as comprehensive as you would like. You probably have a reasonable amount of emotional freedom and discretionary time but still have the potential to benefit in either outward success (such as finances) or inward success (such as your state of mind). Pay particularly close attention to the listening and verbal skills sections in this book. These new skills are likely to give you important insights, which may help you make those subtle improvements that make a big difference. Your opportunities lie in your ability to make subtle, yet important, changes.

62–75: *Relatively Effective.* You probably experience success in some areas, but face challenges in others. It's likely that you have most of the mind-sets and beliefs needed to be effective, but not necessarily all the specific skills. Perhaps your level of emotional resourcefulness is sporadic, and you don't always have true control over the circumstances in your life. Pay close attention to the listening and verbal skills sections, as well as to any other section that seems to hit home. You will know where your opportunities are, so it's just a matter of addressing them. You will probably enjoy this process.

46–61: *Less Effective.* You are likely to be having significant challenges (outward, inward, or both) in at least one area of your life and perhaps in several areas. You probably are having difficulty gaining the emotional freedom you need and may find yourself running on automatic pilot rather than living life with full consciousness of its wonders. If you are open to implementing the skills laid out in this book, you can benefit from all sections. There is a tremendous opportunity ahead of you, and you can make significant changes very quickly. Pay particularly close attention to the section about mind-sets; these will lay the necessary foundation for the skills that follow. Even if you have the signs of outward success, you may be suffering from inward challenges. Don't fool yourself; inward success is just as much a part of success as is outward success, and it's perfectly achievable.

Under 46: *Lacking Effectiveness.* You are likely to be having significant problems with many areas of your life. You may feel that your life is out of your control and that people or organizations in your life are making things extra difficult for you. Accepting responsibility for yourself is likely to be the biggest challenge you face. Your primary opportunity will most likely rest within the mind-sets you choose to live by and in your unequivocal acceptance of the responsibility mind-set. This mind-set may not be easy to accept right away, but embrace it and you will reap many rewards. You have the most to gain from this book. It will show you how to make the changes necessary in your life, but your intentions will be the means to your success. I salute you for your perseverance, and I admire you for your willingness to move forward!

How—The Difference That Makes the Difference

It's a busy world out there, and you might find yourself spinning around in it. How do you slow it down? How can you take control? How do you manage and handle the incredible number of demands placed upon you and still have the emotional resourcefulness you need? These are the questions this book will address.

I was having a discussion the other day with a successful and mature manager. He was expounding on the importance of listening to his employees and explaining how he needed to do more of that. As our conversation continued, we began to speak about the importance of motivating employees. I took the opportunity to share just a tiny portion of the material contained in this book. I shared some ideas about the importance of listening and of creating win-win arrangements, but I also told him specifically *how* to do these things. The longer we spoke, the further down his jaw dropped.

I shared the fact that there were many managers who have worked with people for years but have never taken the opportunity to find out what's most important to their employees about their jobs. Consider that for a moment!

By this time, his jaw had just about hit the floor. He looked at me and said, "You know, I've been a pretty good manager for many years, but it's never even occurred to me that I could, or should, talk to my employees to find out what was important to them.... I've got a lot of work to do, but I want to make sure that we stay here and continue this conversation, because I know that this is far more important than any of the work I was about to go do." He set aside the rest of his very busy afternoon just to talk about motivation in more detail. And we had just scratched the surface of what's contained in this book.

It's important for a manager to know what's important to his employees. That's obvious. And helping people fulfill their values plays a major role in motivation. That, too, is obvious. But since we're rarely taught about these processes, we generally never have the chance to benefit from them. How much better would your work life be if your boss knew exactly what you wanted out of your job and tried to give it to you every day? How much better would your life be if you could do the same kind of thing for each of your employees, friends, lovers, and family members?

There are multitudes of books, tapes, and seminars that give you valuable information about how to live a more fulfilling life. They tell you to do things like control your emotions, make win-win agreements, listen to what others have to say, be a leader, and so on. These books have good things to say, and by following their advice you will likely increase the quality of your life.

However, very few books, tapes, or seminars give you the type of information contained in this book, especially the way it is presented. This book tells you, in a way you've probably never known before, *how* to do what you do. I mean the *real* how, not the *more-of-what-to-do* how. You've probably heard many times that controlling anger is an important part of effectively relating to others, but that's as far as it goes. How do you really control anger? Do you say mantras? Do you take deep breaths? Do you visualize yourself being happy? Or better yet, instead of "controlling" anger, how do you simply *change* your emotional state? Why not avoid having the anger in the first place? Then there's nothing to control. Have you ever been taught how to take any of these actions?

You may already know the value and importance of having win-win agreements in your life. Stephen Covey's best-seller *The Seven Habits of Highly Effective People* has an entire chapter devoted to win-win thinking. Win-win took its place for some years as the buzzword of choice in management circles throughout the world, and it is a highly valued aspect of good management. But have you ever been told the importance of eliciting the specific values of the person you're negotiating with? What specific questions can you ask to help others find out what they *really* want? Which specific words should you use, and which specific words should you avoid because they derail the process? Has anyone ever told you that most people don't really know what they want? It's interesting that oftentimes people don't know going in what a win for them would look like, so aiming for win-win is like trying to shoot a bull's-eye without knowing where the target is. How can you ensure a win for other people if neither you nor they know what they want?

If you're old enough to know how to read this book, then I'm sure you've been told, or have told others, about the importance of being a good listener. It's important as a lover, friend, employee, boss, parent. The traditional "how-to's" associated with being a good listener direct you to ask questions, be attentive, show interest, avoid interrupting, clarify what you heard with more questions, and so on. But how do you really *do* these things?

Instructions such as "ask more questions" don't give you the tools you need to succeed at the task. Have you ever been taught *which* kinds of questions to ask? What specific things to be *most attentive* to? When is it *better* to interrupt? Has anyone ever specifically told you what to listen for and when to listen for it? If your friend calls tonight, would you know which specific questions to ask to find out what motivates him to continue as your friend? Few people do.

These same principles apply to other well-meaning advice. Consider the notions of being a leader, communicating effectively, thinking positively, standing up for yourself, setting boundaries, and looking at things in different ways. What you may not know is that each of these behaviors can be understood, codified, simplified, taught to others, learned, and mastered. These behaviors are not necessarily gifts that only a lucky few people possess—they are behaviors that you can learn.

This book offers specific instructions on how to do many of these things. You will learn specific, concrete skill sets. They work.

When you read about how to be a good listener, you will learn more than just how to listen with your ears. You will learn things to watch for (with your eyes), and you will learn how to make sense out of the confusing, mixed messages people give you nonverbally. You will learn about the role of emotions and their effect on the messages being communicated. You will learn which questions to ask so that you can quickly determine the things a person values most about any given situation, including what specific words are the most important words to remember. You'll learn how to determine which answers are fluff and which answers are vitally important. And you will learn all this within a framework of integrity, compassion, and respect for the other person.

When you read about how to communicate verbally, you will learn specific ways to make sure your message is heard, specific words that can give your message more impact. You'll learn step-by-step techniques for making your words more easily accepted and for steering conversations into useful avenues. You'll learn how to deal with challenging situations so that you succeed, excel, and have maximum fulfillment in each interaction you have.

These are the skills you need to improve the quality of your life. If you are not being the person you want to be, the circumstances in your life are probably making it difficult for you. Change those circumstances to be more to your liking, and you'll find that the very best of you will come shining through. Your ability to change the circumstances in your life is directly related to your level of effectiveness in relating with people.

So the purpose of this book isn't to tell you more about what to do. It's to tell you how to do some of the things you may have been trying to do for years without ever really knowing how. It's about teaching you how to get through some common challenges you may be facing, and giving you specific methods for creating success. And all the while it will provide a solid foundation of principles, integrity, and win-win mentality that will further support your success.

When you find yourself communicating better, taking control over your life, and handling challenging situations gracefully, then you will find yourself living and experiencing the world as the person you really want to be.

CHAPTER 2

GET READY FOR CHANGE

IF YOU'RE READING this book because someone told you to, then you're in for a real treat. If you're reading it to understand the information presented, then get ready for something more. If you're reading it so you can use your new knowledge to "impress" others with your cleverness, then you're going to be surprised. These reasons may get you started reading, but once you see what's contained in this book, you'll start to read with the vigor and excitement of a child opening a present. For you, this book will be a gift.

My hope is that this book will give you more than just something to get excited about. I want to teach more than interesting, intellectual concepts. And my purpose is to do far more than just give you some ideas to show how clever you are. I have designed this book to guide you in making real improvements in the way you function in the world.

Neuro-Linguistic Programming (NLP)

The bulk of the information in this book has its roots in the field of Neuro-Linguistic Programming, or NLP. NLP has origins in diverse fields, including therapy, linguistics, and hypnosis. I've found NLP to be an extraordinary field with largely unexplored potential, and I attribute much of my personal development to my experience with it.

As you may expect, the name was chosen to be descriptive of the field. *Neuro* refers to the nervous system, including the brain and thinking processes. *Linguistic* refers to language, or more holistically, to the process of forming meaning from sensory input. *Programming* refers to a specific set of instructions intended to bring about an outcome. Collectively, these three words refer to the specific behaviors humans use when thinking, speaking, and behaving to bring about specific outcomes.

NLP as an independent field began in the early 1970s through the collaboration of cocreators Richard Bandler and John Grinder. These men attempted to determine exactly how certain people achieved excellence. They combined their studies with information from a variety of fields, most notably the fields of linguistics and hypnosis, and published some of their initial models in four books published between 1975 and 1977: *The Structure of Magic,* Volumes 1 and 2, and *Patterns of Hypnotic Techniques of Milton H. Erickson, M.D.,* Volumes 1 and 2.

Today, the body of information referred to as NLP encompasses not only that original work, but also additional material. Bandler and Grinder have added substantially to their original work, and much of their source material has come to be more widely explored, including that of the linguist Alfred Korzybski. In addition, several other people were trained directly by Bandler and Grinder, and they formed the first generation of trainers and additional contributors. As the field matured, new generations of trainers emerged and have continued to add to the field in significant ways.

For many years, NLP was primarily oriented toward the therapeutic context and thus was neither widely known nor understood by the general public. In a few cases, portions of NLP were brought into the mainstream by other books and trainers, most notably through Tony Robbins' best-selling book *Unlimited Power.* Robbins was the first person to tap into the enormous potential of sharing NLP with everyday people for use in everyday situations.

Today, people have begun to apply NLP to many fields, including business, with trainers throughout the world disseminating an expanded body of information, which they continue to call NLP.

So why learn NLP? What kind of NLP are you about to learn? Are there different kinds of NLP?

One of the fundamental tenets of NLP is a belief that "the map is not the territory."[1] In simple terms, this phrase means that a description (the "map") for something (the "territory") is fundamentally different from the thing itself. Further, if we attempt to represent this thing by a "map," we necessarily make alterations.

For example, if you go to the Big Island of Hawaii, you may want to rent a car and drive around the island; and to do so effectively, you will most likely get a map. However, the map may not show all the roads, it may not identify elevations, it may not describe the quality of the roads. In effect, it will have *deleted* some of the information about the island itself.

Additionally, the map is likely to highlight several points of interest such as the location of certain hotels, restaurants, or tourist attractions. But in order to get these all to fit on the map and keep the information easy to understand, it may be necessary to *distort* relative distances and positions.

It's also likely to include advertising, labeling, legends, and drawings. Of course, the island itself isn't labeled (if you fly overhead, you won't see the letters H-A-W-A-I-I written on the mountains), so the map has certain *distortions* that are additive in nature.

Furthermore, many maps are made for specific purposes and may be very different from other maps of the same place. Many maps of the Hawaiian Islands are designed primarily to show only the location of the resort hotels. Others are designed primarily to help people drive around the island, perhaps to visit the volcano. Any given map will likely be quite distorted to fulfill its purpose and will differ from other maps with other purposes.

So although each map may be a very useful description of some aspects of the island, maps are often quite different

from one another and always different from the actual island. You can't drive on the map!

Similarly, the description most often used for NLP is a
map. It is filled with specific techniques, phrases, definitions,
and terminology; and it is relatively similar throughout the
world, regardless of who is teaching the program. However,
other maps of NLP are quite different. Tony Robbins had a
specific purpose in mind when creating his map of NLP; and
as a result, his map varies significantly from traditional NLP
maps. The map that I will be sharing here is quite different
from both the traditional NLP map and Tony Robbins' map.

My map of NLP results from my personal extension and
utilization of NLP. Although many of the terms and procedures are very similar to those of traditional NLP, others are
derivations of the material brought about by my personal
experience and development with the program.

When I began studying NLP, much of the material was
designed to help me become a better therapist. However, I
wasn't a therapist, and I had no intention of ever becoming
one. So when I started to use this information in my everyday contexts, I had to do some translating and adapting. As
time went on, I began to get excellent results using these
adapted techniques, so I continued to develop and adapt
them even further.

I bring this to your attention so that you know exactly
what you are about to learn— and what you are not about to
learn. The information I present bears enough resemblance
to the source material that I can confidently call it NLP, but
it's also modified enough so that parts of it will seem different from traditional NLP. It is a different map.

My map of NLP focuses primarily on the following
outcomes:

- Expanding your ideas about what's possible in the world
- Enhancing your ability to get results
- Offering mind-sets that support your success using the
  information
- Dispelling commonly misunderstood perceptions that
  thwart success
- Improving your ability to communicate

- Helping you make maximum impact on your life
- Creating that impact with the least amount of effort
- Keeping the learning process easy and fun

Necessary Conditions for Change to Occur

If you want anything in your life to be different, then change must occur. Usually, change begins internally, then manifests externally. In other words, you have to change yourself, and then you play a part in making the world around you adjust to your internal changes.

A model commonly used in NLP states that for change to occur, three conditions must be met:

1. You must *want* to make the change.
2. You must *know how* to make the change.
3. You must have the *opportunity* to make the change.

In addition to these, I add the following:

4. You must have the *disposition* to make the change.
5. You must have the *willingness to do what it takes* to make the change.

Items 1 and 5 address *motivation*. How motivated are you to make the change? If you're not doing well in your relationship, the first question you could ask is, "Do I really *want* to be in this relationship?" (Item 1). If you answer yes, then the next question you could ask is, "Am I willing to *do what it takes* to make this relationship work?" (Item 5). If you don't answer yes to both questions, then the challenges in your relationship may be related to motivation.

Item 2 addresses knowledge. If you're having difficulty making enough money, then you might ask yourself this question, "If someone put a gun to my head and told me to make more money, would I be able to do it?" If you answer yes, then the hindrance is related to motivation or disposition, but if you answer no, then the hindrance is related to knowledge *(how to)*.

Item 3 refers to circumstances that are difficult to control, but that may be under your control more than you realize. If you want to be president of the United States and you were born a French citizen, then U.S. laws prohibit you from being president. That limitation would be one of *opportunity*. This requirement may prevent you from becoming president of the United States, and so you might have to limit yourself to a role as secretary of state, the post that German-born Henry Kissinger held. As chief foreign policy advisor for four presidents, he was one of the most influential people in U.S. government for many years.

If you want to play basketball in the NBA, but you're only four feet tall and have only one leg, then you would not meet the reasonable physical requirements. Thus you would again be limited by *opportunity*. However, as five-foot-three-inches-tall Mugsy Bogues of the Charlotte Hornets proved, the physical requirements of the NBA are less restrictive than most people imagine.

Item 4 relates to your unconscious belief and value system. If you want to run a four-minute mile, but your deep-seated belief system states that a four-minute mile is physically impossible to run, then you probably will never be able to do it. You would not have the *disposition* to do it. If you wanted to make more money, but the only way you knew how was to hold up a bank, then your value system would prevent you from doing so. Again, you would not have the *disposition* to do it with your current level of knowledge.

These five items become important when you start to look at what's possible in your life. If you look at goals you might have, such as making more money, having a fulfilling relationship, or succeeding in your career, you'll find that if you haven't already achieved these things, then it's almost always an issue of one of these items.

This explains the enormous popularity of motivational speakers like Tony Robbins. They do far more than simply get people motivated *(want to* and *do what it takes);* they help people change their beliefs about what's possible *(disposition to).* Many times, simply helping you realize what's possible and motivating you to take action are the only two things needed for you to achieve your goals.

This particular book will first focus on your beliefs about what's possible *(disposition to)* and then will teach you the steps to take *(how to)* to make your goals become a reality. In almost all cases, you will find that you already have the *opportunity* and *physical requirements* needed, so all that will be left will be the willingness to *do what it takes.* This final piece comes a lot more easily when you know how to do it and you're being supported in the process.

Know Your Outcome

I've often found myself in the position of interviewing and making hiring decisions. In interviews, one of the first questions I ask an applicant is "What are you looking for?" It's a simple question. Yet as simple as this question is, you might be surprised at the quality of responses I get.

Roughly 70 percent of applicants do not have an answer to that question! Consider that for a moment. Most people go to a lot of effort to apply for a job. They draft résumés, write cover letters, buy new clothing, set up the interview, and take time off from work to go to the interview. Yet after all that time and effort, many can't even articulate what they want in a job!

Most people don't know what they want. In fact, many people go through their entire lives never even asking themselves what they want. Of the few who do ask themselves this question, many never come up with a clear answer. Of the tiny minority who do have an answer, only an even tinier minority phrase their answer in terms that make their goals achievable.

Most people don't meet their goals in life because they don't have an *awareness* of what they really want. It's almost as if they wake up one day surprised at how old they are and wonder why their life is the way it is. It never dawns on many people that they have been working very hard to get exactly where they are, without ever having had an idea about where they wanted to go. There's an expression often heard in NLP training sessions which is, "If you're not sure where you want to go, then that's where you're going to end up."

THREE-STEP SUMMARY OF NLP

One of the reasons NLP can be so effective is the persistent attention it places on goals. To summarize NLP as three basic steps, they are:

Step 1 Know your outcome.
Step 2 Be aware of the progress you're making with respect to your outcome.
Step 3 With the intention of achieving your outcome, vary your behavior in response to the feedback you get in Step 2.

Throughout this book, and NLP in general, these steps are the building blocks for virtually every process and technique, sometimes subtly, sometimes obviously.

CHAPTER 3

THE MIND-SETS
OF EFFECTIVENESS

I WAS ONCE TOLD a story about change. A woman went to a consultant and described her situation as disappointing and frustrating. She described in detail all the challenges and problems she faced and asked the consultant if he could help. The consultant said, "Yes, I'm sure I can help you." Then he laid out several steps for the woman to follow.

But as the consultant laid out those steps, the woman started to object. She said that she couldn't possibly do what was listed. The consultant knew that what he asked was possible, so he continued, "Do you have any physical limitations that prevent you from doing these things?" She answered that she didn't. "Is there some outside agent or force that is preventing you from doing these things?" Again she said no. "Are you failing to understand what these things are? Are you confused?" Once again she said no.

At this point, he said, "So what's the problem? What could possibly be making you say you can't do these things?" She replied, "The problem is that if I do these things, it just wouldn't be me."

Jubilantly, the consultant replied, "Exactly! The whole purpose of change is to do something that 'isn't you'! Otherwise it wouldn't be change!"[1]

Sometimes our biggest obstacles to getting what we want aren't the obstacles in the outer world; they're the obstacles in the inner world. These obstacles take the form of beliefs, perceptions, and mind-sets. If these are stopping you from changing your behaviors, then learning "how" to behave differently won't do you any good. To reap the rewards, you need to have a supporting framework of beliefs, perceptions, and mind-sets. In this example, the woman's obstacle was rooted in her belief about who she was.

In the next few chapters, we're going to look at some effective techniques. You will learn how to listen in ways that you may never have known existed. You will learn how to be eloquent with words and to encourage people to be more receptive to what you say. You will learn how to gain others' attention and to keep it long enough to make your points. You will learn the basis of persuasion and the basics for helping others understand and accept your point of view. You will learn how to give bad news gracefully and to get positive results from potentially negative situations. You will learn how to eloquently disagree and how to give constructive feedback that is both appreciated and used.

But learning *how* to do these things won't necessarily mean that you will *do* these things! Knowledge is power, but only if it's used. Unused power is called *potential power*, and all of us are gifted with far more potential than we may ever imagine.

Consider for a moment the effects a belief can have. For years management training schools have subscribed to the Pygmalion Effect. *Pygmalion,* a play written by George Bernard Shaw in 1912, revived a concept dating back to Greek mythology. (It was made popular through the 1956 Broadway musical *My Fair Lady.*) In the play, two upper-class gentlemen perform an experiment to determine if they can transform a lower-class Cockney flower girl into an upper-class lady. After the Cockney girl is given the proper training, she is then presented to a group of upper-class persons, who perceive her to be one of their peers. However, to the surprise of her mentors, the girl does more than simply fool these people; her change is so comprehensive that her self-identity makes a full transformation to being that of a legitimate upper-class lady.

In management circles, the Pygmalion Effect refers to the influence a manager's beliefs can have on the performance, and even self-identity, of those who work with the manager. Documented examples abound where the negative beliefs of managers influence employees to perform below expectations, while positive beliefs from managers inspire employees to perform at higher levels and higher capacities.

Consider the story of Roger Gilbert Bannister, the English runner who made track history on May 6, 1954, when he became the first person to run a mile in less than four minutes. For years before Bannister's achievement, doctors and runners alike believed that running a four-minute mile was physically impossible. This belief seems to have been enough to have prevented anyone from doing it, because after Roger Bannister did it, John Landy set a new record (3:58.0) just 46 days later, and Bannister did it again on August 7 of that same year. Once the idea that a four-minute mile was impossible was disproved, the "barrier" became an achievable goal, and four-minute miles were accomplished with regularity.

Such is the power of belief to influence reality. Whether beliefs come to you via external sources (those of other people) or via internal sources (your own beliefs), they can have dramatic impact on your success, your effectiveness, and your life. If you hold limiting beliefs, you will create barriers and obstacles to support those beliefs, thus creating true limitations. However, when you hold empowering beliefs, you give yourself the power to make those beliefs become true, and you give yourself the potential for a fuller life.

NLP places a great deal of emphasis on beliefs and belief systems. Many NLP training sessions begin by describing a key set of the program's beliefs, referred to as the "presuppositions of NLP." Although trainers sometimes vary the content, most of the presuppositions are shared verbatim. The presuppositions are one of the fundamental aspects that define what is and what is not NLP.

Additionally, NLP trainers often begin their training sessions with something they refer to as "setting frames." This is NLP terminology for asking you to make sense of your experiences in ways the facilitators are suggesting. In effect, they are asking you to adopt, even if temporarily, mind-sets that affect how you respond to the training and information. In many cases, the presuppositions and the frames are eventually accepted by the participants as part of their personal belief systems and make significant contributions to their personal growth.

A common frame used in NLP is the "As If" Frame. It holds that your ability to benefit from new ideas can be greatly enhanced by temporarily adopting complementary biases. In the As If frame, you are asked to accept the information being shared "as if" it were true, to temporarily suspend any beliefs that may run counter to the new information, and to "play along" with new beliefs during the term of the training. This frame allows you to have experiences and to evaluate your results while "trying on" the new beliefs. This process greatly enhances your ability to benefit from new ideas.

One of the most devastating impediments to the learning process is the rejection of material before it is understood. Virtually every concept and idea presented in this book, or any other, could be argued with. If you tried hard enough, you could find ways to disagree with almost anything, even this sentence. But the process of disagreeing before understanding (I'm using the term "understanding" loosely, as we will discuss later) prevents you from getting the benefit of the information. By suspending your opposing beliefs temporarily, you allow yourself the opportunity to "get to know" the new beliefs, and to determine for yourself which parts, if any, have value for you. As you gain more experience with the new beliefs, you amass more evidence that may support them; thus, it becomes easier to incorporate all or part of the beliefs as your own, if you so choose.

I believe that the majority of personal development that occurs in people, whether it be through NLP or other fields, is firmly dependent upon an adoption of different, more empowering beliefs. In my opinion, a change in your beliefs is the deepest, most profound change you can create for yourself, and your external world will seem to change in response to your new beliefs.

Let's begin our process of personal development by examining a variety of empowering mind-sets. These mind-sets may already be part of your belief system; you may not even be aware of how they are already helping you. If you don't yet hold these beliefs, you can try them out for a while using the As If frame. Experience each mind-set knowing that your core belief and values system are safe and secure. As you consider and temporarily adopt each mind-set, refrain from trying to determine how each one could be wrong; instead, do your best to accept them first and then direct your attention to figuring out how they can possibly be true. Do everything you can to understand each mind-set from a point of view that makes it true and real, and test-drive it for a period of time. You just may find that some of these mind-sets are beliefs you will want to firmly cement as your own.

Your Life Is the Result of Your Action or Inaction—The Responsibility Mind-Set

The responsibility mind-set is perhaps the most pervasive and most powerful of all mind-sets. It asserts that you are responsible for your life. Your life, and everything in it, is the result of your action or inaction.

This is the exact opposite of the victim mentality, in which people blame others for their situations in life. Those who employ the victim mentality do not change their lives because they believe that others exert controls over them. If you accept the responsibility mind-set, you understand that you have created your life to be the way it is; therefore, you are empowered to make it different.

This concept is not always accepted right away and is often charged with immediate counter-examples. After all, are you responsible for the fighting in the Middle East? Are you responsible for the stars in the heaven? Of course not. In fact, counter-examples to the responsibility mind-set are relatively easy to come by. But, unfortunately, these counter-examples often cause people to overgeneralize the boundaries of their influence. If you're not responsible for the fighting in the Middle East or the stars in the heaven, then it's likely that there are a lot of things in the world that you're not responsible for, right?

Unfortunately, that generalization can move people into a victim-like, powerless state of mind. Are you responsible if you are a victim of a crime? Are you responsible if your company downsizes and lays you off? Are you responsible when people misunderstand you? If you take your lead from the idea that most of what happens in the world is beyond your control, then it is easy to think that these everyday kinds of experiences are beyond your control too.

Are you responsible for what time you get up each day? You may think that your wake-up time is determined by your job, but isn't it really your decision? Are you responsible for the number of friends you have and the quality of your friendships? Are you responsible for the romantic relationship you have and the quality of that relationship? Are you responsible for your personal health? Are you responsible for your spiritual connections? Are you responsible for the quality of your family relationships? Are you responsible for your own emotions? Do you have control over any of these aspects of your life?

The responsibility mind-set asks you to say yes, and to accept responsibility for these matters and many others. It asks you to generalize in an opposite direction. You know there are things in your life you are fully responsible for, things that are fully under your control, so the responsibility mind-set asks you to generalize that observation into the rest of your life.

Remember, test-drive the concept for a while to see how this mind-set could possibly be true!

The responsibility mind-set keeps you empowered. You may not be responsible for the fighting in the Middle East, but you *are* responsible for your reaction to it, for how much attention and consideration you give to it, for how important you consider it to be. You *are* responsible for your own emotional responses.

THE RESPONSIBILITY MINDSET HELPS YOU TO TAKE CONTROL OF YOUR LIFE AND YOUR EMOTIONAL RESPONSE TO IT.

Consider for a moment what this thinking can do for you. If your boss verbally abuses you in front of others, one potential response would be to criticize your boss and feel discouraged. But another potential response would be to follow the responsibility mind-set. You could choose to believe that the abusive action was brought on by your actions or inaction.

This mind-set empowers you. It allows you to consider what you may have done to allow the abuse to happen. Did you fail to stand up for yourself? Did you attack first in some way that you don't yet understand? Did you fail to communicate effectively in a previous encounter? Did you fail to build a strong relationship with this person previously?

Whatever your answers, you've directed your attention toward things that are within your control. You've directed your energy toward things that you can change. You've increased your level of empowerment, and you've increased your ability to respond to the situation.

Consider the possible after-effects of an abusive encounter with your boss. Your coworkers and peers are likely to approach you with a victim mentality and talk about what a jerk your boss is. They might express the opinion that the way he has behaved is an unchangeable aspect of his character and that there's nothing you can do about it except complain. You can get your coworkers, friends, and family to resent your boss for being such a jerk. If you really wanted to, you could go to a lot of effort to spread this opinion and increase the overall level of animosity and frustration in your life. This would be a *destructive* response to the situation.

With the responsibility mind-set, you choose to believe that his being a jerk is the result of your action or inaction. You look for ways to change your actions so that the next encounters come out more to your liking. After all, would your boss have acted that way if he were addressing the Queen of England? Or the President of the United States? Or a small child? Or Gandhi? If these people were temporarily placed in your body, how would they respond to the situation? Would they have made things turn out differently? How would they have done that? When you ask yourself these kinds of questions, you will start to discover *constructive* ways to respond to situations.

Your roles in all interactions in your life have an effect on the outcome of the interactions. The queen and the president are human beings just like you, yet they would most likely be able to do something to make the situation come out differently. You can too.

Getting an unwelcome response is an indication that your behavior isn't resulting in the outcome you desire and that it's time to change that behavior. (Remember Step 3 of NLP: With the intention of achieving your outcome, vary your behavior in response to the feedback you get in Step 2.) The responsibility mind-set says that you are responsible for the behaviors you elicit in others. Communication is not a 50/50 responsibility—it's 100 percent your responsibility. When it seems as if a circumstance is beyond your control, you act as if you somehow played a role in its creation and as if the ensuing steps in the process are within your control too. You look for ways to make your next experience more to your liking. You look for ways to respond, rather than to blame.

Some people have initial difficulty really applying this mind-set. How could you possibly even pretend that the things happening all around you are the result of your action or inaction?

It's helpful to take your attention away from whether or not this mind-set is true and to instead focus on what gets you the best results in life. Which mind-sets allow you to have a better, more productive, more fulfilling life? A wide variety of people, myself included, have found that this mind-set is the *crux* of personal development, emotional fulfillment, and great personal effectiveness. This is not an exaggeration! This mind-set is exceptionally powerful and pervasive.

Over and over again, firm acceptance and application of this mind-set helps people regain control and create fulfilling and empowered lives. Throughout this book, I will continue to refer to this mind-set. If you haven't already incorporated it into your belief system, then I encourage you to review this section each time I refer to it in this book. The first step toward accepting it is understanding it.

ANDROID ASSIGNMENT

I once was given a writing assignment in a personal development course. The assignment was as follows:[2]

At the beginning of a ninety-minute writing period, you are handed a note that says:

> Up until this point in your life, you believed that you were one person, and all the rest of us were other people. You believed that you had your life, and we all had our lives, and that they were separate. That is a lie.
>
> The truth is you are the only person on this planet. All the rest of us are androids, and we were programmed by you. You created our programs to handle the smallest details, then made it so that you would forget all of this.

Everything that we have done up until this point was specifically planned and programmed by you. We have followed your instructions perfectly.

At this point in your life, you programmed me to give you this information. You instructed me to ask you to spend the next ninety minutes writing down the answers to these questions:

- Why did you program the androids in your life to do the things they have done?
- Why did you choose these particular androids for your most frequent interactions?
- Why did you program us to do the things we did the way we did them?

Take the time to do this exercise. For me, this exercise embedded the responsibility mind-set into my experience and allowed me to transform it from a conceptual idea into a living part of my belief system. If you don't have time to do the exercise now, then I encourage you to schedule a time for it in the next few days. Take responsibility for your life to the point where you can create ninety minutes of time for this one exercise.

Replace Guilt with a More Functional Process

When you accept the responsibility mind-set, your own health and well-being will be much better served when you concurrently replace ongoing guilt, blame, and shame with more healthy, useful processes. Taking responsibility for your life is different from beating yourself over the head with your failures. We want to empower you, not bludgeon you!

At first thought, many people think that guilt keeps them from doing all kinds of bad, mean, ugly things. But let's think about that for a moment. What prevents you from stealing? Is it a fear of feeling guilty, or is it a feeling that it's important to be a person of integrity? What keeps you from cheating on your spouse? Is it a fear of feeling guilty, or is it the value you place on your relationship and your not wanting to do anything to jeopardize it? Of course it's the latter.

Guilt may call your attention to the matter, but it's your *integrity* that determines your actions.

When you look at things more closely, you realize that your inner sense of morality is the true inspiration for your decision to act or restrain yourself. When you act in ways that violate some of your morals, that's not an indication you're a bad person—it's an indication of an inability to solve a difficult problem in your life. If you're in that kind of a position, you don't need shame; you need support!

The guilt-control games and the abusive history behind guilt control have given people legitimate cause to question the value of guilt. But what about the natural emotional process that many have become so familiar with? What about when you decide not to do something because you would feel guilty about it?

Guilt is an emotion tied to evaluations of right and wrong. It is a warning bell that lets you know when your action or inaction is out of alignment with your values. It causes you to contemplate the issue before acting. In a positive way, guilt suppresses the potential to act in damaging ways; but in a negative way, it also makes it more difficult to respond to *correct* a problem. People who succumb to guilt often allow it to take over, and then they fail to respond productively to serious situations.

Additionally, the feelings of guilt call to mind previous occasions of guilt and create a situation that often results in senseless self-condemnation, self-criticism, and lowered self-esteem. In most cases these emotions and actions are inappropriate for the situation and become destructive agents. The habitual, debilitating aspect of guilt is something that is pointless and should be avoided. It is unhealthy, and actually *prevents* you from solving the problem.

Another problem with guilt is that some people use it to suppress others' actions, especially those of children and loved ones. The habit is often so ingrained that people are usually unaware of what they are doing. How many parents have told their children that they "should be ashamed"? If you watch the interactions between couples or families today, you will often still see the negatively manipulative, suppressive underpinnings of guilt-control being played out, often in the form of "just joking." Many times, people just don't realize what they are doing, so they default to blaming one another, a form of manipulation that produces guilt. When used responsibly, guilt is a short-term warning sign that helps you recognize a problem. You respond to it, then turn it off. When used in a damaging way, it becomes a controlling device, or it runs out of control, causing needless discomfort and failing to serve any useful purpose.

For example, imagine the following situation. You are considering whether to go to your stepmother's house for Thanksgiving dinner or whether to spend some private time with your spouse over the holiday. You can't do both simultaneously, so you need to have a process for making your decision.

You think about skipping the dinner, but you realize that would be a real disappointment to your stepmother. Guilt kicks in and you feel lousy.

So you think about going to the dinner, but you realize that you do need to spend some quality time with your spouse. You've ignored the relationship for too long, and it is important to you. Guilt kicks in and you feel lousy.

Even worse, the guilt is just getting started. Not only do you feel bad about the idea of skipping the dinner, but you also recall all the times you weren't very nice to your stepmother and feel even worse about them. At the same time, you conjure up every instance you can recall when you've failed your spouse and feel even worse about them.

The net result is that you feel lousy about everything. It's still early November, so you get to continue this torture for several weeks. But at least after all this torture, you can come to a decision, right? At least these awful feelings have helped you solve the problem, right? Unfortunately, they haven't. Instead, you've suppressed your ability to take action of any kind, and your torture has led you avoid the issue entirely. As a result, you fail to come to a resolution.

At the last minute, you make a decision, knowing full well that no matter what choice you make, the guilt has taken over, and you'll feel terrible about either one. You might even choose to really screw things up by deciding to satisfy one person, then making up a *lie* to cover yourself with the other. Isn't that what many people end up doing? They feel guilty about that, too! Such is the destructive power of guilt.

The alternative is to replace guilt with a functional, useful process that helps you solve the problems, not make them worse. When you explore the conflict directly, without negative emotions burdening you, you are better able to determine the source of the problem and then fashion a solution. You allow yourself to address the problem from a state of resourcefulness, freeing up access to useful resources like creativity, motivation, initiative, and pride.

Suppose that in our example of Thanksgiving dinner, you decided to look at the problem from this perspective: Going to your stepmother's for dinner is important because you want to improve the quality of your relationship with her. Spending time with your spouse is important because you value that relationship and want to demonstrate your support of it. These are the pertinent issues. Once you've identified them, instead of feeling lousy, you can turn your attention to solving the problem with full access to your positive resources. You might even appreciate yourself as you realize that your values make you a supportive, loving, caring person.

In the process of solving the dilemma, you may find that you can't satisfy the demands of all your values at the same time, but you will be able to see how to take steps toward addressing each of them. Perhaps you choose to support your marriage by opting for quality time with your spouse. To address the other demand, you let your stepmother know how much you value your relationship with her by sending her flowers or writing her a heartfelt letter. Whatever you may decide, choose an action that helps you achieve your value in another way. The end result is that you take responsible action toward fulfilling your values, and you get to feel good about yourself in the process. I'd say that beats the heck out of guilt!

Toward the end of this book, we're going to examine some processes that can give you a great degree of emotional control. You will be able to choose which emotions you feel at any given time. Perhaps for the first time in your life, you will be able to choose whether or not to feel guilty at all. This can be an amazing process.

However, in that section, I will also emphasize that although the emotions that we call "negative" may not feel good, they can still have a useful purpose. Guilt alerts you to examine a conflict between an action and some aspect of your value system. It's useful to have indicators like that around. But once alerted, you are going to need all of your resources to address and solve the conflict, and you can do it in a constructive, healthful manner. I submit that you are far better at examining that problem and determining a solution when you feel resourceful.

Win-Win Is the Only Real Choice

The mind-set of win-win is something that I believe should permeate every aspect of human relations; it's the only real choice. Win-win is the process of evaluating actions or potential actions and determining if they are acceptable and desirable for all parties involved. The simplest way to evaluate if an action is a win-win is to determine if all parties feel congruently good about the outcome and gain benefit from it (their idea of benefit, not necessarily yours). Win-win is based on the belief that human interactions are cooperative, rather than competitive. For example, I want to get a raise and you want me to take on a difficult project. If I'm happy to take on that project, and you're happy to give me the raise for my efforts, then that would most likely constitute a win-win.

Although the win-win phrase has only two words, be aware that win-win also includes the welfare of other parties who are not directly involved. Win-win is holistic and must take into account the needs and desires of all people who could be affected by your actions or lack thereof. In NLP, this holistic viewpoint is often referred to as "ecology."

Win-win as the only choice is a slightly different approach from others you may have been exposed to in the past. For example, in his excellent book, *The Seven Habits of Highly Effective People*, Stephen Covey suggests that the best approach in relating to others is to strive for win-win, with the alternative to that being "no deal." While Mr. Covey and I would likely agree on the matter conceptually, I choose different semantics to illustrate an important point: Every action or inaction has an effect on the world around you, so even a "no deal" can be evaluated in terms of win-win. "No deal" is an appropriate response only if it creates a win-win. Inaction is action by omission and should be evaluated in terms of the same criteria by which you evaluate action.

If you and your spouse are living in a home that is causing your spouse to have health problems, then the two of you would likely take action. If your spouse's heart is set on buying a new home in the mountains, and you have your heart set on renting a beach cottage, then you are starting with relatively different criteria. If you fail to agree on where to move, a no-deal would be to not move at all. However, that would still be a losing proposition for your spouse, because the health problem would persist. Win-win as the only choice requires you to continue your pursuit of a suitable arrangement until all parties have their needs and desires met.

The holistic sense of win-win requires you to take into account not only the needs and desires of you and your spouse, but also those of others who may be affected by your actions. Perhaps the two of you agree on a specific home, and you decide to make your move. But your choice requires you to make financial commitments, which you can make only if you withdraw money from the account set aside for your children's college education. This could affect the needs and desires of your children and would most likely not be a win-win. Or perhaps the land on which you want to build your house is the burial grounds of a local indigenous people. This could affect the deep-seated spiritual needs of these people and again would most likely not be a win-win.

The concept of win-win is relatively easy to understand; however, the application of the concept is sometimes not straightforward. For example, how do you know when something is a win for someone else? Who gives you the right to make that determination on someone else's behalf? How do you know whom to take into consideration for each action you take? These are difficult questions with complicated answers.

In this book, I will be presenting you with skills and techniques for exploring the answers to these questions. You will find that many times people will agree to a solution, believe that it is a win for them, but not realize until later that it's a losing proposition. Again, this is often a result of not being directly in touch with core values. Cognitively, the agreement is made (an outer approval), but later, when they eventually realize the agreement does not meet with their inner approval (it doesn't agree with their values systems), they may feel manipulated, abused, or tricked. Your best intentions can be foiled by poor execution.

By supplementing win-win mentality with the responsibility mind-set and using the techniques laid out in this book, I ask you to do more than just take responsibility for agreeing to win-win as the only choice. I also ask you to take responsibility for helping flush out the information needed to ensure that the final solution is the win-win everyone thinks it is. Again, by embracing the responsibility mind-set, *you* take responsibility for ensuring that you avoid win-lose agreements in your life, regardless of whether the other people are willing to settle for a losing arrangement.

Keep in mind that throughout this book, the ideas, mind-sets, strategies, and techniques presented are offered to assist you in achieving excellence. And keep in mind that the words *effectiveness, success, achievement, fulfillment, empowerment, influence, persuasion,* and others related to them have an interwoven fabric of win-win philosophy built into them.

No person is successful at the expense of others. I consider that abuse. No person is effective through the process of manipulation or coercion. I consider that failure. No person is a leader who leads people somewhere they don't want to go. I consider that injustice.

True success and effectiveness is not an individualistic process but a holistic process; all related parties are part of the achievement.

People Are the Greatest Asset—The Synergy Mind-Set

Synergy is the process by which several independent parts can work together to produce results greater than would have been achieved if each part worked independently. Synergy is the characteristic that people strive for when they work together as a team.

In sports, it is common knowledge that the overall skill level of All-Star teams (in which the best individual performers are put together on one team, usually without being given the opportunity to practice together and gel as a team) is significantly less than the overall skill level of a good team that has been playing together for some time. At each position, the All-Star team has a member who is individually superior to the member of the regular team; however, the All-Star team is inferior in overall performance. The processes that make average players play collectively better than All-Stars is called synergy.

The trend in business today is to create plentiful combinations of work teams. In many instances, representatives from various departments are pulled together and asked to contribute their skills to the relatively autonomous group. The team is assigned complex and comprehensive tasks and asked to achieve them with excellence. It is hoped, and often realized, that the results of this smaller, representative group will be superior to those that are routinely achieved by the company as a whole.

The sum of the capabilities of the team are far less than that of the entire organization, yet work teams have proven to be an effective way to *increase* productivity and get *better* results. Again, this is the result of synergy.

The process of synergy relates directly to your personal effectiveness. Many people think of their job in terms of skill sets and tasks. If you consider the requirements for being a secretary, you quite probably think first in terms of technical skills: typing, word processing, telephone answering, and so on. The role of design engineer might conjure up images of drafting, designing, problem solving, and so on. Even the role of human relations director is likely to make you think of skills such as labor relations, employment practices, interviewing, hiring, and the like. Again, each indicates a focus on technical competence.

As a society, we know how to help people learn technical skills. If Mary is failing to succeed because she can't perform a technical task, there will probably be training available to address her deficiencies. And the training is likely to be successful much of the time.

The thrust of this book, however, is in people skills, skills that are interpersonal rather than technical; they include communicating, listening, leading, persuading, and other skills related to human interaction. They are the skills that require more than one person to perform.

We don't always know how to help people learn interpersonal skills. If Mary doesn't know how to work with people effectively, there's probably not much you know to do about it. Sure, there are courses available. But do they work? Do you really get results? Do you have the same confidence in them as you do in technical courses? In society today, the information relating to interpersonal skills—and the ability to teach those skills to others—is far less developed and understood than information about technical skills.

The synergy mind-set asserts that your success in the world, be it professional or personal, is most directly related to your ability to interact effectively with others. The area in which most people can make the greatest improvement in their success, effectiveness, and results will be in the area of relating with other people.

While it may seem that we still need to be technically excellent to succeed in a society (our computers won't work if there are bugs in the microprocessors), you must be aware of the synergy mind-set. The results of a group are far better when the group gels as a team than they are when the group is composed of All-Stars who don't work together.

Whether you're starting a new company or organizing a birthday party, the quality of your life is enriched in direct correlation with the quality and functionality (the degree to which something constructively contributes toward a specific outcome) of the relationships you create with people.

Balance Is an Important Part of Life

We've all known people who were out of balance. Consider the extreme case of Don Simpson, a wonderfully talented Hollywood producer, who gained great success while producing movie hits like *Top Gun* and *Beverly Hills Cop*. Some years into his success, at the height of his career, he turned to a life of abusing prostitutes and using excessive drugs. His "success" revolved around his career accomplishments, but after one of his movies didn't do well, he experienced what he described as "a feeling of profound emptiness; a void." He died at the age of 52 with the presence of multiple drugs in his system.[3]

The workaholic may expend inexhaustible energies toward solving the most difficult of problems at work, yet balk when faced with the most superficial of challenges at home. The single-focused homemaker may make unnecessary sacrifices for her family for years, yet fail to provide for some of her own most essential needs, allowing her life to lose meaning outside her family.

Without balance, success in one area of life can be part of an overall calamity. In some cases, extreme "success" is a symptom of imbalance gone out of control.

The balance mind-set asserts that the degree to which you achieve and maintain balance in your life may be the determining factor that measures your success in life.

Many people allow some of life's aspects to atrophy and fail to pay attention to them until they reach some threshold level. Someone who spends many years eating fats and failing to exercise, without caring in the least about personal health, is likely to focus on health after having a heart attack. Subsequently, that aspect of life may begin to overshadow all others.

If you allow one aspect of life to atrophy, you may have to rebuild it. But even then it's common to transfer that atrophy to another area and still live a life out of balance. Total lack of focus on health may eventually require you to focus on it completely; however, what would you have to ignore in order to do so?

So that you won't have to live with a constant imbalance, the balance mind-set encourages you to pay attention to all aspects of your life now. Although there may be times when you will want or need to focus your attention more strongly on one area, balance requires you to ensure that all areas of your life are relatively stable while you are doing so.

The desire for balance is what allows you to leave work at reasonable hours, even when that may not be the optimum thing to do for your advancement. The desire for balance is what allows you to take the rest you need when you need it, helping you to maintain health and vigor. The desire for balance is what allows you to spend your time and money developing yourself and your potential, even when that time and money has other demands upon it. Balance is an important aspect of a healthy, rewarding, productive life.

ASPECTS OF LIFE THAT AFFECT BALANCE

When you consider the totality of your life, you can consider the following categories to have an equal level of importance. Be mindful, however, that equal importance does not equate to equal time. It is the *quality* of each area that's important, not necessarily the quantity.

- Career
- Money
- Sexual relationships
- Nonsexual relationships
- Family
- Physical health
- Emotional health
- Intellectual fulfillment
- Personal development
- Spirituality

This particular model asserts that each area is equivalent in importance to the other areas and that there is no particular order involved. Just like the knights at King Arthur's Round Table, each item has equal stature.

As you consider each aspect, you might honestly ask yourself some questions. First, how balanced are you now? How does the quality of each of these areas stack up with the others? Do you have a great sense of spirituality, but lack career success? Do you have a fulfilling sexual relationship, but fail to have equally strong nonsexual relationships? Do you have excellent physical health, but have extended bouts of depression? These are the types of questions you should ask yourself. In which areas do you want to make changes? For each area, are you being the person you want to be?

And second, how are you currently directing your actions and attentions? Are you busy improving your strengths and ignoring your weaker areas? Are you focusing most of your efforts on your good health, but failing to gain rewarding relationships? Do you spend most of your time improving your career life, but ignore the glaring issues in your sexual relationship or family?

Although this book can't answer these questions for you, it will help you explore many of them for yourself and encourage you to find your own answers. The techniques and

I THOUGHT EVERYONE KNEW WE WERE HAVING
A MEETING - WE'D BETTER ROUND UP THE REST
OF THE KNIGHTS BEFORE KING ARTHUR GETS HERE!

strategies in this book are not directed toward any specific
aspect of life; you will find that they can be applied equally
well to all aspects of your life.

I encourage you to take some time to ask yourself the
questions just listed. Take an objective look at where and
when you could use some assistance, then use this book to
support that part of your development. Your results will improve dramatically when you have specific ideas in mind
about where and when to use the information.

You Can Learn from Anything, Even a Sign on the Road

I was once told a story about learning. A man who was a very
good skier decided to go to the Sugarbush ski area in Ver-
mont. It was his first time there, and he met some people
who recommended that he take a skiing lesson with the
course instructor. Because he was such a good skier already,
he was not inclined to pay good money for a skiing lesson,
but his friends insisted he would gain something from it.
Reluctantly, he decided to check it out. He went to the office, paid his money, then proceeded to the place on the
mountain where the instructor did her training.

The instructor had once been a superb skier, but she
was now in her late forties and was no longer in excellent
shape. Her skills had degraded somewhat, and it showed
when she was skiing. This was immediately evident to her
new student.

Time came for the lesson to begin, and the man began
with an attitude, which was immediately apparent to the instructor, who asked him what was going on. He said, "You
know, I saw you skiing out here just now, and I can tell that
I'm a much better skier than you. I'm not trying to be critical,
but I just don't think there's anything you can teach me."

Unfazed, the instructor replied, "Well, you may be right.
Is this your first time at Sugarbush?" He replied that it was.
She continued, "Have you seen that sign down at the bot-
tom of the hill, just before the turnoff to come up here?"

He replied that he did indeed know the sign, because it was the one that told him how to find the ski area. She then said, "Yeah, that sign has shown a tremendous number of people how to get here. Without it, many people would have missed the turn and gotten lost." He nodded in agreement, but with some confusion, wondering what this had to do with skiing. She then said, "Do you know, that sign has never been to Sugarbush?"

The ensuing lesson turned out to be the best lesson he had ever had.[4] You can learn from anything, even a sign on the road.

Understand That You Will Never Understand

How many times have you heard the expression, "I know exactly how you feel"? Or "I understand what you're going through"? What about "I know, I've been there myself"?

While these expressions generally demonstrate feelings of empathy and support, we intuitively know that they're also far from being accurate. In NLP's model of communication, we start to see exactly how and why it's so very difficult to really understand another human's experience of the world.

Humans experience the world via their senses (that is, through sight, hearing, touch, smell, and taste, with the possibility of extrasensory perception as well). However, the sensory input that goes to our senses and the information we receive in our awareness are transformed. Not only is the volume of data too large to handle, but it is also filtered through our past experiences.

Incoming information is distorted and biased as a result of our life's history. Our attitudes, beliefs, decisions, emotional responses, and values all play a role in helping us to determine exactly what information gets in, and what information doesn't. They help determine which bits of data are changed and in what way they are changed. This process of altering incoming data explains how ten people can all see the same incident, yet have ten different accounts of what happened. NLP categorizes the filtration process into classes of deletion, distortion, and generalization.

After the bits of raw sensory data are filtered and distorted, then we *represent,* or more correctly, re-present, the experiences to ourselves; we create internal images ("I can see her face as clearly as if she were here right now"), internal sounds ("I can't get that song out of my head!"), internal voices ("I keep telling myself that it will get better"), internal sensations ("I felt as if I were going to burst"), and even internal smells and tastes. Just as most of our life's experiences involve multiple senses simultaneously, our internal representations also involve multiple senses simultaneously.

We interpret the filtered data stream and assign meaning to it. We determine which things we like, which things are normal, which things are important, and so on. Then each internal representation is specially encoded in ways that have meaning for us as individuals. For example, some people encode exciting events using larger pictures with bright colors; from this come expressions like "larger than life" and "bold statements." It is not clear how or how much, but time and additional life experiences can cause these internal codings to change as well. This is how those same ten people will have ten new remembrances of an experience after time has passed.

When we decide to tell someone about our experience, we first have to translate the experience from our internal re-presentations (the internal pictures, sounds, feelings, smells, tastes) into this thing we call language. If a picture is worth a thousand words, how many words must our feelings, smells, and tastes be worth? People have written volumes of books just about the single feeling of love. How many words would it take to accurately describe the difference in smell between mint and oregano?

To add even greater variability to the process, remember that your particular encodings mean something to you (such as a larger-than-life picture), but they may not have that same meaning for another person. To you, a bright, bold idea may be exciting, but to someone else, a bright, bold idea may be overwhelming and frightening.

Despite the tremendous amount of information we could share about any given experience, we typically manage to condense our verbal descriptions into a few words or sentences. (Remember, we're still talking about just one experience, and life is a continuous stream of experiences occurring one after the other.)

When we finally speak the words, we have somehow managed to take volumes of filtered data, much of which have particular meaning to us alone, and distill them into a relatively small group of words. And we often think that these few words can accurately convey to another person the entirety of what we saw, heard, smelled, and tasted, not to mention our virtually indescribable feelings about the matter.

The process I just described is a condensed description of an NLP model of communication, intended simply to get you thinking about the complexities involved with communication. Don't concern yourself with trying to "understand" the details of this model at this time. Feel free to just keep the ideas in mind as you consider the following:

You go to a restaurant, and your friend orders a seafood bisque soup and salad with a special house dressing. This friend is an accomplished chef himself, and you know that when he tastes a food, he tastes for very subtle differences. He can tell you within a very close approximation which spices were used, how the food was prepared, which ingredients were used, and how fresh they were. He tastes his soup, and responds with, "Mmm, this is good soup." He tastes his salad and responds with, "Mmm, this is good salad dressing." With the enormous amount of distinguishing data points and refined sensory distinctions at this man's disposal, he's managed to condense his experience into the single word "good." Do you think you can ever really understand what his experience of the food is? No way!

But wait. We still need to consider the person doing the listening. If you are truly listening, which is more rare than you might imagine, you will hear the few words being spoken and begin to create meaning. Just as with any sensory experience, you take in data with many senses, perhaps noticing what facial expressions your friend used, what tone of voice he used, what feelings you got when you heard the words, even what you were saying to yourself at the same time he spoke the words. To reduce the amount of data, this experience is distorted through your filters of values, beliefs, and experience. You draw upon your history of what "good" is and distort his meaning to make sense in light of *your* past experiences. You re-present your results with your own internal representations and encode them so that they have special meaning just for you.

After all this, what do you think the odds are that you and he both have the same internal experiences? What are the chances that you both will have the same internal pictures, sounds, tastes, feelings, smells, and words—and that you are going to have the same internal meanings associated with each aspect of them? Do you think you will know exactly what that soup tastes like the moment you put it to your lips? By the way, did I mention it had anchovies in it?

This is all a very fancy way of saying that people are infinitely different, and the differences are so vast and extended that we can't even possibly hope to understand even a small fraction of those differences.

When you start to look at the processes involved in communication, you may wonder that we can understand anything anyone says, even remotely! In light of this, you may now have a clearer understanding of how awesome a task it is to really understand another human being.

This mind-set does not, however, say that you should not make efforts to understand other people. On the contrary, connecting with others in the way that we call "understanding each other" is a very important process of human interaction, and you should continue to pursue that process. In fact, by understanding that you will never truly understand, you come much closer to the goal.

When astronomers look into the sky from Earth, they understand that light is refracted through Earth's atmosphere. They understand that what they are seeing is not really what they are seeing, and they understand at least some of the ways in which it is distorted. This understanding allows them to use the information they get in more useful ways, to give more accurate results. In the same way, the mind-set of "understanding that you will never understand" can allow you to use the information you get in more useful ways, to give you more accurate results. This will be an especially important mind-set to be aware of when we explore the topic of listening.

People Are Emotional First, Rational Second

If you have ever watched any of the original *Star Trek* shows, you probably remember the character of Spock. Spock's race of people did not experience emotions and prided itself on being very logical. In the series, Spock often called attention to others' illogical and emotional actions and alluded to their inferior processes. Despite his criticism, it was often these illogical and emotional behaviors that ended up saving the day.

Spock was half human and was prone to bouts of emotion himself. However, he chose to squash and deny these emotions and to portray himself as a fully logical, emotionless person. His private struggle was the subject of many episodes. On occasion, and to the delight of his human counterparts, Spock sometimes acted with blatant emotion. The humans took advantage of these occasions to accuse Spock of behaving emotionally—a charge he would vehemently deny.

Our attraction to television often stems from its portrayal of real-life experiences. Spock personified our real-life conflict between logic and emotion.

In our typical way of thinking, emotion is not logical, nor is logic emotional; and logic is the method of choice for making decisions. However, just as in the case of Spock, we often take actions based on emotions, then vehemently deny that our emotions played a role in the decisions. And as exemplified in these many *Star Trek* episodes, decisions based on emotions are often the best decisions available.

The mind-set of "people are emotional first" portrays people as emotional beings first, rational beings second. I'm fully convinced that emotions play a far more active role in human interactions than most people think.

The next time someone does something really silly, ask "why"? Watch for a significant delay, as the person struggles to come up with a reason. He or she will probably conjure up a reason after a moment or two, then swear that's the *reason* for doing that silly thing. Yet, if it were really the reason, then why does it take so long to figure it out after the fact? Many times, our decisions have an emotional basis, and then we fabricate "reasons" to "explain" our behavior. Unfortunately, we sometimes allow these faulty reasons to unnecessarily limit us.

Consider an example that might hit home. Do you agree that people are emotional first and rational second? You

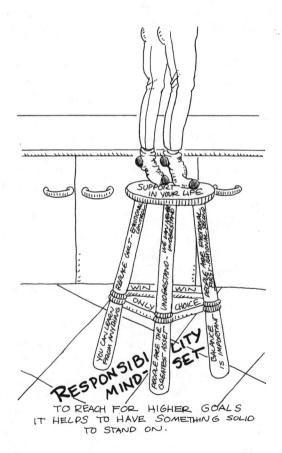

TO REACH FOR HIGHER GOALS
IT HELPS TO HAVE SOMETHING SOLID
TO STAND ON.

probably had an answer right away, the moment you read the statement the first time. Yet, do you know "why" you agree or disagree? That probably takes a little bit longer to determine. Take a moment to think about it. Then let me ask you just one more question. How could you have possibly, logically, rationally, objectively have made that decision before you even chose to read the rest of what I have to say on the matter? I might just have the answers to the mysteries of life on the next page, just waiting for an open, objective, rational mind to come discover with me!

People are emotional first, rational second. And just in case you're wondering, this entire explanation has been a rational explanation for something that is emotionally, intuitively, and subjectively obvious to me.

CHAPTER 4

LEARNING, UNLEARNING, AND RELEARNING

THUS FAR, we've looked at some mind-sets that, when incorporated into your life, can create an increased level of empowerment. However, being empowered doesn't necessarily mean that you use that power. A boulder tied to the top of a mountain has a great amount of potential energy. When released, it can roll down that mountain, transforming its potential into an energy of action.

In this chapter, we're going to look at some of the things required to turn your potential energy into energy of action; and we're going to determine just what it may take to release you from the ties that may be holding you back.

Unconscious Behavior

A significant portion of NLP is related to hypnosis and the unconscious mind. Unfortunately for the legitimate field of hypnosis, stage hypnotists around the world have mystified and frightened people with their unorthodox presentations of hypnosis. From watching them, many people have the perception that hypnotists can cause you to do things you don't want to do or that they can take control of your mind. Listening to them can make you believe that your unconscious mind is a perfect stranger to you, rather than the good friend that it is.

As we begin our discussion about the unconscious mind, please dispel any of these negative images of hypnosis. They're simply hogwash. Stage hypnotism is a show, and the participants take part in that show willingly.

NLP uses a model of the mind, as do hypnosis and a variety of other psychological methods, which states that your "mind" can be classified into at least two parts: the conscious mind and the unconscious mind. These so-called parts are not biological distinctions, but rather functional distinctions. Conscious mind activities include those things that you give your attention to and are limited to a relatively small number of simultaneous items. Unconscious mind activities include the many things that you do but don't have a conscious awareness of doing.[1]

For example, if you decide to walk over to the pool, that is a conscious decision. Your decision to walk rather than run or crawl is also a conscious decision. However, the process of walking is done unconsciously. Hundreds of muscles work in synchrony with one another in order for you to physically walk, but you are usually oblivious to every one of them. It's your unconscious mind that makes sure you bend your knee at the right time, flex the muscles in your toes at the right time, swing your arms at the right time, and do all the other things needed to walk. Consciously, you probably couldn't even identify all the muscles involved, but unconsciously, you coordinate all of them with grace and ease.

Similarly, many of our actions are unconsciously driven. Many people have had the experience of driving their car, getting lost in thought, then somehow finding themselves much further along than they remember driving. Driving a car can be an unconscious process.

In essence, there is a lot going on in your head beyond what you're thinking about. In fact, some researchers believe that you can process only between five and nine things simultaneously with your conscious mind. Consider grocery store visits. How many items can you decide to pick up without having to use a list? Unless you use some sort of special system, you'll probably find that it's fewer than ten items, after which you start to forget things. This is an indication of the limits of the conscious mind.

Alternately, the unconscious mind is capable of handling many pieces of data simultaneously. If you witness a crime, it is likely that you will later be able to recall the general characteristics, facial features, voice qualities, clothing, and distinguishing features of the perpetrator, even though you may not have been consciously noticing those things as the crime took place. With time, you may eventually be able to recall hundreds of different pieces of data, all of which were somehow stored within your brain at the time you saw the event. The information is coded and stored, all without your conscious awareness or approval. Even information that may seem impossible to remember can often be brought back into awareness with the help of hypnosis.

The unconscious mind stores massive amounts of data and carries out tasks that you don't really want to bother thinking about. Right now, you're probably thinking of a few things, but the digits in your phone number are not among them. Yet if I ask you to say your phone number aloud, you could likely do that. You would retrieve the information, then bring it into your consciousness long enough to say it aloud. Similarly, when you go to tie your shoelaces, you probably don't have to think about exactly how to do it; it just happens. You can think about other things while you're tying shoelaces, because your unconscious mind is handling the details of that task for you. If you decide to cross your arms, your unconscious mind goes through the details of the task for you.

Just for fun, cross your arms now. Once you've done that, then cross your arms the other way, with your other arm crossing on top. Even the simple task of crossing your arms can take considerable concentration if you haven't already delegated the process to your unconscious mind.

Your unconscious mind is also the domain of your emotions. If you were consciously able to control your emotions, you could choose to feel any emotion at any time. If you were feeling sad, you could simply decide to feel happy instead. If you were feeling guilty, you could simply choose to be motivated to solve a problem instead. If you were feeling angry, you could conveniently choose to feel supportive instead. However, few people have that kind of emotional control; and even when they do, they still prefer not to make moment-to-moment decisions their entire life about how to feel. Your emotions are almost always determined through unconscious processes. And although the ability to gain emotional choice is available, the methods still rely substantially on unconscious processes.

But what is the point of saying all this? Why does it matter what is conscious or unconscious? What does all this mean to you?

The answer is that your unconscious processes are what determines the majority of your actions. If your unconscious mind does not approve of your conscious decisions, then it's difficult to take action and even more difficult to maintain your behavior.

Consider the "choice" to lose weight. You know what you need to do if you decide to lose weight. It's simply a matter of eating fewer calories and/or expending more energy. Nothing complicated there. Yet people have a tremendously difficult time adhering to their decisions, thus a difficult time losing weight or keeping it off. That's because weight regulation is an unconscious process. You may have noticed that people who go through pivotal life changes often undergo significant weight changes soon thereafter, and these weight changes occur without any conscious effort whatsoever. I knew a woman who struggled unsuccessfully to lose five or ten pounds for years, then dropped twenty pounds after a divorce without even trying, and kept it off.

In your life, you may choose to do certain things, but if those things don't fall in line with your unconscious processes, you won't do them. You might stick with them for a little while; but just when you stop paying attention, you'll either stop doing them or sabotage yourself. Thus, you will never make progress in this way alone.

True progress is made when you put your conscious decisions into alignment with your unconscious processes. In

NLP, this is called congruency. Just like the twenty pounds, goals that once seemed unattainable will be met with an ease and naturalness that you don't quite understand. It certainly makes life a whole lot easier.

So how do you get your actions into alignment with your unconscious processes? How can you incorporate new behaviors and be sure they will become a part of your everyday life? These are good questions, and we'll be looking at them as we continue through this book.

Steps for Integrating New Skills

Our discussion about conscious and unconscious activities leads us directly to the learning process. This book will offer a plentitude of skills, ideas, mind-sets, strategies, processes, and procedures for making your life better. Some will be new to you. Others will run contrary to what you already know. Still others you will already know, but you may need to adjust your knowledge. These possibilities describe the topics of learning, unlearning, and relearning.

Much of this book addresses the topic of persuasion. Many people think that persuasion and influence must be "natural" to be okay. However, we're going to learn that in order to learn skills, if you don't already know them, you will need to be *unnatural* with them for some period of time. It's a part of the normal process of learning that humans experience.

You are going to find not only that it's okay to know what you're doing when you're doing it, but that it's also *imperative* for some period of time.

To understand this, let's look at a useful model often used in NLP. In it, the stages of learning are defined as follows:

Stage 1: Unconscious Incompetence You not only don't know how to perform the skill, but you don't even know that the skill exists to be learned. For example, the first time you sang "Happy Birthday," you may not have adjusted the pitch of your voice to the exact same note as the accompaniment. You probably didn't have the skill for distinguishing subtle differences between sounds that were slightly flat or slightly sharp. Even more, you probably didn't even know that these skills were part of the process of singing—you might have thought you were singing just fine, especially if you were very young.

Stage 2: Conscious Incompetence   You begin the process of learning and immediately recognize that you haven't yet mastered the skill. Your lack of ability is consciously known to you. When you realized that your voice wasn't matching the pitch of the accompaniment, you probably weren't able to correct the problem immediately. You realized it was a skill you had not yet learned.

Stage 3: Conscious Competence   You become proficient with the skill, but your conscious attention is required to use it. After learning more about singing, you may be able to sing perfectly on key, but only by paying very close attention to what you are doing.

Stage 4: Unconscious Competence   You are proficient with the skill, and you can use it without even thinking about it. A song comes on the radio, and you sing perfectly on key as you simultaneously do chores around the house. You might not even be aware that you're singing as you do so.

Learning   The process of learning takes us through Stages 1, 2, 3, and 4 in sequence. This is the process for learning new material.

Unlearning   Unlearning is the process of going from Stage 4 back to Stage 2. When information, strategies, and behaviors are unconsciously integrated, you must move back to Stage 2 and regain conscious awareness of the process prior to initiating an adaptation.

Relearning   Relearning is the process of going through Stages 2, 3, and 4 after having unlearned. The unlearning-relearning process gives you added choices, enabling you to incorporate any of the skills learned to date.

This model supports the observation that the best players in a sport are often the worst coaches. They don't know what they do; they just do it (Stage 4). In human dynamics, you'll likely find that the best communicators and the most successful people are also operating in Stage 4. Thus, they also don't know how they do what they do. Unfortunately, not only are these people unaware of how they do things, but they also often create well-meaning, but incorrect, ideas to "explain" how they do things. This creates a misleading and difficult trail for others to follow, making it seem impossible to learn the skills.

You may be starting to see how communicational and interpersonal skills sometimes seem as if they're gifts, natural talents. The people who are good at these skills typically do not know what specific steps they are taking, and they typically do not have a certain model in their mind that they are following. They are unconscious of their processes and therefore have no conscious awareness of what they are doing. They are often happy to share what they know, but unfortunately they don't know what to share. You either get "I don't know what I do, I just do it," or "Well, you have to understand that the key principle is to make sure that you...." The former approach doesn't help much, and the latter approach actually throws you off the track.

As odd as it may seem, the best person to learn a skill from is probably not the person who is best at the skill, because that person is operating in Stage 4, unconscious competence. The best person to learn from is a person who has analyzed the most talented examples and has maintained his or her awareness in Stage 3, conscious competence. Some of the best coaches in the world can't do the things they are teaching others to do. This is part of the mechanism that supports the mind-set of "you can learn from anything, even a sign on the road."

You may be starting to recognize something about the structure of this book. In the beginning, we started by getting you to examine your life in detail and by calling attention to some of the things that may not be working perfectly for you. In the beginning, you may be starting from Stage 1, unconscious incompetence. You might not have realized that there were things in your life not exactly working for you.

We began with a questionnaire designed to help you identify some of the ways in which you might not be functioning at optimum levels. We continued with a conversation about goals, asking you to look not only at the predominant aspect of your life, but also at the aspects that you may not be paying much attention to. Again, this was to highlight any areas that you may want to make changes in.

Through all this time, you were likely to be in Stages 1 and 2, finding areas in which you were not necessarily as competent as you would like to be and oscillating between not even knowing this (Stage 1, unconscious incompetence) and realizing you would like to make some changes (Stage 2, conscious incompetence). It wouldn't have done you any good to give you some great strategies if you didn't feel you had a use for them, so we had to start in Stages 1 and 2.

As we continued, we began to build a framework of beliefs and mind-sets that would set the stage for what's about to happen next. These were required to help you be receptive to the material and to provide a set of filters that would help you receive the information in the way it is intended.

However, we have not yet addressed the issue of unlearning and relearning. The material we begin to cover in the next chapter relates to listening, persuading, and responding. However, you probably already have some ideas about how these processes work, some of which support you, but others of which do not. So before we enter into the process of relearning that material, it is better to do a bit of unlearning first.

Unlearning is always an interesting process, so get ready to undress some of your previous notions and expose their vulnerabilities.

Unlearning Old Success Paradigms

We're going to begin our unlearning process by looking at some old success paradigms that may be near and dear to your heart. However, this process isn't designed to support those ideas; it is designed to expose what's wrong with them.

They are flawed paradigms that bring about difficulties for large numbers of people.

Remember that unlearning is required before relearning can properly take place. As we unlearn these things, it will help to stay open to some novel viewpoints. You will find that they open up a tremendous number of possibilities for you and even help you start to explain some of the difficulties that you or others have had in the past. It is important to unlearn ineffective paradigms so that you can be fully prepared to relearn better options.

These first examples are directed primarily toward work environments, which is the context I use for many of the examples in this book. I do so for a specific reason; the work environment is often the place where you will have the most opportunity to develop new interpersonal skills.

In a business setting, you are placed in an environment that is unlike most other environments in your life. You are asked to work with people whom you ordinarily would not interact with, you are asked to act in synergy with these people to achieve specific results, and you are pressured to work through problems without quitting or leaving. This just doesn't happen in other parts of life.

If you've joined a country club to play golf, you may run across people you wouldn't ordinarily interact with, but you're free to just avoid them. You aren't asked to synergize with these people, and you aren't asked to achieve any specific results with them. You aren't even asked to get along with them. If you find that the club is causing you more problems than you want to deal with, you will likely quit the club and go to another. No big deal, right?

The business environment is different, and it tends to bring about the most frequent and varied challenges to your interpersonal skills. By mastering this environment, you will find that many other everyday environments are simple by comparison. Although the following examples are work-oriented, you will find that they are fully applicable to other areas as well.

The following paradigms are so ingrained with many people that they can be used to demonstrate a significant portion of the unconscious misunderstandings surrounding effectiveness. Our intention here is to unlearn these paradigms in order to take a look at what we might have been doing and understand the inherent flaws. This is a critical part of the process for acquiring new skills. For each paradigm, I will point out some of the prime faults inherent to the paradigm:

Faulty Paradigm #1   *Work hard and you will be rewarded.* Hard work is often a part of success, and indeed you will often find successful people who work very hard. Yet this hard work often translates into excessive work, and more often creates a lack of success in other areas of life because of imbalance. In other cases, excessive work does not contribute to success at all. In fact, it can be a strong indicator of a lack of success.

For the average person, working hard is generally either an indication of strong motivation or an inability to influence. Usually, it's the latter. People who work excessively are often ineffective in groups and are forced to succumb to external pressures that seem "beyond their control." This lack of control (lack of taking responsibility) creates a feeling of powerlessness that translates into ineffectiveness. After a long period of time, a person may either lash out with resentment and anger or become resigned to "giving up," thus dealing a fatal blow to self-esteem. Often, the person may drift into win-lose thinking as a last resort and seek malice or retribution against the other parties.

Even when you continue to work excessively without malice ("putting in your time" or "paying your dues"), you are accepting an arrangement that is not win-win, most obviously not a win for you.

The skills not being demonstrated here are the ability to influence others and to redirect the pressures that are being directed toward you. (You may wish to read the previous sentence again; it says a lot!) The problems are exacerbated by failing to take responsibility for the situation and incorrectly thinking that the organization is "doing it to you." And most importantly, the acceptance of inappropriate circumstances represents a failure to insist on win-win solutions.

By adopting the skills contained in this book, you will learn how to work effectively, not excessively.

Faulty Paradigm #2   *Respond to feedback and you will improve.* At times, feedback contains some gem of information that, if accepted, will make a difference in your level of success. However, even in those cases, the "gem" is generally feedback like "you need to learn how to manage your time." This is really no gem at all, but rather a nonspecific direction that fails to provide the strategies you need to succeed at the task. As a result, people often get the same feedback year after year and often don't improve.

I once had a conversation with a coworker who was about to give a performance review to a woman who had been with the company for twenty-five years. My coworker had just started in his position, so he was giving this woman a review for the first time. Commenting on the content of the review, he said, "You know, I wrote out this review, and then I looked through this woman's file and saw that she got virtually the same review year after year, often from different managers."

This is the problem when people are not given specific strategies to replace their old ones—they aren't given the tools to know *how* to improve. They're told what to do, but not how to do it.

More often, however, feedback is not filled with "gems" and is based more on opinion than on fact. Adherence to this paradigm places more importance on the opinions of others than on your own; thus, you are necessarily placed in a position of ineffectiveness. If you are directing your efforts toward responding to feedback, you are not influencing others to see your points of view. You are responding rather than directing and influencing. You will always need to respond to the feedback of others; but, in most situations, by the time you resort to responding to direct feedback, it's probably too late.

Another detrimental response can be to take on guilt over the lack of "perfection."

The skill not being demonstrated is the ability to influence others' opinions in a win-win process. This is often exacerbated by unnecessary justifications that the person giving the review is either "wrong," or "doesn't really know what's going on," both of which fail to adhere to the responsibility mind-set and detract from your ability to respond.

Faulty Paradigm #3   *Do a good job, and things like "politics" and "power struggles" won't matter.* So many people wish this were true; they wish they could just "do their job" and leave the politics to others. Unfortunately for these people, they fail to realize that working with an "organization" (an organized group of people) is about working with people, not just about doing tasks.

On some rare occasions, individuals have such exceptional task abilities that they are given a lot of room to operate; however, they still won't succeed and excel in the business environment without sound interpersonal skills. In most cases, they will become isolated and outcast, turned to only for their singular abilities. They certainly won't have influence over their work environment.

Things like politics and power struggles always matter. If you retreat from them into a cocoon of "doing a good job," you are failing to demonstrate the ability to manage, direct, lead, and influence others. Adherence to this paradigm indicates a failure to accept the synergy mind-set, thus reducing both your personal effectiveness and also the effectiveness of the organization as a whole. Politics and power struggles are very much a part of the process for effectiveness.

Faulty Paradigm #4   *Let your work speak for itself.* Again, there will be times when your work is so exceptional that it will speak for itself. But that's not going to be very often, and it certainly won't carry you through to having an overall effective, balanced environment.

This concept follows the adage "Build a better mousetrap and the world will beat a path to your door." Unfortunately, if the world doesn't know you made the mousetrap, or if it doesn't understand how and why it is better, or if it doesn't believe that it really is better, then the path to your door will become overgrown with weeds.

If you let your work speak for yourself, you have indicated that you have resigned yourself to failure in any attempts to persuade others. You won't succeed by letting your work speak for itself, and this trap encourages many people to work longer and harder, only to find that many years down the road they lack the appreciation and respect they deserve. Again, this often results in resentment and anger, a sense of futility and failure. Obviously, this is not a win-win scenario.

The skills not being demonstrated are the ability to direct the attention of others and to encourage others to accept your viewpoints. It indicates resignation to the inability to persuade others; thus, it indicates a failure to take on the responsibility mind-set. Adherence to the faulty paradigm often creates undesirable results, and the failure to deal with them also indicates a failure to create win-win situations.

Faulty Paradigm #5 *Be efficient in your work, and seek to avoid wasting time with excessive talking to others.* Outwardly, this seems to be sound advice. We all see examples of people wasting time just talking and socializing with others. However, just because people can waste time in this way doesn't mean that talking is a waste of time. In fact, talking to others is a necessary aspect of working with others.

The primary skill not being used here is the ability to effectively use and benefit from interactions with others. The personal communications you have with individuals will almost always have the most direct impact on your overall effectiveness in an organization (assuming you have a reasonable technical skill level). When people follow this rule too strictly, they sometimes fail to generate balance in their life, fail to develop any levels of personal relationships with those they work with.

Organizations are groups of people. Far more can be done by ten people working together for the same cause than by one hundred people working for opposite and different causes. People gel together in a synergistic relationship by communicating and developing relationships with one another.

Communications with others can be random and disorganized, but the skills in this book will help you to achieve order and purpose in your communications. You won't always have a directed purpose, but these skills allow you to pick and choose the best times to be effective in achieving your goal and the best times to simply have an enjoyable time with the people you relate with on a regular basis. Both are important.

Faulty Paradigm #6   *Use logic and facts to be persuasive.* We all like to believe that human beings are logical people, but remember our previous discussion about the mind-set "people are emotional first, rational second." There are times when people make decisions based solely on logic and facts, but you may be surprised how rare that is.

Remember that information given to others is filtered through their beliefs, values, mind-sets, and preconceived notions. Just because you present logical information doesn't mean that the person listening to you will receive logical information. The level of distortion, deletion, and generalization is remarkable. This paradigm also implies the faulty assumption that logic is something that can be commonly understood by all (if that were the case, then debate classes would not exist). However, regardless of how well the logic is understood, good decision makers almost always check their gut feeling. Logic and facts are good, but actual decisions are highly influenced by emotions.

If you rely on logic and facts to persuade others, then you're rejecting what may be the most effective tool you have, that of emotional persuasion. If you spend enough time losing debates when logic is on your side, you are likely to become highly frustrated and critical of the group and the people in it—and that just compounds the ineffectiveness.

The mind-set of "people are emotional first, rational second" is not being utilized here. Nor is the mind-set of "understand that you will never understand." If frustration and criticism of the group follow, this difficulty often leads to a failure to use the responsibility mind-set and to take responsibility for the undesirable results.

These perspectives may be new to you. Whether these faulty paradigms are applied to the business context, as they were above, or to the context of relationships and family, they are still equally problematic. Relationships built on "hard work" don't necessarily succeed. When you try to rebuild a relationship based on the feedback from your partner, that doesn't necessarily make things work out. In your family or relationships, you may feel as if you're doing a "good job," but that won't necessarily create great relationships. Your good work won't necessarily "speak for itself," nor will your attempts at being logical help matters much either.

Each commonly accepted "rule" fails to recognize the importance of *influence* and subsequently fails to apply the vital mind-sets of responsibility, win-win, and synergy. By accepting your role in the process of influencing and persuading and by applying each of these mind-sets in your future, it will be easier for you not only to make sense of the challenges you're faced with, but also to empower yourself to respond to them in productive, healthy, supportive ways.

Manipulation—It Just Doesn't Work

We just looked at several faulty paradigms with the intention of unlearning them. These were paradigms that may have been directing your actions, albeit not in very effective ways. Now it's time to unlearn some other faulty paradigms that could be needlessly impeding your success. It's time to address the problems and misperceptions associated with manipulation.

Whenever an effective body of information comes along that can reach people at deep levels, especially when it talks about persuasion and influence, the question of possible misuse inevitably comes up. NLP is one of those effective bodies of knowledge, and this becomes strikingly obvious in a very short matter of time.

Like anything else, NLP can be misused. However, because NLP is related to the processes of interacting and relating with people, it is not as easy to misuse as you might first believe. And the relative minority of people who try to misuse it find out very quickly that negative manipulation just doesn't work.

Although the dictionary definition of "manipulation" is relatively neutral, the common usage of the word has definite negative connotations. In this book, when I refer to manipulation, I am referring to the negative misuse of the process—the deceitful, win-lose, selfish approach of tricking others to do things that are not in their best interest, just for the sake of personal gain.[2]

However, not everything you may have come to associate as being manipulation is necessarily so. In fact, many people have mistaken perceptions about what constitutes manipulation, and these misunderstandings impede their ability to get results in their life. This is unnecessary and wasteful.

Many people mistake the useful process of knowing what you are doing as being negative manipulation. However, these two things are very different. As we just discovered, the process of achieving excellence in any skill, whether it's the skill of communication or that of learning to sing, involves steps that include knowing what you are doing. Conscious competence (Step 3 of the process of learning) is a required part of achieving skill in anything.

When people try to avoid conscious competence with their communication skills out of a fear of being manipulative, they unnecessarily impede themselves from making improvement. They confine themselves to doing what they already do (unconscious competence, Stage 4) and to staying incompetent with the rest (unconscious and conscious incompetence, Stages 1 and 2). They allow themselves the freedom to unlearn (Stages 4 to 2), but prevent themselves from gaining the benefit of relearning (Stages 2 to 3 to 4).

For improvement to take place, an integral part of the process is to perform the skills with volition and to be aware of what you are doing when you are doing it. This is not negative manipulation—rather, it is an important component of achieving excellence.

Another misperception about negative manipulation is that it works. But it does *not* work. In fact, in the overall scheme of things, negative manipulation is one of the surest ways to create failure. It's the only sure way I know of to make every single process in this book fail without question.

It tears the living heart out of every useful part of the communication process and wounds so deeply that recovery is virtually impossible. There are instances where people who are manipulating in this way make short-term gains. They cheat a little here, lie a little there, and before you know it, you're stuck with something that just isn't right. Do you remember when used car dealers were almost universally perceived to be hucksters who passed off "lemons" to unsuspecting customers? Years ago, the public was relatively unaware of these kinds of tactics, and people fell prey to them relatively often. But people soon realized they were being taken advantage of. They noticed that they felt bad about these kinds of deals and that they didn't want to do things that way any more. And the unscrupulous people started to have a more difficult time of things. In the long-term, the people doing the manipulating paid the price for their deeds, and only a tiny few continue trying to do business in that way. In the used car business, companies based on integrity have essentially displaced the used car lots plagued with shady reputations.

Today, we are wise to these tricks. In fact, we have our antennae up at all times, ready to detect even the slightest hint of manipulation. Regardless of your ideas about intuition and gut feelings, you are probably familiar with that gut-level hunch that tells you whom you can trust and whom you cannot. This is almost universal. Although many people still have the idea that they have to be on the constant lookout for negative manipulation, nothing could be further from the truth. Negative manipulation is easy to spot.

In the larger scheme of things, you'll find that the manipulator is actually someone who could use your help and support. Negative manipulation is a symptom of a problem. The person doing the manipulating mistakenly thinks that he or she has to approach the world in a one-sided, selfish, "look out for number one" kind of way in order to get results. This symptom is representative of a skewed sense of the world and actually prevents the person doing the manipulating from getting results. It is a symptom of a problem that the person doing the manipulating does not know how to solve.

The techniques in this book are powerful and effective, but they work only when they are used in conjunction with a supportive set of empowering beliefs and mind-sets. These beliefs and mind-sets are *required* in order to make the techniques work. At the very heart of that supporting structure is the philosophy of win-win. To try to use these ideas and skills in a negatively manipulative way would require discarding the very aspects that make them work. It would be like trying to ride a bicycle without wheels.

Negative manipulation is a desperate, futile approach. When you give people better options, they will choose to *solve* their problems, rather than contribute to them.

As we proceed through this book, you will continue to see how interwoven the concept of win-win is with the process of human relations, and you will continue to be supported in developing your skills with the highest integrity.

GREAT INFORMATION AND GOOD INTENTIONS CAN BE OVERSHADOWED BY FEARS OF MANIPULATION —THIS IS YET ANOTHER GOOD REASON TO CONSTANTLY STRIVE FOR WIN-WIN.

This opens the way for the transition from unlearning to relearning, which we can now fruitfully begin.

Relearning—The Value of Strategies

When the question is "How do you climb to the top of a mountain?" the first part of the answer is "Decide to do it." The second part of the answer is "One step at a time."

This reasoning is particularly true when it comes to reaching your goals. Each major goal in your life involves a decision to reach for the goal. Then the accomplishment of that goal involves a tremendous number of smaller actions, or some inaction, on your part. When your smaller actions are planned and organized, they build together to form a path toward your goal, each action working together with the others.

This organized approach creates synergy. Each independent action is more effective when combined with the other actions. They build on each other.

One of the things that effective people understand is that achievement is a *process*, not an event. If you want to be an Olympic swimmer, you don't wait until the day of the race and then just show up. You pursue a course of action that takes you from where you are now to where you want to be. The same thing goes for getting a raise, developing a relationship, nurturing a friendship, and all the other activities in your life that may be important to you. It also applies to the less understood processes we call people skills.

A sequence of behaviors designed to bring about an outcome is referred to as a *strategy*.[3] Strategies are descriptions that represent and help us understand *processes*.

Many times, the success you achieve is not directly related to how well you perform individual tasks. Nor is it directly related to how well you perform the entirety of tasks in your strategies. In many instances, the level of success you achieve is related to the quality of your strategy.

Consider the following example. Suppose you're a weekend tennis player. You've spent many years of your life playing tennis, and you've developed some very good shots. You're athletic, you've got a good grasp of the game, you're in good shape, and you enjoy it. You have a strong forehand and reasonably strong backhand, a great serve, and a pretty good volley. You can hit long rallies of points with consistency, and you often have as many as ten to fifteen groundstrokes in your points. You do fairly well playing your friends, but you lose more often than you win, and you'd like to improve. How do you improve?

You ask your friends for advice, and they give you some general guidelines. They've seen you play, and they tell you they have a good idea what you need to do. They tell you to be more aggressive and to "work" the points. They say to get a "feel" for when to make your moves and to use your strengths as "weapons." They tell you to look for times to take charge and to "force things" with your opponent. They say not to get so mad and to keep your cool. And above all, concentrate! This is all very good advice, but you're not sure exactly how to use it.

So you talk to other friends. They tell you to work on your strokes more. Make your forehand even better. Make it a true weapon. Fine-tune your backhand. Make it more consistent. Of course, this will take a lot of time. You'll need to practice. But, you're told, you've got the potential to take your game to the next level. Within a year or two, you'll probably be able to play in the next higher division. But again, you'll have to work at it. You can't expect your game to improve overnight. Some people spend years playing the game and never have sound strokes, so be patient. You'll get there. Sound familiar? It may, because it is a very common approach.

But you decide to hire me as your coach. You find very quickly that I see things differently. I tell you that your strokes are already good enough for you to be playing at the next level. Instead of working extra hard on the things you already do well, I counsel you to take a different approach. I give you a new playing strategy.

Up until now, you played the baseline game. You had long rallies and long points. But I tell you to do something different. I tell you to hit to your opponent's backhand and rush the net. Just do that, and your results will improve a level immediately. That's what I tell you.

You try it, and you notice that your opponents don't handle that strategy very well. They feel under pressure to hit a good backhand, and they miss the shot. Or they hit it right to you, and you put it away. Or they try to lob, and your overhead is too strong for them. Within ten minutes, you move up to the next level. Your skill level is the same, but your strategy has just improved, and so have your results.

A friend of mine gave me this strategy years ago when I was playing competitive tennis. He gave it to me in the middle of the first set in a match that I was losing badly. By the end of that set, my game had literally improved to another level. It took only a few minutes! I won the match easily after that.

Sometimes, immediate quantum increases in improvement are possible through the application of more effective strategies. Sometimes, you already have all the skills you need, and you just need an effective process in which to apply them.

In the personal development field, there is one term that is usually condemned and criticized almost as fast as it's said. That's the term *quick fix*. Many of the quick-fix techniques that have been shared do not rest on a sound base of principles and are not effective. For people experiencing real problems, hoping for real solutions, failures resulting from incomplete presentation of material can be disheartening. As a result, just the mention of having a quick-fix technique is enough to draw criticism and condemnation in a hurry.

However, don't throw the baby out with the bath water! There will be times when you already have all the principles and skills needed, and a new strategy is all you need. I've had numerous examples in my life where I turned a losing situation into a winning situation just over the course of a few minutes—through being told about and applying a new strategy. It's just as possible in the field of human relations as it is in tennis.

Some of the different processes you learn in this book might give you immediate results. It may be that some of these strategies are exactly right for you, and you already have everything else in place to use them right away. When that's the case, take advantage of the strategies to their fullest extent.

In the earlier tennis example, I described four common methods of attempting improvement. The first is typified by the "be more aggressive, and work the points" advice. While this may be a useful way of approaching the situation, it routinely fails to create the desired improvement. It's like saying, "be a better listener, and ask questions." It's good advice, but it doesn't give you the steps you need to succeed at the task.

The second method is the "don't get so mad" approach. This is an example of the confusion between symptoms and results. Anger is a result of ineffective play, not the cause. Being able to control your emotions is certainly an effective strategy for solving certain problems, but it won't necessarily address the weakness in your game. (Interestingly, top professional athletes often try to get angry before a big game, reporting that it helps their performance.)

The third method is the "work harder on your game" approach. It advocates that you do more of what you're doing and do it better. Many people believe this concept will lead to improvement. But it's like telling a manager who's a poor communicator to "talk to your people more." If his communication is causing problems, then telling him to do more of it won't help the situation. This approach drives people to dig a deeper rut, whether it's effective or not.

The fourth method is the one that I ascribe to. It's to provide a sound strategy (perhaps a different strategy from the one in place) and to describe it in understandable terms. It is to give you a level of detail that is easy to understand, in a way that makes it easy for you to apply.

For example, here is a more detailed description of the strategy of hitting to the backhand and running to the net:

1. Rally from the baseline until you get a short ball on your opponent's backhand side of the court.
2. Hit a deep, low approach shot down the line to his backhand.
3. Charge the net.
4. At the time when your opponent is about to hit the shot, slow down your momentum, and take a split step.
5. Hit the first volley deep and down the line.
6. Close in on the net after hitting that volley.
7. On the next volley, look for an opportunity to hit an angled volley to win the point.

If you're not a tennis player, this strategy may not make a lot of sense, but you can still see the level of detail involved. This strategy worked so well for me because (1) it was a good strategy, (2) I understood it, (3) I knew specifically how to apply it immediately, and (4) I already had the incremental skills required for each step (I already knew how to hit groundstrokes and volleys and so on).

In the pages that follow, you're going to start to see a lot of numbers. But these numbers won't have anything to do with math; they will be the numbers identifying steps in a variety of very useful, very important strategies. I think you will find that this is an effective approach for helping you improve your specific results.

Three Steps in Effective Communication

The first new strategy that we are going to examine covers the overall process of communicating effectively. In a nutshell, the process can be condensed into three distinct elements. They are:

1. Know what you really want. Get in touch with your true core.
2. Find out what the other person really wants. Go beyond the surface words.
3. Use influence and persuasion skills to help both of you get what you really want.

This is the model of communication that I subscribe to, and it is the basis upon which the rest of this book is built. It applies equally well whether you are interviewing for a new job or deciding where to go for dinner. If you organize your strategies of communicating around this framework, you may find it easier to see how each specific activity contributes to the whole.

Steps 1 and 2 are two facets of the same process, and both are addressed in the next two chapters. With Step 1, you are asked to get in touch with your core feelings and your core desires. You are asked to be clear about what you want, not so much with words, but with body, mind, and spirit. There is a difference between intellectually wanting something and wanting it with your heart and soul.

I'm sure that you've found that you don't always know what you really want, at least not until you take the time to ask yourself and listen to the answer. In addition, you've probably found that sometimes you act as if you want something that you know in your heart you really don't want. This lack of clarity is the first thing you'll want to address when increasing your ability to communicate. This is what Step 1 is meant to call your attention to and help you address.

And as much as you may fail to clarify things to yourself, it's helpful to realize that other people do it too. Step 2 is the process of gathering information from other people, while offering them the opportunity to explore and become exceedingly clear about what they really want.

Step 3 addresses the processes involved in getting from where you both are to where you both want to be. It includes an underlying reliance upon the mind-set of effectiveness; and despite the fact that it involves "influence and persuasion," you'll find that it is cooperative, not controlling. This step involves a greater number of specific skills than Steps 1 and 2 and these specific skills are the topic of five upcoming chapters in this book.

This model of communication is a process that can help you change the circumstances in your life. The next several chapters will give you the details about *how* to do this.

CHAPTER 5

NONVERBAL LISTENING SKILLS

WE'RE ABOUT TO SPEND a lot of time learning about something that you might think you already know how to do. We're going to give a lot of attention to the details of something you might think you've been doing your whole life. But unless you've already been trained in the field of NLP, it's a safe bet that you're about to find out a lot more about the process of listening than you ever thought possible.

An effective listener is more prone to be a great lover, a good friend, a star employee, even a smarter person. However, listening *more* and listening *more intently* do not make you a better listener. Many people think listening is simply a matter of hearing words with your ears and paying attention. However, there's a world of communication that can't be reached with your ears, and it eludes even the most heightened sense of awareness.

As I refer to listening in this book, I will continue to expand the definition to include processes that ask you to use all the senses available to you. When you listen to others, you will use your eyes to see things, your ears to hear both words and tonality, your kinesthetic awareness to sense things, your intellect to analyze sentence structure, and perhaps even your nose and taste buds, too. When you listen to yourself, you will use each of these things as well.

This is the fuller process of receiving and interpreting communication from another human being—and also from yourself. It entails an entire body of information that you may never have realized existed.

All the processes you are about to learn are designed to make you a better listener and to create higher quality win-win arrangements in all aspects of your life. These processes are likely to be different from what you are consciously aware of doing now, and they will make you conscious of very important information that may seem "hidden" or "subtle." In a society where it's inappropriate to stare or to probe, sometimes we don't feel comfortable paying close attention to others. Reservations of this kind are natural and may even be heightened during the consciously incompetent and consciously competent stages of listening, when you're not quite as fluid as you will be in the later unconsciously competent stage. However, remember that these processes we are learning are used every day by ordinary people. They just use them unconsciously. Your ability to learn these techniques and use them will benefit both you and those around you.

I've seen hundreds of people go through the relative clumsiness of the unconsciously incompetent and consciously competent stages, and the ones who maintain constant sight of win-win and respect for other people always succeed—regardless of their level of fluidity. People want to be listened to, and they want to be understood. When you do these two things better, you communicate more effectively, get better results, and increase the quality of your relationships with others. You also know much more quickly if someone does not particularly care for this depth of communication, so you know when it's appropriate to adjust your behavior accordingly. You become more responsive to people, and they appreciate that.

In short, it's time to take your blinders off and explore an entirely new realm of human communication. We begin by learning how to recognize nonverbal communication, which we loosely call "listening."

Nonverbal Behaviors Are Related to Emotional States

Nonverbal communication provides a great deal of information about a person, much of which is related to emotional states. We know this intuitively. Consider the state of sadness. People who are sad almost always tilt their head down and look downward. They don't look up at the sky with open arms and a smile on their face. Even more interesting, if you ask sad people to look toward the sky and tilt their head upward, and if they can do it, they will almost always start to feel better. Instantly!

Le Penseur (The Thinker), by Auguste Rodin, is another example of a commonly observed physical stance, this one commonly representing deep thought. Visionary thinking often manifests itself in a position of looking upward and outward. Fearful states often are manifested as a body that is closed and moving away. Someone who is interested tends to move closer and lean forward. Someone who is angry most likely scowls. We all have everyday experiences of emotional states that are linked with physical bearing and facial expressions.[1]

In addition to these outer manifestations of emotions, there are internal physiological changes that have to do, in part, with natural processes in the body and how it reacts to certain stimuli. These changes include such unconscious responses as an increased heart rate, deeper breathing, or blushing. Consider the relationship between the following emotional states and the inner physiological and outer physical changes associated with them:

- Anger—The heart and breathing rates jump up, and blood flows to hands, preparing the person for a strike. Overall energy jumps up immediately.
- Fear—The heart and breathing rate go up, but blood leaves the face and surges to the legs to allow for fast escape. Momentarily, the body freezes, making it possible to determine if hiding would be better than running.

- Sadness—An overall drop in energy, accompanied by a
  sunken posture and deep breathing, making it easier to
  access contemplative processes.
- Disgust—A response indicating a shun by the senses,
  such as squinting the eyes, turning the face away, curling
  the lip, and wrinkling the nose.
- Love—A relaxed state, increasing blood flow to the lips
  and hands accompanied by an open physical bearing
  and deep breathing, facilitating arousal, contentment,
  and cooperation.
- Curiosity—An increase in energy with a widening of the
  eyes and an increased attention to the senses, facilitating
  the acquisition of more information and interpretation
  of the information given.

These kinds of responses are beyond the control of most
people. Most people never learn how to make their heart
beat jump up twenty beats per minute in an instant or how
to send blood to their face and lips in a moment. Most people
have no idea of how they are breathing—not only how fast,
but also how deeply and from where in their body they are
taking breaths. Most people have no idea that they squint,
stare, fix their vision, look in different directions, widen and
close their eyes while they are talking. Nor do they realize
they turn their ear toward some things and withdraw their
face (both ears) from other things, or that they curl their
lips, wrinkle their nose, flare their nostrils, open their mouth,
lick their lips, and roll their tongue while they are communicating. Most people have no idea when and why they move
toward or away from something, lean forward or back, shift
sideways or face squarely, sink their chest or open it, shift
the weight on their feet from front to back or side to side.

Emotional states are also related to tonal voice characteristics. When people are angry, you can generally hear it
in their voices, regardless of what words they are saying. They
may yell loudly or speak with a forced restraint. When people
are in love, you can often hear that in their voices. They
might speak more deeply and with more resonance. Ten-
year-olds can tell what mood their parents are in just by their
tones of voice. However, as adults, we sometimes forget about

voice tone and instead rely on the words people use, which are often misleading.

Consider the tonal voice characteristics associated with the emotional states we've already described:

- Anger—Volume and projection increase to allow the instillation of fear in listeners.
- Fear—Volume and projection lessen to minimize the potential of drawing attention.
- Sadness—Vocalization becomes breathy and disjointed, inhibiting the ability to communicate verbally, thus encouraging internal thought.
- Disgust—Vocalization is staccato and marked by quick, short outbursts of breath, similar to the process of spitting out unwanted food.
- Love—Vocalization becomes more resonant, perhaps to soothe and charm a would-be lover.
- Curiosity—Vocalization becomes louder, higher-pitched, and staccato, thus helping to gain attention.

Most people are not aware of these responses. How smooth, breathy, staccato, resonant, and high- or low-pitched a voice is generally reflects a person's emotional state. Even loudness is more routinely determined unconsciously than consciously.

Physical bearing, facial expressions, physiological reactions, and tonal voice characteristics are reflective of the kinds of nonverbal characteristics that constitute communication. They reflect changes in emotional states and can clue you in to what experiences a person is having.

So what can we do with this information? How can we use it? How can we make sense of it all? That's what we cover in the next section.

Approaching Objectivity in Your Listening

NLP identifies two distinct processes in nonverbal listening activity. The process of hearing, seeing, and feeling the communication from another person is referred to as using *sensory acuity.* It involves fine-tuning your attentiveness, giving you the ability to detect a whole range of information that is supplementary to semantic communication. Sensory acuity gives you a tremendous amount of information that can be applied in the other distinct part of the listening process, that of *calibration.* Calibration helps you to use and interpret the data gathered in the sensory acuity process. It involves making interpretations based on patterns of behavior that are relatively consistent for a given individual. It is intended to be a relatively objective method of interpreting the data you receive.

Through the applications of sensory acuity and calibration, NLP introduces a new kind of objectivity to the listening process. Although the term *objective listening* is really a misnomer (all human experience is subjective), this phrase serves to highlight our true goal—to gather the most accurate understanding of the information possible with minimal distortion and bias.

To appreciate this attempt more fully, let's look at three pervasive communication problems. All three occur when someone tries to form meaning from a communication received. However, these attempts fail because of an overabundance of subjectivity—that is, a lack of objectivity.

First, many people think that words mean the same thing to everybody. They do, don't they? Don't we have dictionaries that tell us the absolute meaning of words? No, not really. The real meaning of a word is the individual meaning that each person ascribes to it. That means ten different people will have all have different meanings for any given word.

In humans, meanings are not based on a collection of more words (as in dictionaries). Rather, meanings are based on a collection of internal representations of the word, including things like emotional responses; gut feelings; visual images; even internal sounds, smells, and tastes (we'll be discussing this topic in later sections). While a word like *dog* is likely to have a fairly universal meaning, a word like *integrity* typically will not. Consider the words that are really important to us: *love, inspiration, hope, fear, pride, communication, strength,* and so on. Each of these words will have different meanings to every person you meet. Every person!

I've seen a group exercise done many times, always with the same results. A facilitator puts a word on the board and asks each person in the room to say what that word means. The chosen word is an intangible, usually something like *love*. Very quickly, you get to see how incredibly varied our definitions of words can be. For some people, love is a warm fuzzy feeling. But for others, it's an aching pain in their chest, coupled with burden and animosity (that was one person's experience of the word). For others, it's a steadfast commitment. For still others, it's an intellectual decision. You would be amazed at the definitions people have of the words they use every day, and you'd be amazed at how different they are from your own. Reliance upon the semantic meaning of words to establish another person's meaning is a surefire way to create confusion and misunderstanding.

The second pervasive communication problem is that other people try to make sense of your experience using their own experience as a guide. You tell your friend Bill how hurt you are about what your lover said, and he says, "Yeah I know exactly how you feel. That happened to me a bunch of times." Of course, he has no idea how you really feel; you've got an entire life's history of experiences, beliefs, and ideas on which you base your responses, none of which are available to Bill, though he may be well-meaning. Additionally, he received only a tiny amount of data from you on which to base his opinion about your situation.

Yet Bill assumes that the experiences he picked from his own life are very much like the one you started to describe. He assumes that your response to similar circumstances is very similar to what his own response would be. He even assumes that things are so similar that you don't even need to go into all the details, because he's already figured it all out! And after all these assumptions, he actually believes that he really knows *exactly* how you feel!

Reliance upon your own emotional responses to interpret another person's experience is a surefire way to create confusion and misunderstanding—even resentment.

The third recurring communication problem is that of mind reading. Mind reading is the process of describing another person's experience with your own map of reality.

Someone says she's mad, but you decide that there's really sadness under that anger. Someone says a cross word to you, and you decide it's because he thinks you're not paying enough attention to him. Someone takes a deep breath, and you decide that it's because she's discouraged about her circumstances.

The commonly misused "body-language" models are further examples of mind reading. In many body-language models, people who cross their arms are identified as having closed minds. However, most of us have come to realize that people cross their arms for many reasons. Some people cross their arms when they feel cold, or when their shoulder starts to hurt, or when they don't feel comfortable saying what's on their mind—and for many other reasons as well. And they may do different things at different times under different circumstances.

Whether the mind reading comes from our attempts to make sense of the world (using maps, models, or concepts) or whether it comes from our emotional responses (often mistaken as intuitive responses), using mind reading to determine what others are saying is a third surefire way to create confusion and misunderstanding. Each of these communication problems results from a process of being subjective, rather than objective.

FORMING MEANING FROM NONVERBAL BEHAVIOR

Objective listening is much different from the kind of listening that most people are accustomed to. It involves the process of forming meaning from communication; however, it is designed to avoid glaring mistakes and pitfalls, such as those just described. For nonverbal communication, the conceptual process of objective listening can be summarized as:

1. Making precise observations of the person doing the communicating—especially observations of shifts in physical bearing, facial expression, physiology, and voice tone
2. Calling attention to specific shifts that may have meaning
3. Gathering more data about the shifts identified in Step 2, with the intention of eventually determining what meaning they may represent

4. Drawing conclusions based on patterns of behavior
unique to the individual doing the communicating

Step 1 is essentially equivalent to developing and using
your sensory acuity. Steps 2, 3, and 4 constitute the integral
elements of calibration.

Back in the days of the Wild West, some people came to
be known as legendary poker players. They made their live-
lihood, and risked their lives, playing a card game, and they
became exceedingly good at it. The game itself is rudimen-
tary; however, the human interactions that became a part of
the game could be complex. Much of the success of a card
player depended on his ability to know whether someone
was bluffing (attempting to mislead) or not.

The great poker players were legendary in their ability
to notice fine distinctions in physiology. If an opposing player
was sitting across the table, and he raised the bet, you would
want to know if he was bluffing or not. If you noticed that at
the same time he made the bet, his left temple made a slight
twitch, you might want to pay attention to that. Would the
twitch mean he was bluffing? Maybe. Would it mean he was
not bluffing? Maybe not. Would it mean his pants were too
tight? Maybe. In short, you wouldn't know what it meant the
first time you played with him.

"YOU KNOW JESSE, I'VE GOT THE FUNNY FEELING
THAT YOU'RE NOT BLUFFING THIS TIME."

However, if you played poker with this man for several hours, you might start to notice a pattern. It might be that his left temple would twitch each time he bluffed. That would be an important conclusion, which, if consistent, could make a tremendous difference in the outcome of the game.

This example illustrates the processes of using sensory acuity and calibrating. Sensory acuity is used to see the twitch (Step 1 of the conceptual process of effective listening). Calibration is the process of deciding to pay attention to the twitching, to look for a pattern, then to determine whether a correlation exists (Steps 2, 3 and 4 from the conceptual process of effective listening).

Here also is where calibration is different from the commonly understood body-language models. If you play poker tomorrow with a new guy in town, and he has that same twitch in the same part of his left temple, you won't know what it means until you go through the entire process of calibration again. You'll have to play some period of time with this man to see if some pattern exists. The twitch itself doesn't have meaning, but a twitch from a certain person in a certain situation might.

Far More Than Just the Words

Thus far, I've made distinctions between overall communication and nonverbal communication. With sensory acuity and calibration, we are paying attention primarily to the nonverbal aspect of communication. Let's take a closer look at why this may be important and at how important it actually may be.

CATEGORIES OF COMMUNICATION

Three pertinent categories of communication warrant our attention:

1. Words that we use—a small but important percentage of communication
2. Tonal characteristics of voice—a relatively large percentage of communication

3. Body communication—the largest percentage of communication (different from "body language")

Category 1 is about the words that we use. It may surprise you to know that many people consider the semantic meaning of words to convey the least amount of information of each of the three categories of communication. As little as 7 percent of communication may come from the specific words being spoken.[2] Whether that's exact or not, the fact that some experiments show the percentage to be so small is quite surprising to most people.

Category 2 is about the tonal characteristics of the voice. Most people have had experiences where they knew someone was lying or someone was upset or angry just by the tone of voice used. However, experimental results showing that tonal characteristics of voice can constitute as much as 38 percent of conveyed information are surprising to most people.

Category 3 is about body communication. This category is the most significant at as much as 55 percent of communication. Body communication is different from what is commonly understood as body language. (So much questionable material has been passed off as body language that I prefer to use different sets of words to describe the two.) Body communication, as used in this book, is the communication made through bodily movements and changes. It's the communication given by a person's physical bearing, facial expressions, and physiology.[3]

Tonal characteristics and body communication provide a surprising amount of information from sources that don't include the semantic meanings of words. As much as 93 percent of the information you gather in any verbal interchange can be from these two categories. This is specifically what I mean by "nonverbal communication." The term *nonverbal* does include voice characteristics, but not semantic meaning.

We all communicate, and we all know how to communicate, so it should not be a surprise that we communicate extensively in ways that don't include semantic meaning. However, our communication patterns have become unconsciously competent (Stage 4), so most of us are no longer aware of exactly how we communicate. This is why we are surprised when someone tells us that as much as 93 percent of our communication does not include words.

So what kinds of things are we talking about here? How can we recognize nonverbal communication? Are we talking about twitches in the temple? In a way, yes. Let's look at some examples of raw data.

There is a world of things that people do when they communicate. In the face alone, they will clench their jaw, lick their lips, tremble in the mouth, flicker an eyelid, move their head side to side, squint off into the distance, move their eyes all over the place, flare their nostrils, tilt their head, shut their eyes, shake their head no, nod their head yes, wrinkle their forehead, open their mouth, and all kinds of other things. That's not to mention the more subtle things you might see, like a sudden flush, a newly protruding vein, a swelling of the lower lip, a rise in heart rate (observed via the pulsing vein), and so on. In the course of just a fifteen-minute conversation, a person is likely to exhibit many of these behaviors. And that's just in the face.

Breathing is another interesting phenomenon. We all breathe, but did you ever notice that people breathe from different places in their body? Some breathe from high in the chest, others from deep in the abdomen. Breathing rates change frequently; people hold their breath, gasp, take occasional deep breaths, change from nose to mouth, change from smooth breathing to staccato. Even something as simple as breathing can be full of interesting dynamics.

The incredible thing is that any of these observations can end up meaning something very important.

The way people use their body is also interesting. They shift weight from one leg to the other, lean forward, cross their arms, shake their hands back and forth, hold parts of their body, step backward, turn to the side, lean back, put their arms above their head, wring their hands, cover their mouth, cover their eyes, scratch their head, play with their hair, rub their neck, bite their nails, push on their cuticles, shift their weight on their chair, tilt, turn, shake, and even dance, all the while carrying on a fluid, natural conversation.

These are things that you can see; however, there's also more information coming to you from another angle. That's the angle on the side of your head, where your ears are. The tonal characteristics of voice can also vary tremendously. Again, you may not notice this, but right in the middle of a conversation, people will raise their voice, whisper, change to a nasal sound, speed up, slow down, change their method of enunciation, momentarily speak with an accent, increase their resonance, vary their pitch, speak from the diaphragm, speak from the throat, speak with breath, speak while holding the breath, emphasize certain words, smooth out their sounds, speak in a staccato manner, speak out of the side of their mouth, project their voice, hold back their voice, talk sing-song, speak with rhythm, enunciate every syllable, slur their speech, and so on, all the while carrying on a natural, easy conversation and being totally unaware of doing any of these things.

And remember, you're a person too, so everything that I just mentioned is something that you do as well. As we continue our discussion, keep in mind that it is very useful to apply your sensory acuity and calibration skills to yourself just as much as to other people.

What do all these things mean? What does it mean when people speak from their throat? What does it mean when they clench their jaw or squint off into the distance? Well, it depends. It might mean nothing, and it might be the indicator you need to achieve the communication breakthrough of a lifetime. However, you won't know that until you calibrate!

Correlating Behavior with Meaning

The process of using our senses to gather information is something we all do. But we don't always know how to distinguish the important data from the unimportant data.

Sensory acuity simply recognizes data. Calibration begins the process of assigning significance and meaning to the data.

IMPORTANT CATEGORIES OF DATA

There are three situations in which it is especially useful to pay close attention when gathering data:

1. The gathered data seem to be in conflict with other parts of the data set.
2. The gathered data seem to be related to emotional states.
3. The gathered data seem to be related to a sudden change in emotional state (a response or a reaction) related to the circumstances.

In each of these cases, you will generally want to focus your attention on that connection. To think of this in pragmatic terms, imagine yourself at work, where you're about to make a presentation to a group of people. Your goal in the presentation is to sell the group on your idea. Your idea is good, and it's very creative. Selling this idea is very important to you, and this may be your only chance to pitch it.

If you're like most people, you will prepare for this presentation. You may do research on the problem, pull out statistics and data. Perhaps you will graph this information so that it's easy to understand, and you'll present the information in an organized manner. You want people to understand the idea and to follow what you are saying, so you will practice your wording and the sequence in which you present your facts. You might even decide to psych yourself up. Maybe you will wear your lucky suit, which always gives you extra confidence. In short, you may go to a lot of trouble to make your presentation top-notch. You know that the quality of your presentation can make or break your idea.

However, you may overlook some things. Will you take the time to really get to know your own reactions to the material? Are there things you're planning to say that you don't fully believe in, with your heart and soul? Do you feel uncertain about certain parts of your presentation, but not enough to have taken action toward addressing them? Are you sure you really want to sell your idea, or do you have an underlying agenda running in the background that you haven't quite addressed? Do you really believe things will be better for you if you sell your idea, or have you even taken the time to think about that? Depending upon your answers to these questions, you may have some problems brewing that will undermine your entire presentation—at an unconscious level.

But wait, other issues could come into play as well. When you start to make your presentation, will you take special notice of the emotional states of people in the room? How will you know if people are ready to listen to you? Will you notice if people are feeling hostile, close-minded, or fearful? Will you notice if people have hidden agendas? Will you take into account the moods of the people in the room? Do any of these people have vested interests in seeing the project fail? Or in seeing you fail? Will you pay special attention to these kinds of things?

But wait again! What about once you get into the presentation? Are you going to be attuned to how people are responding? How they are changing? Will you notice when people come across something that causes them to react? How will you know if people are having objections or concerns? How will you know if they are paying attention or understanding what you have to say? And with all this going on, are you going to be paying attention to your own emotional states? Would you notice if you started to get angry? Or confused? Or if you started to lose your confidence? Would you remember to make sure you *stayed* psyched up? Would you be aware of how you were responding to the situation?

So let me ask you another question. Don't you think these things are at least of equal importance to the quality of the factual data in your presentation?

Myriads of great ideas get lost in the shuffle because the originators don't persuade others of their worth. Many solutions fall prey to inner conflicts and confusions. Others fall victim to the personal hidden agendas, fears, and power plays. Others get overshadowed by emotional reactions, from both sides.

With all the effort you go to in preparing a presentation, if you are like most people, you will put virtually no effort into really addressing your deeper responses to what you're doing and saying. Nor will you put any effort into getting the group *ready* to consider and accept your ideas. Nor will you address your attention to handling emotional responses. But in one very important way, you are not like most people. You are one of the small minority of people in the world who have already read to this point in this book. This just may be the difference that makes a difference!

To be an effective listener, of both yourself and others, you need to have some important skills:

1. You need to know when a person has internal conflicts regarding a situation (this applies to both yourself and others).
2. You need to know when someone is open to receiving your information.
3. You need to recognize changes in emotional states, and respond to them (this applies to both yourself and others).

People generally don't offer this information verbally. Many people are oblivious to their internal conflicts until they reach extreme levels. Others get so caught up in their emotions that they really aren't aware of what they're doing. (Awareness requires a removed perspective, which is not always easy to come by when someone is in a strong emotional state.) Others just don't feel comfortable or don't feel it's appropriate to express their emotions verbally, if they even know how to verbalize them. Someone in tears, speaking with a trembling voice is far more likely to say "I'm okay, don't worry about me" than to say "I feel so bad that I'm crying and I can't even talk without trembling."

So you won't be able to rely on verbal communication alone. You will want to get the information in other ways. Let's look at each listening skill in isolation.

Incongruencies and Mixed Messages

In the circumstances of our lives, striving toward win-win is predicated on the assumption that you are able to identify a win. That is a big assumption. The Three Steps of Effective Communication begin by asking you to find out what you really want and also what the other person really wants. The word *really* implies that it's not always a straightforward process. And it's not.

In your communications, you will need to know when a person has internal conflicts regarding a situation. That person may be the one you are talking to, a third party who is going to affect or be affected by the process, or you yourself. Your communication will be far more successful when you make sure that all conflicts are cleared throughout the process of communicating.

NLP models of communication support the observation that communication is received through multiple data sets concurrently. When you hear the semantic meaning of words, that is one data set. Simultaneously, you hear the tonal characteristics of words, which is another data set. Also simultaneously, you observe body communication, which is at least another data set. These are examples of *simultaneous communications*. When each of these data sets supports the same interpretation, or meaning, then they are termed *congruent*. When there is a discrepancy between one or more messages, they are termed *incongruent*. Any one data set has the potential to be incongruent with any other.

In addition to simultaneous messages, distinct messages can be conveyed sequentially. This can happen with each type of communication, be it semantic meaning, tonal characteristics, body communication, or combinations of each. *Sequential communication* may be marked by quantum, sudden shifts in how the communication is being offered. This is often exemplified by the "on the one hand…, but on the other hand…" description (which you may notice is often accompanied by equally distinct changes in tonal characteristics and physiology), but can be vastly more subtle as well.

When the sequential messages are supportive of an equivalent meaning, they are termed congruent. When they are discordant with each other, they are termed incongruent.

A useful method of describing certain incongruencies brings into play the concepts of the conscious mind and unconscious mind. Consider what happens if the conscious mind does not necessarily agree with the unconscious mind. What if the conscious mind wants to communicate one thing, and the unconscious mind wants to communicate another thing? Sounds strange, but this description seems to explain some very common observances.

This process results in the delivery of mixed messages. A common example is that of a person consciously wanting to say one thing and expressing it through the semantic meaning of words ("I'm not disappointed"), but unconsciously wanting to communicate another thing and expressing that through body and tonal communication (eyes starting to water, voice wavering, lip quivering).

With these types of incongruencies, the semantic meaning of the words is usually reflective of the conscious mind, and the nonverbal behavior is almost always reflective of the unconscious mind.[4] For most people, their body communication and tonal voice characteristics are primarily a reflection of unconscious communication. As those great poker players of the Wild West came to realize, only a small percentage of people can consciously control things like facial muscles and subtle voice qualities.

You've probably seen incongruencies many times. You ask a friend if he wants to eat Chinese food; verbally, he says, "Yeah, that would be okay," but from the tone of his voice you know he would really rather not. You ask your sister if she's angry with you; verbally she says, "No, I'm not angry," but you notice that her jaw is clenched and she's glaring at you as if she could burn a hole in your face. You ask someone who just fell down a flight of stairs if he's okay; verbally he says, "Yeah, I'm okay," but you notice he's having trouble walking and he's holding on to his arm with a wince of pain so extreme that your arm starts to hurt just looking at him. You ask someone if she understands the instructions you just gave her; verbally she says, "Yeah, I think I got it," but you notice that her face has lost all color and she looks as if she would have trouble telling you her name, much less doing the task at hand.

These are examples of incongruent communication. While I've made some generalizations here, it's still pretty safe to say that some responses are almost universal. When people are gritting their teeth and glaring, and when they have locked up most of the muscles in their body, it's a pretty good bet that they aren't relaxed. It may not always be true, but it will certainly be so a high percentage of the time.

It's a rather interesting aspect of human communication. Someone can say she's not angry and really believe what she is saying. But at a deeper level, she may be communicating another message loudly and clearly for everyone to hear. She will be fully unconscious of her anger.

If you approach her later, after the situation has subsided, in many cases, she will have gained a conscious awareness of that anger and will be able to confirm the alternate communication verbally. The woman may say, "Well of course I did that, I was so angry!" even though earlier, she may have vehemently denied being angry at all.[5]

Recognition of the mixed messages is relatively easy when you simply have a model for the process. Once you realize that there are different messages being conveyed simultaneously and sequentially, it becomes very easy to identify possible incongruencies. However, identification is just part of the process; you need to know how to respond to these incongruencies as well.

So in the case of mixed communication, the question is "Which communication are you 'listening' to, and which communication are you responding to?" If a person says he's "fine," but his body and voice suggest he's upset, which do you "listen" to and which do you respond to (assuming, of course, that you begin to notice the incongruencies)? You've probably noticed incongruent messages many times before, but you've probably never been told how to respond to them. Responding to incongruencies is a vitally important part of listening.

GOOD-NATURED ROVER ALWAYS IMAGINED
THAT HIS SIGN SAID:
"WELCOME TO OUR HUMBLE HOME"

The most respectful thing you can do for people when they provide you with an incongruency (and it happens a lot) is to continue the communication until they become congruent. Continue until they give you the same message both verbally and nonverbally, both consciously and unconsciously. You can do this in a very unassuming way and make it seem natural.

Helping someone become congruent is best done by helping bring the unconscious communication into conscious awareness. You give the person an opportunity to become aware of the conflict and to address it. Conflicts are much easier to clear when both sides are sitting at the negotiating table! Bring the unconscious aspect to the table, and offer it a comfortable, safe chair.

Please take notice of the wording I chose in the previous paragraph. I said to give the person an "opportunity." This means it is an opportunity that others are fully empowered to decline. Just because you offer to help mediate, that doesn't mean that your offer will be accepted. There is no room for unwelcome probing here, and there is no reason to use your new skills to bully the people you are speaking with. If you ever get a congruent message, or a nonverbal message, that indicates that your line of communication is not welcome, then gracefully move on to a different subject and be satisfied with that. (However, do not agree to take action based upon incongruent communication.)

With your refined sensory awareness and your understanding of the process of incongruency, you have the ability to listen and see things that others may not be aware of. This can feel intrusive to some people in some situations, even though they are the ones giving the communication to you. You must be respectful of people at all times in your communication.

However, most of the time, your offer to help mediate will be a welcome one. Most people appreciate it when others take a genuine interest in making things better, and they are appreciative of your taking the time to offer your encouragement. There are a variety of ways to call conscious attention to an unconscious communication. For example, Heather says she really wants to take a new job, but her voice tone and body communication don't seem to be supporting that message. Here are some ideas about how to respond:

1. Match the incongruency, slightly exaggerated: With the same tone of voice and same body communication, say, "Yeah I can see that you do. You definitely want to get going right away on that job and pour your heart and soul into it." Often, seeing the incongruency externally is enough to call attention to it internally.

2. Call direct attention to the incongruency: "Oh come on. Who are you trying to convince? Me or you? You can't even say that without cringing at the thought." This response may draw immediate denial (exemplifying the conflict), but if you stay with it, you are likely to help this person bring resolution to the incongruency.

3. Call direct attention to unconscious processes or inner self: In a compassionate way, say, "Are you really sure about this? When you reach down deep, is there anything that you need to look at? Is this really something that is going to inspire you and give you the fulfillment you deserve?"

4. Offer your intuitions about encompassing processes: These are hunches or guesses, but they sometimes help bring the other person's awareness to a higher logical level in which they can see things from a larger perspective. "Aren't you just running away from the problems at your current job?" "Aren't you just looking for some excitement and change in your life?" "Aren't you just avoiding the fact that this profession isn't really the best for you?" It's not a matter of guessing right, it's a matter of being close enough so that you motivate the person to think more holistically about what's going on.

5. Temporarily speed up or accelerate the process: An incongruency will almost always make itself known at some point; however, that point is often later in the process. By giving the perception that the process is speeding up, the incongruency often surfaces right away. "You definitely want that job? Great. Let's go ahead and write your resignation letter, then take the rest of the afternoon to go look for a new apartment closer to your new office."

In many cases, an incongruency is a simple matter to clear up and can be done right away. Given a little prompting, Heather will get in touch with what's going on and be able to respond in a way that is more representative of her true desires and needs. Once the incongruency is cleared, or the unconscious messages are brought into conscious awareness, the words will start to be congruent with the body and tone. In other cases, this takes more than one conversation or takes a period of time. Regardless, it's important to continue to address the incongruencies until they're resolved.

Agreements and actions based on incongruent verbalizations are not win-win. They often break down in later stages or result in feelings of having been taken advantage of, regret, or anger. If you fail to achieve congruent communication from others or if your offers of assistance toward resolving incongruencies are not accepted, then I encourage you to avoid taking action or making agreements based on the incongruencies. Such agreements will almost always lead to difficulties and problems down the road. You will be far more effective when you base your agreements with others on *congruent* communication.

This process applies equally well to you. If you have unresolved incongruencies, then the actions and agreements you consciously accept can also lead to difficulties and problems down the road. Helping others resolve their incongruencies is Step 2 in the Three Steps of Effective Communication, but resolving your own is Step 1.

Incongruency is a natural part of human communication (natural, but not necessarily effective), and it contributes to making the communication process somewhat more confusing. That's okay. You can deal with it effectively, and by doing so, you can make your process of communication much better, much more respectful, much more gratifying.

EXAMPLES OF POSSIBLE INCONGRUENCIES

Although I've mentioned that incongruencies occur frequently, I haven't yet given you many examples, and these can be important in helping you identify incongruencies. In the following list, I have identified some things that often reflect incongruent communication; however, these examples are not based on hard and fast rules. People are different, and they respond differently in varying circumstances. The more accurate meaning of their behavior is best obtained through your thorough and objective calibration. These examples identify situations in which you may want to pay extra attention to a *potential* conflict. They could be inapplicable as often as they are applicable; however, they will give you some ideas about the kinds of things you might look for:

> **Denial of emotions** *He says he feels fine, but you notice:* a clenched jaw, a tremble in the mouth, a shake of the head no, a tremble in the facial muscles, holding of the breath, a gasp, waving of hands back and forth, a step backward, a movement backward, water coming to the eyes, covering of the mouth, increased nervous movements, a holding back of the voice, a lowering of volume of voice, and increased tension around the eyes.
>
> *Or you notice the same sensory observations that you have previously calibrated for this person as:* pain, sadness, hurt, fear, feeling upset, confusion.

Portrayal of emotions   *She says she feels great, motivated, excited, energized, happy, fulfilled, but you notice:* her tone of voice is bland, her face lacks color, her jaw is clenched, she has a slack jaw, she momentarily closes her eyes, she holds her breath, she waves her hand back and forth, she steps or moves backward, she covers her mouth, she covers her eyes, she has tension around her eyes.

Or you notice the same sensory observations that you've previously calibrated for this person as: boredom, disappointment, sadness, hurt, a feeling of being stuck, pain, depression.

Yes/No   *He says yes, but you notice:* he simultaneously shakes his head no, or says no but simultaneously nods his head yes.

Decisions   *She says she's made up her mind, but you notice:* her voice wavers; her mouth trembles; she shakes her head no; she covers her mouth; she has excessive tension around her eyes, nose and mouth; she continues to verbally explain her choice, even though you don't need an explanation or convincing; she is pausing as if to keep thinking about it.

Or you notice the same sensory observations that you've previously calibrated for this person as: indecisiveness, confusion, regret, or anguish.

Demonstration of behavior   *He says he wants things to be a certain way, but you notice:* he simultaneously demonstrates an opposite behavior (that is, he says he wants to get going, but he simultaneously sits back in his chair as if he's not going anywhere).

Evaluations   *She says that something was good, enjoyable, nice, great, super, fine, wonderful, but you notice:* a clenched jaw; a tremble in the mouth; a shake of the head no; a tremble in the facial muscles; a holding of the breath; a gasp; an extra breath in the voice; water coming to the eyes; a holding back of the voice; a lowering of volume of voice; a momentary closing of the eyes; tension around the eyes, nose, and mouth; increased redness of face; loss of redness to face.

Or you notice the same sensory observations that you've previously calibrated for this person as: displeasure, disappointment, resentment, fear, anger, detachment, regret, boredom.

Desires   *He says he'd rather not have, do, take something, but you notice:* his eyes and attention are fully fixed on that something.

Or you notice the same sensory observations that you've previously calibrated for this person as: desire, excitement, anticipation, hope, delight, motivation, jealousy.

He says he would really like, want, desire, enjoy, hope for, value, appreciate something, but you notice: a voice quiver, loss of attention, a move backward, a holding back of the voice, a momentary shutting of the eyes, a slackened jaw, a loss of color in the face.

Or you notice the same sensory observations that you've previously calibrated for this person as: boredom, withdrawal, detachment, displeasure, fear, restraint, indecisiveness, low energy, confusion.

Compliments *She says you are loving, caring, charming, passionate, daring, colorful, funny, sexy, sensitive, vital, a good friend, sensual, but you notice:* a clenched jaw, a tremble in the mouth, a shake of the head no, a tremble in the facial muscles, a holding of the breath, a gasp, extra breath in the voice, a holding back of the voice, a lowering of volume of voice, a momentary closing of the eyes, tension around the eyes, nose, and mouth, loss of redness to face.

Or you notice the same sensory observations that you've previously calibrated for this person as: withdrawal, detachment, displeasure, disappointment, boredom, or restraint.

Obviously, this is not an exhaustive list, and it may raise more questions than it answers. The important thing to remember is to avoid creating your own brand of body language, where you interpret any one behavior to always mean a certain thing. Instead, look for things that *might* mean something, then communicate with the person to find out what's really going on.

Rapport

Whenever you communicate with someone else, you will be cognizant of the level of rapport established, especially with people you deal with regularly. This will give you some ideas about how open this person is to receiving your information. On the flip side, you will also need to be aware of how much rapport you are feeling and should monitor your own level of receptivity as well.

To understand and benefit from the process of rapport, you must first know what it is; second, recognize it in others; and third, be able to help create it. Let's begin by clarifying what I mean when I use the word *rapport.*

Rapport is the state of feeling in harmony with another person. It means that you are receptive to hearing what the other person might have to say, and it involves being comfortable with the other person on an unconscious level. NLP posits that people are most comfortable with those they perceive to be most like themselves, and rapport is generated by reducing the perceived differences at an unconscious level.

Rapport is usually necessary for creating receptivity to communication. When you are in rapport with other people, you will be open to hearing what they have to say, to considering their new or different ideas; and you will be willing to understand things from their point of view. If you lack rapport, none of these things are likely to apply, even when you think you can be rational about communication. Remember that people are emotional first, rational second. An emotional state, such as a feeling of disharmony, can affect perception in ways beyond conscious awareness.

While rapport is an emotional state of harmony, it isn't the same as liking someone. Rapport is the means by which two people who don't necessarily like each other can communicate with each other in a functional way. When you communicate, you will have occasion to deal with people whom you like very much. When you are feeling particularly amiable and friendly, you will most likely be very responsive to their communication. The rapport and the liking will go hand in hand. These are not the times in which you need to have excellent communication skills. In fact, in these situations, you can use relatively lousy communication skills and still be effective with your communication.

But this will not be the case all the time. There will be times when you need to communicate with someone whom you don't particularly like, who may not particularly like you. In these cases, the skill level you have in communication will be critical in determining how effective you are.

Many of the situations in your life will necessitate functional communication with people you don't know, people you don't particularly care for, and people you may not like at all. However, by reducing the perceived differences between the two of you at an unconscious level, you pave the way for allowing functional communication. Rapport is not about getting a warm and fuzzy feeling when you talk to someone; rather, it is the means by which functional communication can be achieved in a respectful way. It is the means by which two people can start a communication from different places, but allow themselves to come closer together. It is the emotional state that assists us in feeling that it is safe to communicate, and from which permission to influence and persuade is freely given.

Once you are very clear about what rapport is, then you can start to be very clear about knowing when rapport has been achieved.

In your own experience, you can recognize a feeling of rapport just as you would recognize any emotional state. You feel it. This feeling will generally be akin to feelings of safety, receptivity, open-mindedness, willingness to listen, and willingness to consider another person's viewpoint. When you search your own feelings about and emotional responses to another person, you will easily know whether you feel in rapport or not.

However, the process for knowing if another person is feeling rapport is different. Since you can't read another person's mind, nor ever really know what another person is feeling, you need to have other ways of gauging the level of rapport. This is done through the methods of calibration already discussed. To speed things up, and to give you a starting point, I'd like to call attention to certain observations that are often related to levels of rapport.

*When people are **not** in rapport, they are likely to be experiencing emotions such as:* distraction, agitation, boredom, unconcern, annoyance, anxiety, embarrassment, fear, frustration, resentment, anger, bitterness, contempt, restraint, spite, or irritation.

The sensory observations that indicate these emotions will vary, but you might look for: a shake of the head "no"; a wince or grimace or other sign of tension in the facial muscles; a failure to maintain eye contact; darting glances; yawning; wandering eyes; tension in the muscles around the eyes; knitted eyebrows; constricted pupils; a waving of hands back and forth; a leaning backward; more distance being kept between you than normal; an interruption or attempt to interrupt; objects being placed between the two of you (such as the other person's sitting in a chair backwards); a turning away; a running away; tones of voice that sound harder, sharper, shriller, less resonant, more strongly projected, or louder; tightly crossed arms; tightly crossed legs; tension in the jaw; a clenching of the teeth; chewing motions; hands made into fists; energetic movements and tension in the hands (wringing, squeezing, pressing); kicking motions; pacing back and forth; frequent shifting of weight; expressions in the mouth; flaring of nostrils; increased blood flow to the face (more red color); decreased blood flow to the face (less red color); increased blood flow to the hands (more red color); swallowing harder than usual; and many other things.

When people are *feeling a state of rapport, they are likely to be experiencing emotions such as:* harmony, comfort, interest, curiosity, relaxation, attraction, security, delight, satisfaction, acceptance, sympathy, empathy, forgiveness, affection, approval, delight, graciousness, thanks, love, tenderness, even sensual attraction.

The sensory observations that indicate these emotions will vary, but you might look for: a nodding of the head "yes"; relaxed facial muscles; steady eye contact; a licking of the lips; breathing through the nose; relaxed muscles around the eyes ("soft eyes"); a twinkle in the eyes; dilation of pupils; relaxed eyebrows; relaxed forehead; hands in open positions (palms up or directed toward the body); gesturing toward the body; leaning forward with the body; leaning forward with the head; slight tilting of the head (often adjusts ear positions); relaxation of the jaw; a mouth slightly open; moving closer than usual; verbal utterances of agreement and understanding ("uh huh," "yeah," "right," "okay," "mm mm"); keeping the space between you open and clear; turning to face you; opening of arms; opening of chest and shoulders; tones of voice that sound softer, more resonant, less strongly projected, or reduced in volume; open and relaxed arms; open and relaxed legs; massaging of self; playing with the hair; shifting of weight which seems more measured; deep diaphragmatic breathing; increased blood flow to the lips and mouth (enlarged lips, more color); increased moisture in the mouth; and many other things.

Although none of these observations may be related to levels of rapport at all, in many cases they will have some correlation. Remember that physical bearing, facial expressions, and physiology are directly related to emotional states, so all these observations convey some meaning; however, the specific meaning you choose to correlate with your observations should depend upon your observation of consistencies and patterns. In the case of rapport, you will want to correlate your sensory acuity observations with your observations of the acceptance that you gain from your messages, ideas, and proposals.

Changes in Emotional States

The final aspect of objective listening that I'd like to call your attention to is that of noticing responses. Communication is an adaptive process of taking action, noticing responses, adjusting behavior, and taking more action. In your dealings with others (and yourself), you will want to take special notice of the *changes* that occur (these are the responses) and gear your communication toward them.

Suppose you're making a sales presentation to a prospective client. You talk about your product and its benefits, and things are going along swimmingly. But you mention something, and suddenly the client leans back in her chair, takes a deep breath and moves her hand to her chin, covering her mouth. She does all this without saying a word. Verbally there is no communication; however, these sudden physical changes indicate a sudden change in her emotional state. Wouldn't you like to know what's going on? Wouldn't you like to know if this means she suddenly discovered a major problem, or if she just determined a much broader use for the product? Don't you think it will be important to your interaction?

Suppose you're speaking to your boss about your future with the company. You're having a fairly reasonable conversation, until he says that you're next in line for a promotion. At this point, you notice that his voice wavers, he discontinues eye contact, and he shakes his head no at the same time. Don't you want to know what's going on here? Don't you want to know if there's a problem, or if you've been blackballed in some way? Don't you want to know if there's a problem that might hinder your promotion?

Although both of these situations indicate incongruent communication as well, the more important aspect of the interactions is the sudden changes that occurred. Sudden changes in nonverbal communication can be your clue that there's something that really needs to be addressed. Verbally, you aren't always offered the quality of communication that you may wish to have. However, nonverbal communication supplements the words very well, and together, they can help you get more of the messages that you need to get.

When there is a sudden change in the nonverbal message being given, you may wish to explore that message further. This involves the process of creating a receptive, safe environment for the other person to explore the unconscious meaning (if he or she is not aware of it already) and to share it with you.

If your sales client changes state suddenly, you probably should respond to it. You might momentarily stop your presentation, and ask, "Did I say something that we need to talk about?" If you get an incongruent, "No, you can go on," then you might say, "Well okay, we can continue [pacing the conscious, verbal communication], but sometimes these kinds of presentations will bring up issues that need to be discussed. For example, if a client hears something one way and thinks it might be a problem, then sometimes that indicates a misunderstanding or a lack of information. Sometimes I just don't explain myself exactly the right way, or I just make a mistake. Other times it means that there's a problem to be solved, but it can't get solved unless I know about it. You know what I mean?" You give the client an opportunity to think about what's going on and to share what's going on in a space of receptivity and win-win.

If your boss becomes incongruent when talking about your next promotion, you might focus your attention on that subject. You might say, "Well, you know that's an interesting thing to say. You know, I really do want to get that promotion, but sometimes I wonder if it will ever really happen. You never really know. There may be some things I'm not doing right that could get in the way. Things I don't even know about. Or I may have pissed off the wrong person and not even know it. Or maybe the company's going to restructure or get bought out or something. I might be looking for a job sooner than I get a promotion. Do you ever feel that way?" Again, you give your boss an opportunity to think about what's going on and to share what's going on in a space of receptivity and win-win. It certainly is easier for people to talk about a difficult subject if you bring it up and genuinely want to talk about it!

We'll cover more about how to structure your words in very effective ways in later chapters. For now, it's primarily important to realize that you need to respond to the nonverbal and unconscious communication, and often need to flush it out more.

Listening to Yourself

This chapter directed our attention to a wide variety of concepts and methods for communicating. Although much of it may seem to have been directed toward your ability to receive information from others, it was also intended to address your ability to receive information from yourself. This is a large part of Step 1 of the Three Steps of Effective Communication (Know what you really want—get in touch with your true core).

Let's briefly review some of the ideas presented in this chapter, now with a total focus on listening to your own *nonverbal* communication.

It's very helpful to use sensory acuity and calibration on yourself. Now that you have specific things to look for (voice characteristics, body gestures, breathing shifts, body movements, and so on), you are better able to notice your own nonverbal communication. The calibration process is much easier for yourself, too, because you have direct access to recognizing your own emotional states. If you notice that your temple is twitching every time you bluff, you may not be able to stop the twitch (although the process of anchoring later in this book may help with that, too), but you can immediately recognize whether or not you're bluffing at the time. The guy sitting across the table will need "to play several hands" to make that determination!

Incongruencies seem to be a part of many people's lives, and you probably experience them on a regular basis. When you continue to use your sensory acuity with yourself, you will have a better idea about when you are communicating incongruently. Again, the process for addressing it is the same as it is for others; bring the unconscious communication into conscious awareness. Each time you notice yourself acting incongruently, become introspective and honestly ask yourself what message that nonverbal behavior may be trying to communicate. When you explore your internal processes in this way, many or most of your incongruencies will clear up very quickly, and your future communications on the topic will likely be highly congruent.

Ongoing congruence in your communication is one of the fastest, most effective ways to increase your effectiveness in communicating and your overall results in life.

Monitoring your own levels of rapport with others is also very useful. If you feel out of rapport with someone, there is a good chance that the other person will be feeling that way, too. Monitoring your own level of rapport with another person and taking steps to keep it appropriate for the situation at hand will help keep the overall atmosphere more receptive.

In addition, being in rapport with yourself is also important. Beating yourself up, criticizing yourself, and feeling bad about yourself are surefire ways to hinder the process of communicating with others. In Chapter 11, we cover methods to address these issues directly; however, the framework adopted in this chapter is equally helpful. Give yourself the space to freely and safely explore the issues, and address them in a conscious way. You are the most important person you will ever know, and you can allow yourself the space to be human.

And finally, changes in your physical bearing, facial expressions, physiology, and tonal voice characteristics are going to indicate changes in your emotional states as well. Again, when you direct your sensory acuity toward yourself, you will have another channel for noticing your emotions. We live in a society where emotions are generally not valued as much as intellect, so it's natural that many of us have learned to ignore or squash our emotions. However, they're still there, and it is important that we address them. Using sensory acuity with yourself is a great way to enhance your natural ability to be aware of your emotions so that you can call attention to your own important emotional state changes.

As you work with these skills, you will find that your success rate at various tasks is generally very closely related to your level of congruence.

CHAPTER 6

VERBAL LISTENING SKILLS

UNTIL NOW, our focus on the process of listening has not included words. What an interesting way to begin relearning how to listen! In many cases, nonverbal listening will be of primary importance. However, verbal listening is important too. In this chapter we are going to look more closely at language itself and begin to discover that the words people use and how they use them convey far more information than you may ever have realized.

The Meta Model

NLP provides an excellent model of language, called the Meta Model. It can help you to get more meaning and make more sense out of the words people say. It can steer your attention to a person's unconscious assumptions, beliefs, and perceived limitations; and it can help you gain a much greater understanding of how a person perceives the world.

The Meta Model was inspired in large part by a formal model in the field of transformational linguistics,[1] and was originally developed to be useful in therapeutic interventions, where communication skills are extremely important. Two of the first books about NLP, *The Structure of Magic,* Volumes 1 and 2, by Richard Bandler and John Grinder, introduced and described the Meta Model in comprehensive detail; they continue to be excellent reference books for detailed study of the work.

Initially, the Meta Model was designed as an elicitory tool, and it was used to gather information quickly. According to rumor, it was so powerful and it reached so deeply that the FBI once considered using the process for interrogation. This may give you an indication of how thorough the process is. When used properly and with respect for others, the Meta Model can be the basis for exceptional verbal listening skills.

My presentation of the Meta Model is nowhere near as exhaustive as the original work and doesn't focus on training you to be a therapist (for that, I would refer you to the original works). Instead, I have simplified the information and distilled the portions that I have found to be of greatest value.

The Meta Model refers to spoken words as *surface structure* and to the more complete thoughts behind the words as the *deep structure*. There is often a vast difference between the surface structure and deep structure, and the Meta Model codifies the processes by which these differences occur. For example, the sentence "You should brush your teeth every day" might be spoken by a mother to her son. Because it is spoken, it is the surface structure. If you examine the sentence closely, you will see that some information is not provided by the sentence. For example, it does not state who created the expectations that teeth should be brushed every day. Was it the mother? The dentist? The American Dental Association? Who?

By asking the mother the question, "According to whom should I brush my teeth every day?" the son would have the opportunity to elicit the full thought from her. Other items of information are also not fully expressed by the surface structure. What specific process is she describing when she says "brush your teeth"? There are many ways to brush one's teeth, and she probably has specific criteria in mind. What specific idea does she have about "every day"? Must it be at the same time? How many times per day? The Meta Model assumes that the mother's sentence is backed up by a complete thought in which all the information is available. That full linguistic representation from which the surface structure is derived is called the deep structure.

The universal processes people go through to go from the deep structure to the surface structure are categorized as *deletions, distortions,* and *generalizations.* These are necessary parts of communicating; if you always expressed every thought in complete form, you would spend a tremendous amount of time speaking when it really wouldn't be necessary or useful. Legal terminology is one example of language that attempts to reduce the number of deletions, distortions, and generalizations; and it's so cumbersome that even simple legal documents encompass many pages of fine print.

Each pattern in the Meta Model can be presented with an accompanying response that is used to gather more information or to direct a line of questioning. In the case of deletions, the responses are directed toward helping recover the deleted information. For distortions, the responses are directed toward challenging or exposing the distorted information. For generalizations, the responses are again directed toward challenging or exposing the generalized assumptions. In many cases, the responses are very revealing, bringing up information that is important to the communication process.

Many NLP students can attest to the fact that improper use or overuse of Meta Model questions can be a real problem. One of the fastest ways to alienate someone and create annoyance and anger can be to misuse Meta Model questioning techniques. As NLP students have striven to learn the Meta Model, many have been labeled "meta-monsters" for their insincere, penetrating, and inconsiderate use of the techniques.

For this reason, and for general reasons of respect and win-win, I must stress that the Meta Model responses are to be used only when you have a strong rapport and when you have true win-win intentions in mind. When we get to some of the linguistic patterns in later chapters, you will learn how to soften the Meta Model responses and to use them with grace and elegance.

The processes of deletions, distortions, and generalizations are so natural and necessary for us that we couldn't realistically avoid them. There are times, however, when they create problems, usually in the form of falsely imposed limitations. Consider the following sentence spoken by your fictional friend, Fred:

> Sentence #1: "I can't be promoted until there is a job opening."

If you accept this sentence at face value, then it would seem that Fred's future is at the mercy of the movements within the organization. If there's no job opening, then there is no chance of being promoted. This is a limitation.

Now consider this admittedly awkward sentence:

> Sentence #2: Someone determined that someone or something is preventing someone from promoting Fred until someone somehow opens up some kind of a job.

Although you will probably never hear a sentence like this, it is qualitatively the same sentence as Sentence #1. But with Sentence #2, you might be prompted to start asking some pertinent questions:

- Who are these someones? What are these somethings? Are they credible? Do they have the authority or power to determine this? Do they know what they are talking about?
- What is the source of this information? Did Fred hear it from the president of the company or from the receptionist? What leads Fred to believe this person is both knowledgeable and also telling the truth?
- Who is this someone, or what is this something, that is preventing the promotion? Does this person or thing have the authority or power to prevent it?
- Who can promote Fred? Is it the same person who is might be preventing the promotion, or is it another person?
- Who can create a job opening? Can Fred create a job opening? If not, what is preventing him from doing so?
- How can the job opening be created? Can a new job be created? Can a department be expanded? Can Fred's boss just make a decision to create a new job? What kind of a job must this person open up?

There are a lot of questions there, all just simple responses to the single sentence, "I can't get a promotion until there is a job opening." Yet the answer to any one of those questions might indicate that Fred's limitation is not really a limitation at all. You may find out that Fred isn't really limited at all by the organization; rather, he is limited by his beliefs about the organization. You may find out that Fred doesn't understand the real needs and processes of the organization, and he doesn't understand who is actually making these processes happen. You may be able to help Fred investigate these perceived limitations, and perhaps he will realize that he has more options than he thought. He might even find out there are things he can do today to help him get promoted regardless of whether a job opens up.

People routinely stifle their potential through false limitations, and these false limitations are routinely expressed in their speech patterns. When Fred says a sentence like, "I can't be promoted until there is a job opening," he is saying a lot more than just what the words mean. Through effective listening, you will hear more than just the words; you will hear the process behind the words. Fred thinks that being promoted is impossible unless a job opening exists. Fred thinks that his promotion is done by someone else, rather than by his taking responsibility for the process. These perceived limitations were explicitly expressed by the structure of Fred's sentence. You can learn to hear these underlying expressions as well.

Once you understand the specific processes of the Meta Model, you can easily transform a Sentence #1 into a Sentence #2. (And that awkwardness will even start to make sense to you!) You can identify the limitations inherent in Sentence #1, and investigate the further options implied by Sentence #2. You can pinpoint the critical processes and direct your attention to those.

NLP, and specifically the Meta Model, place greater attention on the *processes* of human behavior than they do on the specific content of human behavior. If Fred is feeling limited, you might address the content of his situation; you could talk about the specifics regarding the rule, such as whom the rule applies to, the wording of the rule, the conditions of the rule, how long the rule is in effect, and so on. However, that would still imply acceptance of the premise that the rule is something that is limiting Fred. If you chose to address the process instead, then you would look at the process by which Fred feels limited and would help him to see more choices. You might come to realize that Fred is distorting and generalizing what's happening in the world and that there is no limitation at all, except the one Fred creates. By calling attention to this process, you can help Fred to realize that he has more opportunity than he realized. Even more, when the undesirable process is exposed, Fred might realize that he's been using that process in other situations as well and that he might see more opportunities in many areas of his life.

In listening, the Meta Model is used to extract information, but the information does not always present itself as facts and figures (the content). It also presents itself as ways in which people make sense of the world (the processes). The processes behind the words are often far more important than the specific words themselves. As you continue, you will be amazed at how many things people are "saying" without really saying them. You will be astonished at how a simple sentence can have multiple, complex messages. And you will probably be entertained too, because it's not every day that we get to learn new ideas about something we've been doing naturally all our lives.

Presuppositions

Have you ever had the experience of talking to other people, and hearing the words, and knowing that there was another message there? Perhaps they were making fun of you, and you weren't sure how. Or they were making things difficult in some way, but it was just a hunch. Or they just made you feel a whole a lot better, but you're not sure what they said to do it.

Most people intuitively know that human language communicates messages without words. They know that there is more meaning to a sentence than the words imply. They know that the logical, semantic words do not convey the entire meaning of a sentence. Even when all body communication and tonal communication is removed, there is still more information being conveyed than just the words. This may not be something you're accustomed to thinking about.

The added meaning often comes through the subtle, yet powerful process of presuppositions. Presuppositions are sometimes taught separately from the Meta Model and are sometimes presented as part of the model (as a form of distortion). My preference is to present presuppositions as an encompassing pattern, which forms a broader description of each of the Meta Model patterns. In this book, I will refer to presuppositions with this wider application as one of the underlying foundations of language. When thought of in this way, each linguistic pattern in the Meta Model can be thought of as a special type of presupposition.

So what is a presupposition?

Presupposition is a relatively uncommon word for a relatively common idea. The words *assumption* and *implication* are common words for the same idea. *The Random House Dictionary* (1980) defines *presupposition* as "to suppose or assume beforehand." Simply put, presuppositions are the things that are assumed and implied by your language, but not specifically stated. They are the unstated thoughts represented by the wording in your language. For example, consider this sentence:

Thank you for your consideration of my proposal.

On the surface, this very simple sentence just says "thank you," but there are three key presuppositions underlying it:

Presupposition #1: A proposal exists.

Presupposition #2: The proposal is owned by the speaker of the sentence ("*my* proposal").

Presupposition #3: The listener has considered or will consider this proposal ("your consideration").

None of those three presuppositions was specifically stated. The sentence did *not* read:

Alternative Wording (awkward): This letter contains a proposal. I am the owner of this proposal. I am asking you to consider it. If you do consider it, I will feel appreciative toward you.

Presuppositions convey meaning without specifically stating it. In natural language, presuppositions are the result of expediency and simplification, and they are made unconsciously. Few people have the linguistic training to be aware of the presuppositions they make, much less the interest in doing so. For example, every time I say something about "my job," I am presupposing that I have a job to begin with; otherwise, the phrase would not make sense. If I had to specifically say "I have a job" every time I referred to it, the speaking process would be far more tedious and difficult. When presuppositions imply things that are accurate, they can be a very useful, helpful way of speaking effectively. However, when presuppositions imply inaccuracies and falsely imposed limitations, problems start to occur.

An incredibly important aspect of effective listening requires you to recognize presuppositions in ordinary communication. You can do this very well through a combination of practicing and increasing your linguistic awareness. To help you with the process of recognition, I will be referring to a wide variety of presuppositions throughout the rest of this book.

There are a broad number of ways in which presuppositions naturally occur (twenty-nine are listed in the appendix of *The Structure of Magic*, Volume 1), each of which is distinctly different from each other. However, rather than getting you bogged down in the intricacies, I prefer to distill and simplify the information and allow you to see many examples. This is an excellent way to learn the thrust of the material and enjoy the process too.[2] Once you see some examples of presuppositions specifically identified and described, you will start to be able to notice them in everyday speaking.

The importance of presuppositions lies in their subtlety. They are a mechanism by which people say things without actually verbalizing them. Here are two simple sentences, with corresponding explanations highlighting some of the things that are presupposed:

Example 1: My success has been primarily due to my strong integrity.

> *Presuppositions:* "My success" presupposes that there is such a thing as success and that I am successful; "success" presupposes that I am being successful at something; "has been" presupposes that this success has occurred for some period of time; "primarily" presupposes that there is at least one additional reason that the success was created besides the integrity; "due to" presupposes that there is a cause-and-effect relationship between strong integrity and my success; "my strong integrity" presupposes that I have strong integrity.
>
> *Meta-presuppositions:* I am knowledgeable enough to determine *why* I am successful; I am knowledgeable enough to determine that I am successful; I am knowledgeable enough to determine that I have strong integrity; I am knowledgeable enough to determine that this cause-and-effect relationship is applicable.

Example 2: We can't have a true relationship without having a pure sense of trust in each other.

> *Presuppositions:* "Can't" presupposes there are possibilities and impossibilities associated with having a true relationship; "have" presupposes that a true relationship is something that can be possessed; "true relationship" presupposes that there are types of relationships other than true ones; "relationship" presupposes that the "we" has the potential to relate in some way; "can't... without" presupposes a cause-and-effect relationship between a pure sense of trust and true relationship; "having" presupposes that this sense of trust is required to exist on an ongoing basis; "pure" presupposes that there are senses of trust that are other than pure; "sense of" presupposes that someone is having a sensory experience; "trust" presupposes that someone is trusting another; "a pure sense of trust" presupposes that such a thing exists.

Meta-presuppositions: The person speaking is knowledgeable enough to determine what is required to have a true relationship; the person speaking is knowledgeable enough to identify a true relationship; the person speaking is knowledgeable enough to determine the applicability of the cause-and-effect relationship between relationship and trust; the person speaking is qualified to make these determinations on behalf of the other person/people included in "we."

Isn't it amazing how many things we mean that we don't actually say? Our words communicate far more than just their meanings! In the previous analysis, I referred to both presuppositions and also to "meta-presuppositions." *Meta-presuppositions* is a term I use to refer to deeper levels of presuppositions, those typically more removed from awareness. They address a different level of abstraction and identify something *about* the situation.

Here is a partial list of some of the other types of presuppositions. This time, I've kept the explanations minimal, and I call attention only to the named presupposition. I suggest that you avoid trying to memorize the labels and instead focus on the underlying process common to each type:

Existence: Your strength is that…
Presupposes that you have a strength.

Possibility: Becoming an enlightened being is just a matter of…
Presupposes that becoming an enlightened being is possible.

Cause-effect: If you read this book carefully, you will…
Presupposes you will have an effect from reading this book carefully.

Complex equivalence: Working hard every day means that…
Presupposes that working hard every day has an equivalent meaning; such as, you love your family.

Awareness: You may not realize that…
Presupposes that whatever comes next exists and is true.

Subordinate clause of time: While you were busy getting rich...
Presupposes you were busy getting rich.

Comparative: If I were as angry as...
Presupposes I am not as angry as the person yet to be described.

Qualifier: Being smart would have enabled me to...
Presupposes the speaker is not smart.

Exclusive "or": Either we make a lot of money or we have a lot of time.
Presupposes we can't have both.

Inclusive "or": Either you can call a meeting or I can.
Presupposes a meeting will be called.

Time: When you finish reviewing this proposal...
Presupposes you will finish reviewing the proposal at some time in the future.

But: I'd like to find a new job, but...
Presupposes that something is preventing the 'speaker from finding a new job.

In addition to these types of presuppositions, there are presuppositions inherent in other Meta Model patterns. In later sections, we explore more about presuppositions and their relationship with the misuse or abuse of language. We'll look at ways to recognize this abuse and how to stop it in its tracks. We'll look at bait and how it can distract a listener from the important presuppositions. And we will look at how interchanges between people can either validate or call into question presupposed statements. Presuppositions are a key element in understanding the meaning behind words, and we will continue to pay attention to them throughout both the listening and the speaking sections of this book.

Mind Reads

We first addressed the topic of mind reading in Chapter 5 and identified it as one of three surefire ways to create problems in communication. This problem can become even more prevalent, and more serious, when it is confused with the process of understanding presuppositions. When people first learn about presuppositions, the tendency is to read more into the sentences than is semantically presupposed, which, of course, is mind reading.

Much of communication happens at unconscious levels, including body communication, tonal communication, and presuppositions. In addition, people filter (delete, distort, and generalize) the information coming in, and so it's no wonder that communication can seem so difficult to understand. Mind reading is the process of *interpreting* the communication, usually through the filters of one's own experience. However, these interpretations are usually severely biased and limited.

At some level, all communication is an interpretation, and any attempt to understand another human being is a form of mind reading. We can never really know what goes on in someone else's experience; we can only make assumptions and educated guesses. But there comes a point at which the accuracy of your guesses will be much closer to the mark. If someone points his finger at me, yells loudly with a scowl on his face, and tells me to "Back off!" I am likely to interpret that communication as anger. In most cases, I would probably be right, but it's still a mind read. But if someone calls my name and looks at me with a curled lip just like my Uncle Joe used to do before he spanked me as a kid, I'm likely to interpret that communication as a warning that a spanking is about to occur. But in this case, my bottom is probably safe.

Much of the meaning we derive from communication is created at unconscious levels. Today, it would be ludicrous for me to fear that someone would spank me; but in a scenario like the one I just mentioned, it would be natural for me to become fearful just at the sight of someone's curled lip. It's logically ludicrous; however, human behavior isn't always logical.

When we are beginning to study language, it is useful to make clear distinctions between logical, semantic meaning based on linguistic models and personal interpretations or extensions of that data. Because we've spent our whole lives

THREE YEARS INTO A DIFFICULT INTERACIAL MARRAIGE, ENOK AND MARYLOU GOT DIVORCED. THEY FELT THEY JUST DIDN'T UNDERSTAND EACH OTHER.

interpreting the data we receive, distinguishing the linguistic meaning from the interpretation is a practice that can be quite revealing.

Consider the sentence:

> If I don't learn how to communicate, I'm going to lose my wife.

With that as the semantic communication, consider the following observations and mind reads, and notice what distinguishes one from the other:

- The speaker doesn't know how to communicate now—this was specifically presupposed by the sentence.
- The speaker wants to learn new ways to communicate—this is an interpretation; it was not specifically stated in the communication.

- Some aspect of communication has a direct effect on whether or not he loses his wife—this was specifically presupposed by the sentence (cause and effect).
- If he improves his communication, he will keep his wife—this is a mind read; it was not specifically stated in the communication.
- He feels frustrated—this is a mind read; he has not communicated how he feels in a congruent manner.
- He communicates with his wife now, but it's just not good enough—this is an assumption; he has not described his current situation.

It is very useful to be able to distinguish the difference between mind reads (assumptions, interpretations, hints, insinuations, presumptions, implications, clues, allusions, and so on) and sensory-based observations (including presuppositions). It's useful both in listening and speaking.

Let's consider some other examples. The following items are examples of either sensory-based observations or mind reads. As you read each one, take a moment to consider how and why it falls into the appropriate category:

- The woman on the television is angry—mind read.
- The vein on his neck is pulsing faster, he's started to form sweat on his forehead, and his face is red—sensory-based observations.
- She's visibly upset—mind read.
- His eyes are watery, his voice is trembling, and his lip is quivering—sensory-based observations.

For the following, imagine you are speaking to a friend, and when you mention the idea of going into business together:

- His face got white and his eyes widened—sensory-based observations.
- He suddenly leaned backward and raised his hands to place his palms toward you, as if to push you away—sensory-based observations.
- He grunted—sensory-based observation.
- He began to stutter and had visible difficulty forming a sentence—sensory-based observations.
- He held his breath momentarily, then took a deep breath—sensory-based observation.

- The idea surprised him—mind read.
- His hands indicated body communication that said he didn't like the idea and wanted to push it away—mind read/interpretation.
- He dissociated himself from the idea by leaning backward—mind read/interpretation.
- His grunt was indicative of a negative reaction—mind read.
- He didn't like the idea—mind read.

There are tremendous differences among observing someone's actions (sensory-based observations); determining additional meaning from linguistic structures through the use of a linguistic model, such as the Meta Model; and interpreting someone's actions (mind reading). It's helpful to keep each clear in your mind. I suggest that, over the next few days, you practice noticing when others are using mind reads to try to understand you and others. There's no need to point these things out. Just take notice of how different people relate to each other. You will probably find that some of the people you interact with rely more on mind reads than others do. It's interesting to notice the differences in communication effectiveness.

Words of Necessity/Possibility

Words of necessity and possibility often represent our beliefs about what's possible in the world. They describe pervasive limitations people attempt to impose on others or themselves. The presuppositions associated with these words represent rules and beliefs that limit behavior or open up worlds of possibilities.

The more common words of necessity are *must, should, have to, need to, got to, it is necessary to, it is required, it is forced upon, it is demanded that, to be obligated to, to be compelled to.* (The negative versions must also be included, such as *must not, should not,* and so on.)

These words each indicate a perceived need. Of course, true needs are few and far between. We need to breathe to

live. We need to eat to live. At some point, we need to have
sex to reproduce (even that's changing). However, after that
list is exhausted, we start running out of true needs.

Do we need to have companionship? Do we need love?
Do we need respect? Although these things certainly improve
the quality of life, they're not needs in the truest sense of
the word.

Do you need to be at work on time? Do you have to get
that birthday card out on time? Are you required to keep
your car tuned up? Is it necessary to clean the house? Do
you have demands placed on your attention? Are you compelled to be a certain kind of person? Are you obligated to
be honest? Shouldn't you reconsider these things?

In these cases, and most other cases, words of necessity
indicate a perceived loss of choice. They indicate a person
is no longer functioning under the premise of actions and
consequences and is rather functioning under the false generalization of need.

Words of necessity are very important words in several
contexts:

- When you're listening to others speak and you hear a
  word of necessity, it usually indicates either a self-
  imposed limitation or a method of self-motivation,
  usually the former.
- When you hear yourself use a word of necessity, that
  indicates the same thing.
- When speaking to others, you can use words of necessity
  to motivate or direct their actions, to impose restrictions,
  and to limit choices.

The important thing to remember is that words of necessity are almost always used falsely. They displace the
processes of choice and consequences. They create false limitations. When you or others use words of necessity, it is often
helpful to explore the potential limitation inherent in the
presuppositions. Bring back into awareness the realization
of choice. What would happen if you didn't do whatever it
is? Would life continue? What would be the consequences?
These are answers worth considering. You may discover more
options than you knew you had.

Words of possibility are similar in nature to those of necessity; however, they deal with the realm of what's possible and impossible.

Some of the more common words of possibility are *can, will, might, could, would, may, to be possible, perhaps, consider, choose, to be able to, to be capable of.* Their negative versions are called words of impossibility and include *can't, won't, couldn't,* and so on.

These words each indicate a perceived option or lack of option. Of course, much of life is about options and consequences, so the words of impossibility are the ones that deserve significant attention. True impossibilities do exist. You can't change your racial background and heritage. You are not able to make yourself taller. You're not capable of making eighteen holes-in-one in a row. It's not possible to fly to the next solar system. Some things just aren't going to happen.

Can you become the top manager in your firm? Would you be able to lose twenty pounds? Will you ever meet that perfect someone? Are you capable of making it work? Have you considered devoting more time to your family? Is it possible that you've been limiting yourself?

While not all these things may be easy to do, they certainly fall into the realm of possibility. In most cases, a person who uses words of impossibility is no longer functioning with the responsibility mind-set. He or she has failed to understand that one's life is the consequence of one's own actions and inaction, to understand that life can be changed and re-created.

Words of impossibility are very important words in several contexts:

- When you are listening to others speak and you hear a word of impossibility, it usually indicates either an unexamined assumption about the world or a decision that limits potential action.
- When you hear yourself use a word of impossibility, that indicates the same thing.
- When speaking to others, you can use words of possibility and impossibility to create or limit perceptions of choice and possibility and to inspire or inhibit the actions of others.

The important thing to remember is that modal operators of impossibility are often used falsely. They represent beliefs and mind-sets that limit choice, limit response, and thwart the responsibility mind-set. When you or others use modal operators of impossibility, it is often helpful to explore the potential limitation inherent in the presuppositions. Reacquaint the speaker with the realization of possibility. What's preventing you from doing whatever it is? What would happen if you did it anyway? How could you do it anyway? What would it take to make it so that you could do it? What would have to be different to allow that to happen? These are answers worth considering. You and those you communicate with just might find out that there's a lot more possible in the world than meets the eye!

NLP NOMINALIZATIONS

Nominalizations encompass words that create lasting impressions. They're the things we fight for, the things we die for, the things we strive for, the things we sacrifice for. They are the things we value most and despise the most. We often don't know exactly what they are, but we know they reach deep into our core. Mention a few nominalizations, and you're likely to inspire strong emotional responses from those around you. Let's take a look at what these incredible things are.

Nominalizations, as defined in NLP, are words in which an action, process, emotional state, value, or feeling is linguistically frozen in time and treated as a noun.[3] For example, the word *love* is classified as a noun, but in reality, *love* describes an active process, that of someone loving someone or something. When we represent an activity as a nominalization, we freeze the process in time (*love* seems like something we can obtain or measure), and we delete information (*love* deletes information about who is doing the loving and what is being loved). Here are some additional examples of NLP nominalizations, calling attention to the underlying activity and the deleted information:

- Success: Someone *succeeding* at something
- Honesty: Someone *being honest* about something

- Commitment: Someone *being committed* to something
- Happiness: Someone *feeling* the emotional state of being happy
- Motivation: Someone *feeling* the emotional state of being motivated
- Belief: Someone *believing* something
- Value: Someone *equating* value with something

Each of these words is probably familiar to you. You probably use many of them on a regular basis, but you probably didn't realize the significance of their true nature.

People often create limitations in their lives by failing to recognize and re-energize their processes. The word *decision* is a nominalization; it's a static word, implying that the decision is fixed, and it deletes information about who made the decision. If someone says, "a decision was made that ...," you are likely to feel as if the decision is final and there are no options left. If someone says, "I've decided that ...," then at least you know whom to speak with if you want to have the decision overturned, even if it's implied that the process has already happened. And if someone says, "I am deciding to...," you are likely to see that you have a good opportunity to have an impact on the final outcome, because you're right there as the process is unfolding.

These different expressions are distorted descriptions of the same process, that of a person *deciding* something. By recognizing that each describes the same activity, you can start to see how there is no tangible thing as a decision (you can't put it into a wheelbarrow), and that all decisions are actually mental activities performed by people. When you realize that an NLP nominalization is more accurately a description of an activity, you empower yourself to make an impact on that activity.

Additionally, reactivating a nominalization removes the falsely imposed limitations of time. With the same example, a decision is more accurately the process of deciding on a regular basis. Every time you honor a decision, you are redeciding in favor of that same decision. A "decision" that being in a relationship is better than being single is something that must be decided upon over and over again. As time goes on, people forget that this deciding is a process;

they lock it up as a decision and then sometimes forget to reevaluate later. Naturally, a decision you may have made ten years ago may not be the best decision for today.

When you use a nominalization, you also delete information. For example, *success* is a well-recognized word, and you may use it very often. Whenever you use the word *success*, you are saying that *someone* is succeeding at *something*, but you're not specifying the someone or the something. In the following example, notice how a simple sentence can seem to mean so much, yet fail to provide even a moderate level of specificity:

> *Statement:* Communication is important.
>
> *Deleted Information:* Whose communication? Who is communicating? Who is receiving the communication? What is being communicated? How is it being communicated? Important to whom or what? How is it important?

"Communication is important" is vague, but people will think they know what it means and either agree or disagree. When you make a statement about success, one person might think that it means succeeding at one's job. Another person might think it means succeeding at meeting company objectives. A third person might think it means the company's success at improving profits. People create their own definitions. Very few people ever ask for clarification of a nominalization.

NLP nominalizations play a vital role in the communication and relating process. When a person accepts the presuppositions inherent in a nominalization—namely that the action is fixed and cannot be altered—then there is a corresponding inability to respond. For example, words describing emotions are often NLP nominalizations. Anger is the process of feeling angry. Yet by misrepresenting the process, it seems as if anger is something that exists outside of our choice of behavior; for example, "My anger got the best of me." That sentence implies "my anger" is something that exists external to me, and that I have no control over it. But we do have control over our emotions.

NLP nominalizations can represent the most important, and most unchanging, aspects of a person. Core values are usually expressed as nominalizations: Honor, honesty, compassion, faith, and so on. Even integrity can be considered a nominalization, illustrated by the common expression, "Integrity is defined by action."

When used to represent core values, NLP nominalizations can encompass a wide system of accompanying definitions and beliefs, which are often quite rigid. For some people, love is a commitment. For others it's a swirling in the head. For others it's work.

If you love someone, you may never even consider having another lover. If you have pride in your country, you could be willing to kill and die for it. If you honor your parents, you might feel obligated to take care of them even at great personal expense. If you respect someone, you may value his or her opinion. These ramifications can form an integral part of your definition of each nominalization.

NLP nominalizations delete information, and Meta Model responses can help you to elicit more information. If people say that loyalty is important to them, then you may choose to ask questions to get more information. Which people are expected to be loyal? How is that loyalty shown? To whom should they be loyal? How do they know when a person is being loyal? What sensory-based observations indicate loyalty? How long does loyalty last? How long before it starts?

This line of questioning can be very useful in a variety of circumstances. By recognizing NLP nominalizations, you can identify the underlying activities, remove falsely imposed limitations, clarify communication, and empower yourself to make impacts on the processes affecting your life.

OTHER PARTS OF THE META MODEL

There are at lease five other parts to the Meta Model. Each of them calls attention to specific words or specific sentence constructions. These aspects of language can provide you with a great deal of insight into how you and others perceive the world, and can specifically help call your attention to unnecessary limitations. Sometimes, simply recognizing the limitation and questioning it are enough to create important changes.

We'll cover the remaining items in less detail, highlighting the most important aspects of each.[4]

1. *Cause and effect:* People in our society are trained from early ages to understand the concept of cause and effect—that events and actions have consequences. One of the first questions a child will ask (over and over and over!) is "Why?" Why is that?

   This is generally a positive aspect of humanity. However, our cause-and-effect interpretations are often inaccurate generalizations and distortions, rather than accurate descriptions of causality, and they can lead to unnecessary limitations.

   Semantically, a cause and effect is composed of two parts, a cause and an effect, linked together by a word or structure to indicate the causality. This linking word or structure is your indication that a cause-and-effect relationship is being communicated. Here are some examples:

   - I can't get a job because I'm not educated enough—"because" is the linking word
   - If I start making more money, then I'll end up with too much responsibility— "if ... then" is a causal construction
   - My professional attitude is responsible for my success—"responsible for" are the linking words
   - When you do that, I feel sad—"when" creates a causal construction

   When we consider a cause and effect to be applicable, for example, when we think a relationship causes our happiness, we sometimes lock ourselves into a limiting perception. First, the perception may be wrong. Perhaps a relationship doesn't cause happiness, but only intensifies the happiness we already have inside. Second, the perception may lock us into one avenue or approach. Maybe a relationship can cause happiness, but we could find other ways to be happy, too. And third, cause-and-effect perceptions can detract from the more useful cause-and-effect generalization, that of the responsibility mind-set, which proposes that we are in control of our own happiness.

2. *Universals:* Universals are words such as *all, none, every, never, everyone, no one, nobody, forever, always, nothing, everything,* and *without exception.* All of them are overgeneralizations all the time. Of course, that's an overgeneralization! In some cases, the use of universal quantifiers is appropriate and correct. *All* of us are human. We *always* have more we can learn. *Nobody* has *all* the answers. These are relatively safe generalizations.

   However, those generalizations are of a different logical type than the following: *All* jobs are demoralizing. Women *never* enjoy sex as much as men do. *Nobody* can help me with my problems. Relationships are *always* a lot of work. In this job, I will *never* get ahead.

   As is the case with many of the other patterns, universals indicate a perceived lack of opportunity and often a failure to take on the responsibility mind-set. Some Meta Model responses are used to identify the perceived limitation, bring extra attention to it, and find counter examples. *All* jobs are demoralizing? Are you sure? I have a job that's not demoralizing; how can that be? My uncle Hubert seems to have a job that makes him feel good.

   These responses can help a person reconsider the generalization, and perhaps increase his or her level of choice and responsibility in the matter. This again brings about empowerment.

3. *Unsupported conclusions:* Unsupported conclusions specify a conclusion, but fail to specify the person who has made that conclusion. For example, "It's a good thing to create a lot of love in your life" is an evaluative statement (declaring something good), but does not mention who made the evaluation. According to whom is it good?

   When a person proclaims that something is good, bad, important, trivial, necessary, wasteful, right, wrong, smart, stupid, sexy, pretty, ugly, pure, tainted, and so on, it is often useful to know how the person arrived at that conclusion. If wearing a blue suit to work is foolish, it's nice to know if it's foolish according to your bosses, or if it's foolish according to the groundskeepers. One group is likely to be more significant in your career than the other.

   Unsupported conclusions often indicate that a person has lost sight of his or her own evaluative processes. By paying special attention to unsupported conclusions, you will identify judgments, decisions, and opinions that may be incorrect, inapplicable, and unnecessarily limiting, at which time you can call special attention to them, thus helping the person regain sight of how such conclusions can be constructively drawn.

4. *Equivalences:* An equivalence is a structure that indicates that two or more experiences are perceived to be equivalent. It interprets one experience as being essentially the same as another. For example, "When she pays extra attention to me, it means she's feeling insecure." This sentence equates extra attention to a feeling of insecurity. As you can imagine, these equivalences are often not equivalent at all, and result in serious misinterpretations.

   Equivalences are also structured in two parts with a linking word or construction. Common linking words are *means that, shows that, signifies, denotes, is, proves,* and so on.

   The Meta Model response to an equivalence calls attention to the questionable relationship, and generally serves to help the person reevaluate. This is done primarily by asking for more information and by exploring potential counter-examples. How does paying extra attention mean that she's feeling insecure? Has she ever paid you extra attention and not felt insecure?

   Most equivalences indicate misperceptions about the world, which can either limit responses or instigate inappropriate responses.

5. *Unspecified verbs and simple deletions:* These are the most common of all Meta Model patterns, and usually the most trivial. They support the premise that we can never fully understand the experiences of another person, and that the information they provide us is limited. In the preceding sentence, I have failed to accurately and fully define the verbs *support, understand,* and *provide.* In this case, they are unspecified verbs, and probably mean something different to me than they do to you. Simple deletions inundate language, and provide yet another reason why legal documents (which try to be complete) are so long and cumbersome. In the previous sentence, I haven't explained exactly what I mean by *inundate, language, reason, legal, documents, so long, cumbersome,* and so on. These are cases of simple deletions.

These last few sections have described in some detail the parts of the Meta Model that I consider to be most useful.

The learning of Meta Model patterns can help you to get more meaning and make more sense out of the words people say. It can help you to clue into the most meaningful, most restrictive, most important, most problematic aspects of a subject, and allow you to get a much better idea about how a person thinks and how a person views the world. It can help you listen with more depth and effectiveness than you may ever have listened before. And it can take you directly into a very personal and private world of the person you are relating with, which is his or her world of beliefs, values, and thinking processes.

In later sections, I will cover ways in which to make your words and questions more easily accepted by others, and you will learn techniques by which you can explore with grace and eloquance the patterns described in this chapter. And continue to keep in mind that respect for the people you relate with, permission to relate with them, and constant sight of win-win are always (yes, always) required (yes, required) for effective and supportive listening to take place.

The Meta Model

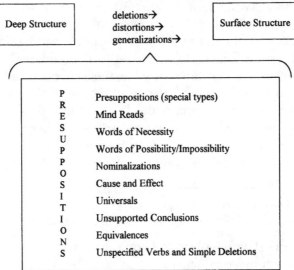

adapted from *The Structure of Magic*, Volume 1, John Grinder and Richard Bandler

Setting Direction with Your Questions

So far in our discussions of listening, we've covered what to look for and certain words to listen for. We've briefly covered some of the kinds of questions you can use to get more information, but we haven't yet defined a strategy for truly effective listening. We have a few mind-sets, and some great tools, but we haven't yet discussed what kind of process you might choose to use when listening. These next three sections start bringing it all together.

Many people think that listening is a one-way process. They think it involves just using ears to hear words. However, people are getting more accustomed to the idea of active listening. They're starting to realize that listening is an interchange and that all parties are involved in the process. You listen to the radio, but you relate with people.

I'm going to take the idea of listening, and take it a step further than you may be accustomed to. I'm going to take the approach that effective listeners play an active role in determining what is said in an interchange. Sounds odd, doesn't it?

Let me say it again. *Effective listeners play an active role in determining what is said in an interchange.* As a listener, you will be a part of determining what is said, how it is said, and in what way it is said. Have I teased you enough yet?

Consider for a moment what the process of asking a question does. We know that good listeners ask questions. But what does a question really do in the listening process?

We tend to think that questions are used to help us gather more information; however, questions perform at least three critical roles in the listening process:

1. Questions help elicit information.
2. Questions set direction.
3. Questions encourage the accessing of emotional states.

The first item is obvious. People ask questions when they want to get more information. People can ask a question to get information, whether they're a good listener or a lousy one, whether they're a considerate listener or an intrusive one. Simple.

The second item may be somewhat new to you. What does "setting a direction" mean? Questions set direction. We know that the questions you ask will generally direct a speaker's attention toward the topic you asked about. If you ask about dogs, the conversation may move toward the topic of dogs. If you ask about cats, it may move toward cats. That's setting a direction. Is that what I mean when I say questions set direction? Partly yes, but not fully.

Questions certainly direct the speaker toward a certain body of information. However, the *way* you ask a question influences the way in which the speaker answers the question.

Let's use an example. Suppose your friend wants you to go out on a blind date with a friend of his. (And to make my writing easier, further suppose you're a man so I can use "he" instead of "he or she.") You don't know whether or not you want to go out with this person, so you decide to ask your friend some questions. Consider the different ways in which you might choose to phrase your questions. For these examples, imagine using one question *or* the other question, and what response each would elicit:

You want to know more about her:

- What makes her special? *or*
- What's wrong with her?

You want to know if she'll be physically attractive to you:

- What are her nicest features? *or*
- Will I need to put a bag over her head?

You want to know if you'll enjoy her company:

- What makes her the kind of person you think I would get along well with? *or*
- What's wrong with her?

Each question in the pair is directed toward getting the same class of information as its counterpart. However, with the first question in each pair you direct attention to the positive side of things. These questions are likely to encourage thinking about things in a positive light; thinking about things that are pleasant, nice, special; thinking of ways in which this blind date will be enjoyable, fun, rewarding.

The second question in each pair is likely to bring about negative thoughts and to create defensive posturing, to make you think of things that are unattractive, unappealing, problematic and then to consider whether or not those things will be present. They are designed to make you think of ways in which this blind date might fail.

A question gives the listener an opportunity to direct a speaker not only toward a certain subject, but also toward a certain perspective on that subject. Would you rather hear what might be disastrous about a blind date, or would you rather hear what might be wonderful about it? The choice is partially yours, because you can guide your friend to give you either perspective.

Consider which type of question is going to be more useful and respectful. Imagine a routine conversation with a fellow employee. You ask her how she's doing, and she says she's frustrated with all the work she has to do. You could ask her, "Frustrated? What's wrong?" or you could ask her, "Oh really? Well, what's the best thing going on for you right now?" or "Oh really? Well, have you accomplished anything good yet?" There are times and places for all types of questions, positive and negative, but these examples let you see how questions can have a dramatic influence on the listening process.

Once you understand how questions can affect the direction of a conversation, you can start to ask yourself what you want to do as a listener. Do you want to elicit to the fifteenth degree not only what's wrong with the world, but also every detail of what's wrong, and how long it's been that way? Or do you want to find out what kinds of limitations are being imposed on this person to make things go wrong and perhaps offer some perspective on how to deal with it? Or do you want to change the perspective, and perhaps her mood, by bringing everything into a more positive, optimistic light? Again, there are times and places for each of those, and it will usually come down to a determination of what would be most respectful and useful for each given situation.

The third thing that questions do in the listening process is to encourage gaining access to emotional states. By setting a direction, you will be starting this process; however, specific questions can be very powerful instigators of certain moods.

I was once told a story that illustrates this point perfectly. A man who was knowledgeable in NLP was at a family gathering. After a time, his young niece approached him to ask what NLP was. The man thought for a moment, then told her that he would prefer to show her NLP, rather than tell her about it. He pointed to his elderly aunt and asked the girl to go to her and ask how old her grandchildren were. The little girl followed these instructions perfectly and waited for a reply. The grandmother thought for a moment and seemed somewhat taxed by the question. She counted and figured and added and subtracted and eventually managed to give a fairly reasonable response, which the niece reported back to her uncle.

Her uncle then gave the niece new instructions. He said to go back to the grandmother and ask her which was her *favorite* grandchild. The niece again followed the instructions perfectly and asked the grandmother this new question. In an instant, the grandmother developed a warm smile and a beautiful twinkle in her eyes. She seemed to glow at the prospect of answering such a beautiful question.

Later, the uncle explained to his niece, "That's NLP."[5]

Now that you have learned to receive nonverbal communication and to appreciate the emotional states of others, it is only a natural extension of your communication skills to ask questions that will start to influence the emotional states of others.

Elicitory Listening

We began our investigation of listening many pages ago with a focus on all of its aspects except for words. After a time, we started to pay more attention to words themselves, especially those that indicated certain processes or perceived limitations.

As we narrow our focus even more intently on words, we come to perhaps the most important words people will ever share with you: The words that represent their values.

Most people think that listening is a passive process. And for most people, it is. However, there's more to listening than just hearing and paying attention to what people are saying. There's even more to listening than calibrating and using advanced Meta Model techniques. When listening skills are directive and interactive in nature, they are elicitory.

Effective people listen interactively. They ask questions of the other person. They help set direction for the conversation, either keeping the other person on track or guiding the other person to the appropriate topics. They set direction for the other person's perspectives, bringing out the information from different viewpoints. They encourage different emotional states, sometimes negative, but usually positive. We've already learned these things, but there's still more to learn.

Successful people listen with a purpose; they seek out information that is important. There's a time and place for letting people ramble on without a purpose, but there's also a time and place for finding out what's really important to other people and how you can help them achieve it. This is what I refer to as elicitory listening.

Elicitory listening distinguishes what's important to someone from what's inconsequential to that person. Re-read that sentence because it is important. *Elicitory listening distinguishes what's important to someone from what's inconsequential to that person.*

Elicitory listening requires you to ask questions of the other person. It requires you to keep the other person on topic. It requires you to pay attention to more than just his or her words. It requires you to constantly evaluate each word, movement, and tone of voice that the person exhibits and to respond to it. It requires you to be far more active than when you're talking.

When your listening skills are honed, you know exactly what's important to the person, what objections he or she might have, what things he or she needs to know, and so on. You can get this information only through interactive listening. Elicitory listening allows you to find the truly important aspects of the person's communication and focus on them with pinpoint accuracy. Instead of using buckshot, you narrow down your verbal interactions to a precisely directed approach, moving directly toward the core values of the person. When done with respect for the other person, with permission, and with a strong focus on win-win, this process creates tremendous rapport.

How do you elicit high-quality information? What specific questions do you ask? What specifically are you "listening" for? How specifically do you know when something is more important than something else?

The magic words we are looking for are words that represent values. In NLP, values have many levels and hierarchies, with the most pervasive usually expressed as nominalizations. A person's most important values will encompass a large number of more detailed items. A car would not be an encompassing value, but freedom could be. A house would not be an encompassing value, but security could be. A relationship might be valued, but more likely love, trust, care, and companionship would be more encompassing values.

When people take actions, they are typically acting in ways to attempt to fulfill intangible values. If a person values security, then that person might stay in a despised job for years just to fulfill that value. People who value excitement might risk their life on a regular basis just to fulfill that value. Values affect people so deeply that they will die for them, kill for them, sacrifice for them, and strive for them. Many soldiers have fought and died in the name of honor and pride in their country. People have given up fortunes in the name of integrity. People have left the loves of their lives in the name of pride and self-respect.

So when you decide to create a win-win arrangement with another person, it is your duty to pay close attention to whether or not that person's values will be fulfilled. You may ask, "Well, why is it my responsibility? Why don't other people just take care of themselves? I take care of myself!" I have two responses to that line of thinking. The first is, I advocate use of the responsibility mind-set, which calls on you to be responsible for everything in your life. The second answer is, you have tools at your disposal to help elicit values, and these tools are better than those most everyone else has.

Most people do not have a conscious understanding of their own core values. They take action in their lives in almost a random way; then afterward, they evaluate their actions in the context of their values. This is often done unconsciously and is the source of the guilt scenario. This process is not the best one available, and it results in people doing things that just aren't right for them.

You, on the other hand, are more fully equipped to use a better process. With your calibration skills and your ability to pick up unconscious communication, you are often in a better position, one where you know what's going on with the person you're communicating with. With your understanding of congruency, you are in a position to continue negotiating until you get a clearly congruent response from both yourself and the person you're negotiating with. With the elicitory skills you are about to learn, you are in a position from which you can effectively troubleshoot incongruencies and internal conflicts and help get them resolved *before* action is taken. With all these skills at your disposal, you are the one responsible for making your arrangements 100 percent win-win all the time.

When interacting with another person, each of you is in the position of taking action and having those actions stay in alignment with core values. Agreements and relations break down when people are not acting in alignment with their core values. If you are a manager, you should know what your subordinates feel is important about their jobs. Then you can help them obtain their goals. If you are married, you should know what your spouse feels is important in your relationship. Then you can help fulfill those values. If your career is influenced by the actions of others, like your bosses, then you should know what's important to them about the work you're doing. Then you can help them achieve those goals.

NLP places much emphasis on values, and with good reason. Although the process of eliciting values is relatively straightforward, it requires verbal dexterity. When you're trying to reach people at deep levels, rapport and permission are required, and maintaining those things while doggedly asking questions is sometimes not the easiest art. However, you can become skilled at it relatively quickly.

So how do you elicit values? What questions do you ask? What process do you use? Essentially the process is quite simple. There's really only one question to ask, but for variety you create as many different versions of that question as possible.

> *Question to elicit values:* What's important to you about [blank]?

If a person wants to buy a new house, you ask, "What's important to you about buying a new house?"

When you take this line of questioning, you are looking for a pattern. You are looking for the responses to your questions to become more general and more encompassing. In NLP, this is referred to as "chunking up." If Gina says that buying a new house is important because she can move to the New Balogosta neighborhood, she may not be chunking up. But if she says that it's important so that she can feel a sense of security, then you're probably making progress. There are many ways Gina could gain security; buying a house might be just one of them, and so security would be a higher chunk than buying a house. Buying a house in the New Balogosta neighborhood would be a more specific aspect of buying a house, and so would not be chunking up; rather, that might be chunking down.

Or buying a house in the New Balogosta neighborhood could be chunking laterally. Perhaps the house isn't the issue: Perhaps living in a certain neighborhood or having a certain status or having certain friends or creating a certain lifestyle is what's at issue here. In any case, you continue your line of questioning until you find a clear path to a nominalization.

To illustrate the process, here is a simplified example:

> *Gina:* I'm going to take all my savings to buy a house. *(You could begin by saying that this is a dumb thing to do, that*

Gina is going to squander her savings and then regret it later. You might notice some incongruities about what she's saying and might determine that she's making a big mistake. Or you could ask some questions to see what's going on for her.)

You: That's a big step. What's important to you about buying a house? *(starting the process of eliciting values)*

Gina: Living in New Balogosta. *(either chunking down or chunking laterally)*

You: Really? What's important to you about living in New Balogosta?

Gina: They've got great streets to take walks on. *(probably chunking down)*

You: Walks in the street? What's important to you about that?

Gina: It's important to me to be around people and to meet people. In my apartment, I don't meet anyone. I feel like I'm in a jail cell. *(starting to chunk up to a value)*

You: What's important to you about being around people?

Gina: Well, mostly just to have people to do things with and talk to. *(chunking up)*

You: What's important to you about doing things with and talking to people?

Gina: Companionship. *(there's the value)*

You: What's important to you about companionship? *(checking to make sure it wasn't a bogus answer)*

Gina: Well ... It just is. *(there's the confirmation)*

This is an example of the process, and you might see that it can be quite tedious if not done with grace. However, regardless of how tedious it might seem, if you maintain rapport, you are likely to end up knowing something very important about this person. For Gina, companionship is very important.

Let's say you are a concerned friend, and you think Gina is making a bad decision. You want the best for her, and you want to be a resource to her. By helping her assess her true values, you can then look for alternative ways to fulfill those values. Joining a fitness club might be a much more cost-effective way to find companionship, and it may work better, too.

Of course, in the real world, people have many values operating simultaneously, and it would not be as cut-and-dried as this. However, by helping Gina to bring into consciousness what is really important (her values) and the different ways there are to fulfill those values, you are likely to help her come up with a much better, much more effective, and much more empowering line of action to take.

Let's say you get to the point of eliciting a solid value, and now it's time to help focus on getting that value fulfilled. For Gina, that value is companionship. We've got a problem here. We have no idea what companionship means to Gina. We know what it means to us, and we know what it means in a dictionary sense, but we don't know what it means to Gina. For you, companionship might be a dog and a cat, but for Gina it might be a houseful of party guests every night. This is where we start to elicit information about Gina's model of the world.

Criteria and equivalences are the qualitative descriptions of how values are fulfilled. If you want to help someone feel loved, you can either do things that would make *you* feel loved, or you can do things that would make *that person* feel loved. There is a big difference! The former sometimes works, the latter always works.

To elicit criteria,[6] we again have a simple question to ask:

> *Question to elicit criteria:* How would you know if you had [value]? What would you see, hear, feel, and say to yourself?

In another simplified, descriptive example:

> *You:* How would you know if you had companionship in your life? *(starts the process of eliciting criteria)*
>
> *Gina:* Well, I would have someone to talk to every night. *(a good start)*
>
> *You:* Would that be the same person, or different people, or some combination? *(getting more specific)*
>
> *Gina:* It would be both. It would be someone I could be very close to and share my most personal thoughts with. But it would also be a variety of people whom I could just say hello to and have some pleasant conversations with. *(Gina has started to give us at least*

two criteria here. One is sharing of personal thoughts, another is variety. Another might be pleasant conversation. At this point, you could choose to focus on one particular criterion and get more specific, or you could more broadly search for more criteria.)

Options:

You: (To get more specific with "personal thoughts"): How would you know if you really had someone to share your personal thoughts with?

You: (To get more criteria): What else would you have in your life if you had companionship?

You: (To check to see if "pleasant conversation" is a bogus criterion): Oh come on, since when have you ever just had pleasant conversation with people on the street?

This process could go on for some time, but I'm sure you get the point.

When you elicit criteria in this way, you draw a road map that will help someone get his or her core values met. For example, if you want to be a "true friend" to someone, part of the process is to know what's involved in being a "true friend" for that person. You need to know what his or her criteria are for true friendship. But you also will be making sure you know your own criteria, and helping the other person to meet those. This creates true win-win relationships that serve both of you.

The processes for eliciting and identifying values and criteria are simple and can be done with little or no experience. It helps to have some verbal skills to keep things light and pleasant, and it helps to have a variety of questions to ask. Here are few examples of different versions of questions to ask:

To elicit values:

- What's important to you about [blank]?
- What would having [blank] mean to you?
- What would you have if you had [blank]?
- How would [blank] make a difference to you?
- How is [blank] significant for you?

And so on. (Notice that none of these questions start with the word *why!*)

To elicit and verify criteria:

- How would you know if you had [value]?
- What would you see [hear, feel, say to yourself] if you had [value]?
- What kinds of things would be different if you had [value]?
- How would you be sure that you really had [value]?
- Could you have [test criteria] and still not have [value]?
- Come on! Are you really trying to tell me that [test criteria] would make you feel as if you had [value]?

And so on.

Although the process of eliciting values and criteria can seem somewhat tedious, think in terms of how easy it really is to find out the most important things in a person's life. In just a fifteen-minute conversation, you can have a better understanding of a person than you might have had after years of doing things together. It's certainly a process worth getting good at!

An Overview of the Listening Process

Much of what you have just read about is likely to be new to you. Here's a simple overview of the process, with some added information, to help you keep it all straight in your mind:

To be an effective listener:

1. *Have a purpose in your listening.* Each time you listen, you must focus on your purpose for listening. If you're listening because you want to hear what someone is saying, then you are listening either to gather information or to be entertained. If you're listening because you want to form a bond with the person, then that's your purpose. If you're listening to determine how to arrange a win-win agreement, then that's your purpose. You should know what your purpose is and keep it in mind. If (or, more appropriately, when) you get off track and are no longer fulfilling your purpose, it is your responsibility to get things moving in

the right direction again. When you have a purpose, you learn how to meet your goals in a shorter amount of time and in a more productive way.

2. *Maintain the highest level of respect, appreciation, and permission at all times.* Sharing things that are important is an incredibly kind and generous thing to do. Let the other person know you understand this. If you ever sense you may be losing rapport, stop the process and get back in touch with the person to see what's going on. Maintain rapport to the highest degree. When you maintain respect, appreciation, and permission, you will find your level of rapport increases very fast.

3. *Ask "what" or "how" rather than "why."* Although I didn't cover this specifically, this is generally good advice. "Why" questions tend to elicit beliefs from people, and they're generally inconsequential to the conversation. They tend to make people become even more stuck in their position, which can be detrimental if the position is not a win-win or is falsely limiting. If people disagree with an idea, and you ask them why they disagree, they will oblige you and start to come up with reasons "why" they disagree. These are "reasons" that a moment ago probably didn't exist (remember, people are emotional first, rational second). Once people create these bogus reasons, the reasons can take on a life of their own and imprison their creators in a limiting or win-lose position. This makes it far more challenging to bring about worthwhile solutions. The question "Why are you angry about the new attendance policy?" is likely to elicit a barrage of negative emotions and detrimental justifications for feeling angry. But the question, "What would have to happen for you to feel better about the situation?" has a much higher likelihood of eliciting high-quality information. It sets a direction and starts the process for creating more positive emotional states.

  "What" and "how" questions are generally a bit more awkward in their wording; however, the benefits are far-reaching. Play with them, and see how creative you can be in avoiding the word *why* in your questions.

4. *When appropriate to the context, and to your purpose, elicit values and criteria.* Always have strong rapport, and maintain permission and respect for the person when doing so.

5. *Calibrate for emphasized words.* The things that are really important to people are usually expressed with different tones

of voice and with more regularity. If the CEO continues to tell people that "customer satisfaction" is the most important aspect of the business, pay attention to that. Efficiency, cost savings, increased production, better quality, employee satisfaction, integrity, and all those other things may be important too; but if the CEO keeps stressing "customer satisfaction," then that's the value that's worth exploring more fully, especially by eliciting specific criteria that you can help meet. Always trust body communication over the words! When you get two different messages, keep investigating until you are sure you understand what the deepest response truly is.

6. *Clarify the individual meaning of the important words*—whether they're values or criteria or stressed words. For example, if your interviewer says he's looking for someone who can be *effective*, you ask "How would you know if you hired someone who was effective? What would let you know that this person truly was effective?" Once you find the key words that are important to a person, you then investigate to determine what those words mean to that person. Dictionary mentality asserts that words have discrete, specific meanings, and they are the same for everyone. Effective listening asserts that words have vastly different meanings for different people. Don't assume you know what any word means; always ask for clarification in more tangible terms.

7. *Stay with the process.* Keep going until you get clear, congruent ideas about what you want to know. "Is that really what you want? What do you really want?" People are unaccustomed to knowing what they want and what they value. Many times, you need to give them time to figure out what's important to them, then give them the space to share that with you. If you get a fast answer to a deep question, it's usually a sign that people are not really accessing their core values. Stay with the process and have patience.

8. *Use history as an indication of criteria and values.* If *loyalty* is a word your boss stresses, then ask her, "When was the last (best) time you had a 'loyal' employee? What made that person more 'loyal' than the others?" Elicit the information that tells you how your boss makes her determinations about loyalty. You might think loyalty means working long hours, while she may think loyalty means telling others what a great person she is. Stay with the process until you determine which observable behaviors constitute the nominalization.

9. *Get the fine distinctions.* Suppose you're interviewing for a position, you ask what the company is looking for, and they tell you they're looking for a person who has a certain college degree, can start in two weeks, has a certain amount of experience, and can do the job adequately. Get the finer, more important distinctions by asking, "There are lots of people who have that kind of college degree, that amount of experience, can start in two weeks, and can do this job adequately. What will be the deciding factors? What are the differences that make a difference? How will you determine the one who stands out from the crowd?" Answers to these questions will give you tremendous leverage for use with the verbal patterns we'll be covering in the next chapters.

10. *Bring out difficult issues.* Later in this book, you will learn how to bring out difficult issues with ease and comfort. Until then, remember that difficult issues are difficult only because they affect people at a very deep level. When you explore challenging issues, you are able to elicit some very important and deep values in a person and create deeper, more meaningful communication.

11. *Reciprocate for the gifts you're being given.* Bonding and interacting with people are two-way processes. You receive, but you also give. Most people will never have the skills you will learn from this book. This offers the potential for one-sided interchanges. You can quickly elicit another person's core values, but that person may not have the skills to do the same with you. You can calibrate the internal conflicts of others, but they may not have the skills to do the same with you. So offer this kind of information about yourself. Reciprocate at levels as deep or deeper than, as meaningful or more meaningful than, as vulnerable or more vulnerable than the levels of the other person. Your gifts will be well received.

We've discussed why it's important to listen effectively, what to listen for, and how to listen. Now it's time to conclude our discussion about listening by answering the question, "When do you listen, and when do you talk?"

Listening is very important, but it isn't the same as persuading. The skills for influencing and persuading are presented in the next chapter. Listening simply prepares you for those important activities; and because it's preparation, it needs to be done first. Always listen first. If during your later relations and communications, you find that your information may not have been accurate, go back and listen again. Listening is a wonderful, empowering process. Do it well, and do it often.

CHAPTER 7

INCREASING THE RECEPTIVITY OF YOUR WORDS

HOW WOULD YOU LIKE to become incredibly elegant in your communication? What if you were never at a loss for words? How about being able to make your ideas incredibly appealing? What if you could do all those things after just reading this chapter?

Well, don't get too excited, because achieving that kind of eloquence takes time. It takes more than fifteen minutes to develop, and most people never attain it in their entire lifetime.

However, if you'd like to have skills like these, read on! This chapter contains excellent strategies for increasing your current level of eloquence. All of them can be carried out with a minimal amount of practice, and all of them will help you to be much more effective in your verbal communication.

In a nutshell, you'll find a distinct difference in the way you approach the process of speaking. Most people think that what you say, the words you use, are important. And they are. But even more important is *how* you say what you say. Your nonverbal communication, your presuppositions, and the emotional states created in the communication process all play very important roles in communicational excellence.

We all know people who are gifted with words. They express themselves with ease and comfort, no matter what the topic. They share their difficult feelings with grace and elegance. They soothe you when you're hurt, and they animate you when you're happy. They always know the right thing to say. Even if they have bad news to share, it somehow isn't as bad coming from them.

Some people have it, most people don't. But for those who don't, is there hope? Is there a chance? Can you learn how to present yourself in this way?

There's a long-standing debate about how we acquire these types of skills and how we develop our personality. It's the classic "nature versus nurture" debate. The position for nature states that you're either born with the skills or you're not. If you're not, there's no chance of learning them. Just like your hair color, it's pointless to try to change certain aspects of your personality. You can use dyes on your hair, or bleach it, but its natural color is always unchangeable. The people who support this argument are constantly looking for the gene or gene pattern in your DNA structure that determines each given characteristic. You can't change your genes in the same way you can change your jeans!

The position for nurture states that your personality is determined by your experiences. Since you learned everything once, it opens the possibility for learning something again, perhaps in a new way. You can change your personality. The people who support this argument are constantly looking for the critical parental, sibling, or peer behaviors that create each given characteristic.

The debate has been so long-standing because there is no simple answer. Plenty of studies have been done on the subject, but the plain truth is that we don't know the answers; it's doubtful that we will have much more of an answer in any of our lifetimes, but it's helpful to look at what we do know. We know for certain that people who are linguistically trained become more effective in communicating. We know for certain that people who make core changes in their strategies for interacting with others become more effective in communication. We are certain that there is a significant amount of progress and improvement available for each of us.

I suggest that the way to do this is to learn new strategies, and the next several chapters are filled with some great ones—

many of which you probably haven't come across before. I think you'll be surprised at how many simple and elegant strategies are available, right now, to help you succeed.

Timing—Let the Game Come to You

So far, we've paid attention to how communication occurs and looked at the importance of nonverbal communication. We've looked at the importance of emotional states, and we've learned about unconscious communication. We've explored how to notice incongruencies in communication and how to notice changes in the emotional states of others. We've explored the process of gaining and maintaining rapport. Throughout these discussions, we've placed much of our attention on other people and paid special notice to what is going on with them. These are some of the fundamentals for being a great listener.

This brings us to the aspect of timing. I once had the pleasure of working with a talented man, whom I'll refer to as Joseph. He was an expert communicator, and he was especially gifted in getting things accomplished in the workplace. He had a natural ability to sell others on his ideas and to get them implemented with minimum resistance and maximum support. For him, two things were critical. The first was something he referred to as "reading people," which we refer to as calibration. The second was "timing."

One afternoon, Joseph had a meeting with his immediate superior. This was a relatively rare occurrence, mostly because Joseph had acquired so much freedom that he rarely interacted with his boss. However, when he did, it was often the kind of meeting that would set the direction for the next several months. This time, Joseph had about five things he wanted to get approved, and he had prepared things accordingly. He went to the meeting with the intention of getting each one approved.

Later that same day and after his meeting, I asked Joseph which of those things his boss had approved and which he did not. To my surprise, he said he didn't bring any of them up. He said that his boss just wasn't in a *receptive* mood.

So Joseph spent the meeting doing things other than asking for approvals.

About a week later, Joseph had another meeting with his boss. He still had three things in particular he wanted to have approved, and again he prepared things accordingly. He went to the meeting with the intention of getting three things approved.

After this meeting, I again asked Joseph which of those things were approved. This time, Joseph surprised me in a different way. He had not only managed to get approval on all three of his items, but he had also gotten approval on about six other things that he wasn't even planning to talk about. Joseph said that his boss was in such a *receptive* mood that Joseph just decided to keep presenting things. Joseph got everything he asked for, even things he thought would take much longer to make happen.

Joseph was a master at applying the concept of timing. Great sports competitors use timing too. If you ever listen to great athletes talking about how to perform better, you're likely to hear the expression "letting the game come to you." They understand that the dynamics of human relations flow.

" Now MAY NOT BE THE BEST TIME TO
ASK FOR THAT RAISE. TRY AGAIN
TOMORROW. "

You can either move with the flow, or you can try to fight against the flow. You can either let things come to you, or you can try to force them to come your way.

Oceans are that way too. If you've ever gone swimming in the ocean, you've probably spent some time getting in and out of the water from shore. When the waves are big, you'll notice that there are good times and not such good times to try to go into the water. If you plan to swim out past the waves, you had better notice when the waves are coming in first. And once you get out there, you'll need to pay attention to the waves if you want to come back in.

Near the shore, oceans have something called an undertow. When a wave comes in to shore, there is a flow of water moving toward the land. After the wave breaks onto shore, there is a returning flow of water moving back into the sea. This returning water is what creates an undertow; and it can make swimming in to shore difficult or impossible. If you're swimming in an ocean with a strong undertow, you had better either know about timing, or you had better start waving toward the lifeguard fast!

Getting to shore is easy when you know timing. Rather than frantically trying to swim against the current of the undertow, you simply let yourself go with the flow. The currents may carry you out somewhat, but that's okay. You let the undertow take you where it will. Then shortly after, a wave will come. As it gets close to you, you can start swimming toward shore, using the flow of the wave to supplement your efforts. You and the wave will be moving in synchrony, and your efforts will move you farther and faster than you may have expected. After just a few cycles of swimming with the wave, and not fighting the undertow, you will probably be surprised that all of a sudden you're standing waist-high in the water, wondering how you got there so soon and so easily.

Human relations have flows just like the ocean, just like a basketball game, just like Joseph's boss. Sometimes things will be going your way; other times they just won't. The skills described in this book will give you the ability to compensate for times when things aren't going so well, but you should still keep in mind that it's a lot like a strong swimmer fighting an undertow—it's a lot of work and there's an easier way.

With each process and technique listed in this book, you will find that there are times when things just flow, and other times when they're a bit of a struggle. When you wish to establish rapport with someone, there will be occasions when you have permission and it works great, and there will be occasions when the timing just isn't right. With your ability to calibrate and to understand others' unconscious communication, you are far better equipped to understand the flow and to move with it.

Calibration of unconscious communication is one of the best indicators for determining if there's a wave coming in or if the undertow is going out. Because so much of what you do as a listener and a communicator is based on permission, it is important for you to be cognizant of the flowing process of human relations.

We're about to discover some very penetrating, very powerful linguistic patterns. When implemented poorly, or without rapport, these patterns can wreak havoc. When implemented properly, respectfully, with permission, and with rapport, these patterns can open doors that you never even knew existed. So as we continue, I'd like you to assume the frame of going with the flow.

Reaching Common Ground

In an earlier discussion of values and criteria (Chapter 6), I mentioned that elicitation of criteria helps you get information about a person's model of the world. The phrase "model of the world" is relatively common in NLP, and it speaks to one of its underlying themes.

Having Regard for Another Person's Model of the World

As you interact with people, your effectiveness will be dramatically increased when you have regard for another person's model of the world. This process has two distinct aspects to it:

1. Recognizing that other people have a right to their own beliefs, values, and mind-sets
2. Recognizing that people function in the world in accordance with their model of the world

The first item brings up distinctions that are important to mention. We all have different perspectives on life and different understandings of how the world works. Sometimes our ideas will be very similar to those of others. Other times, our ideas will be very different. Regardless of whether we like or dislike, agree with or disagree with, value or don't value another person's ideas about the world, it is important to maintain respect for that person and his or her ideas. Respect is different from agreement. It is different from support. Respect is simply an acknowledgment that each person has a right to his or her own opinions and ideas.

In addition, acknowledging that people have a right to have their own ideas is different from condoning behaviors that stem from them. At this point, we're talking about behaviors that are almost universally considered to be detrimental to others or society, which brings us to the second item—recognizing that people function in the world in accordance with their model of the world.

In management circles, it is common practice to differentiate between beliefs and behaviors, and the distinction is often referred to in situations of difficulty. For example, when an employee feels prejudice toward a certain group of people, it is inappropriate to fire or discipline that person for his or her belief. However, if the employee acts in ways that compromise or injure a member or members of that group, then discipline is in order. Standard management practice subscribes to managing behavior rather than ideas. This is sound advice in the typical context for which it is applied; however, more comprehensive processes are available.

Because NLP is built upon addressing process, rather than content, it is naturally drawn toward addressing the *source* of behaviors, rather than the specific behaviors. And this brings us back to ideas, beliefs, and a person's model of the world.

By recognizing that people function in the world in accordance with their model of the world, you open your mind up to understanding the processes involved with another person's behavior. Getting caught up in whether some behavior is good or bad, right or wrong, can only take you down the path of passing judgment on others. That's not very useful, nor is it your role to be the judge of others. Instead, when you investigate the processes that lead to a given behavior, you put yourself in a better position to affect that behavior.

This idea is related to the NLP presupposition, "Behavior is geared for adaptation, and present behavior is the best choice available for an individual." In plain terms, this is a mind-set that people are doing the best they can with the knowledge, skills, and resources available to them. It leads to the conclusion that the behaviors which seem to be inherently negative are really adaptive behaviors by people responding to situations that are challenging for them.

Applying this mind-set to real-life contexts means responding to "negative" behaviors with assistance rather than punishment. One of the best ways to assist others is to gain a fuller understanding of the processes that lead to undesirable behaviors. The roots of those processes usually rest in the domain of mind-sets, perceptions, beliefs, perceived limitations, and so on. In other words, to offer assistance, you must first have regard for the person's model of the world.

In terms of the communication process, this requires you to reach common ground with the other person. It is from this common ground that you can begin to influence and persuade, and so have an effect on, the behaviors of others. Your level of influence is much greater when you deal with the process level (that of mind-sets, beliefs, and perceptions), rather than the content level (that of behavior). The best managers today realize that leadership is far more than just controlling the "negative" behaviors of others—it's about supporting and assisting others in making desirable change.

So the first process we're going to cover in the area of speaking involves reaching a common ground with your listener.   The process I am going to suggest is one that comes directly out of the field of hypnosis and comes more directly from the NLP Milton Model. Milton Erickson was one of the world's foremost hypnotherapists and was known for his extraordinary success helping others. His work involved inducing trance states in his clients and giving them useful and applicable suggestions. Two of the more important aspects of his success were his ability to create deep levels of trust with his clients and his ability to persuade clients to be highly receptive to his ideas. His expertise was built on his mastery with words and his voice tonality.

The Milton Model is a distillation of the verbal and tonal techniques that Erickson used to achieve his great success. The intricate details of this model are discussed in the books *Patterns of Hypnotic Techniques of Milton H. Erickson M.D.,* Volumes 1 and 2, by Richard Bandler and John Grinder, published in 1975 and 1977, respectively. These excellent books are especially useful if you wish to practice therapy or hypnotherapy. Our purposes will restrict us to a fractional but important portion of the Milton Model, modified for use in everyday applications. In NLP terms, we will cover an applied process of verbal pacing and leading, which helps us reach common ground with our listeners.

Verbal pacing is the process of verbalizing aspects of another person's experience. In simpler terms, it's about saying things that both of you recognize to be true. It sounds simple, but you may find that it requires conscious effort, at least initially. Verbal pacing requires you to see the world through the eyes of the person you're speaking with and to vocalize the things you see. It is a means by which you can enter into the world of the person you are speaking with. It helps you share perspectives and come closer to understanding each other. When done with integrity and respect, it is a process that creates rapport and strong feelings of trust (for both of you).

In order to understand verbal pacing, we must distinguish among truth, perception, and perspective. Consider for a moment a scenario where a company president gives a speech. There are four people we are going to focus on.

One is the janitor who is happy in his job. He's worked for the company for twenty years, and he's very glad that the company has given him a job during that time. He is very appreciative of the president, and he is glad that he works so hard to keep this company going.

The second person is a mid-level manager who is frustrated with her job. She feels she has been lied to and cheated by the company, and she blames the president. She suspects he is corrupt, and she harbors animosity toward the man.

The third person is an upper-level manager, who works closely with the president. She knows a great deal about what the president is going through, and she is aware that this particular speech was mandated by the Board of Directors. It was something that the president did not want to do, because he felt the information was misleading; however, he was pressured into doing it anyway. She understands that the president had a very difficult time making the speech, but he tried as much as possible to give the impression of total support for the information.

The president, the fourth person in this scenario, felt that if people knew of his disagreement with the Board, then it would be very difficult for them emotionally; he felt the employees needed to see strong, unified leadership. The upper-level manager respects the president's strength and integrity and values him for going through such a difficult process while keeping the welfare of his employees foremost in his mind.

These people all hear the same speech, but they hear it from different perspectives. They have different mind-sets about the president, about the company, and about the event. Through their personal perspectives, they will filter and interpret the data they receive in order to create meaning.

Now consider the statement, "The president showed great leadership by making that speech." Is that a true statement?

From the perspective of the janitor, it is a true statement. The janitor noticed that the president acted very presidential, and he explained the information so that people could understand it. The janitor doesn't usually get to hear about the topics covered in the speech, so he found the entire speech to show great leadership, from a man who is obviously helping keep this company alive and growing. The janitor perceives that this man is a great leader.

From the perspective of the mid-level manager, the speech did not show leadership at all. It was a misleading and deceitful speech, shaped by the evil and ugly traits that have characterized the president's behavior. She could sense deceit from his body language and his tone of voice. It was just one more example of his lack of integrity and his efforts to trick and deceive others to get things done his way. She perceives that this man is not a good leader, and she has a strong desire to thwart his efforts.

From the perspective of the upper-level manager, the speech showed great leadership. Despite the challenging circumstances, the president was able to present himself in a professional manner. He demonstrated a unified leadership position, despite his misgivings about the information. His restraint and strength are an inspiration to her. She perceives that this man is a great leader and is now an even stronger supporter of his actions.

And finally, from the perspective of the president, the speech did not show leadership. He felt he sold out his own principles due to coercion. He wasn't willing to stand up for his internal values and instead took the easy way out. He showed cowardice in that speech, not leadership. The president perceives that he is lacking in character.

Consider the following sentences from these four perspectives, and consider who would agree with them, and who would disagree with them:

- The president gave a good speech.
- The president is a great leader.
- You can trust the president.
- The president has a strong sense of values and morals.
- The president was wrong to yield to the whims of the Board.
- If the president were a better man, he could have solved this dilemma in a more honorable way.
- Whatever the president said, it didn't matter. What mattered was his leadership presence.

- The president has a character flaw that makes him difficult to believe.
- The president lied during the speech.
- The president did the best job he knew how to do.

If the four people mentioned had a chance to discuss each of these statements, they would have very different ideas about what was true and what was false. That's because we can never know what's really true and what's really false. We can only have our own *perceptions* of truth.

You might start to see some patterns forming in this book. Earlier I said it's not very useful to think in terms of right or wrong. I said the same about thinking of things as good or bad. Now I'm even saying that truth and falsity are matters of perception. Are the walls shaking yet?

Some people are very rigid about these concepts. However, each of these things is more effectively understood in terms of individuals' perception. It's our perception of what's happening in the world that allows us to have opinions. We don't know what really exists in the world; we just know what we gather from our senses and what we interpret from the massive amount of data that we gather.

The process of pacing requires that you avoid trying to impose your mind reads, conclusions, judgments, value judgments, and opinions on others and instead to speak about things that will be perceived as accurately describing the other person's experience—from the other person's perspective. It forces you to change your perspective, and to bring yourself into *his or her* model of the world.

So far we've discussed conceptually how to pace current experience. But how do you do this? What specific processes can you use? How do you know what words to use? Or what experience to pace?

Let's begin by learning several different ways to structure sentences so that they more closely pace the current experience of other people. While I present these techniques as near universals, it is helpful to keep in mind the caveat that this is an individual process for each person. Generally, the more you customize your words for your listeners, the more effective you will be with them.

EXAMPLES OF INTERPRETATIONS VERSUS SENSORY-BASED OBSERVATIONS

The first way to pace current experience is to speak in "sensory-based" terms. This means that you will verbalize the observations you make—observations that are equally accessible to the other person. The observations can come from any of your senses but require you to forego the process of making interpretations. If you are unaccustomed to making the distinction between observations and interpretations, then this can be an eye-opening experience. With a little practice, this process becomes quite easy. For example, notice the differences in the following examples:

You're on a golf course ...

> *Interpretation:* It sure is a hot day today. ("Hot" is relative.)

> *Sensory-based observation:* I have sweat running down my forehead.

> *Interpretation:* This is a long hole for a par 4. ("Long" is relative.)

> *Sensory-based observation:* It says here that this hole is 552 yards.

> *Interpretation:* What a beautiful day for golf. ("Beautiful" is relative.)

> *Sensory-based observation:* The sky is very clear; I see only a few clouds over on the horizon.

The distinctions between interpretations and sensory-based observations are very important. Interpretations force your listeners to consider *your* model of the world and fail to let them know that you're willing to understand *their* model of the world. Alternatively, sensory-based observations make statements that coincide with your listeners' ongoing sensory experience and let them know that you are seeing things that coincide with how they perceive the world. The effects are dramatic.

By stringing together a series of sensory-based observations (SBOs), you create a stronger and stronger perception that you're on common ground with your listeners. This perception will be accurate, because you will need to think of things from their perspective in order to succeed. Let's consider a simple business example:

> **Situation:** You're in a meeting, and it's your job to present some bad news about a project that is far behind schedule.
>
> **You:** Now that we're all here *(SBO)* and it's 8:35 *(SBO)*, I am going to talk about the Conveyor Project. *(You have already started, so this is pacing their experience and is an SBO.)* We met last Friday to discuss the project *(SBO)*, and almost everyone was concerned about our failure to meet schedule *(SBO)*; and as a group we expressed the need to do a better job *(SBO)*...
>
> **Analysis:** You begin with six SBOs in a row, and then you might introduce some measurable data and facts, which would also be SBOs. With this kind of groundwork laid, it is very likely that you will have established yourself as having reached common ground. This will likely prepare the group for the ensuing process that hints of leading, in which you introduce statements that we are going to cover next— observations, conclusions, judgments, values, and opinions.

Pacing is as simple as that. It takes a bit of practice, but just the process of reading this book will most likely attune your awareness so that the process becomes quite easy for you. Once you've learned pacing, you're ready for leading. We'll begin the transition by looking at some methods of presenting your observations, conclusions, judgments, values, and opinions that fall somewhere in the middle of the two.

The following five categories of language patterns can make or break your ability to share common ground with another person verbally. They all focus on the outcome of pacing current experience and avoiding disagreement from the listener. This is the true testament to whether you are on common ground with your listener. In addition, these statements allow you to introduce glimmers of your model of the world.

SAMPLE SENTENCE CONSTRUCTIONS

In each category, I begin by listing an example of an ineffective statement (one likely to create disagreement), then

describe the major problems associated with it. In subsequent examples, I begin to make subtle changes in the wording to make it more universally acceptable (more universally likely to create agreement). Pay close attention to these constructions and the subtle changes in wording—they are the crux of creating communication that is understood and received. I recommend you go over this section in detail; many of the changes are subtle but significant. The descriptive name for the type of statement is listed first, followed by the statement and then an explanation:

Observations

Mind read observation: "I can see this is making you sad." Because nobody can truly know what someone is feeling, it is impossible to truly know if someone is sad. Many people see a frown and equate that with sadness, but that is a mind read. A frowning person may not be sad or may be sad and not be attuned to it. In either case, the person would disagree with the statement, saying it was false. Mind reads should be avoided except in rare circumstances, which we will cover in a later section.

Interpreted observation: "I can see that you are frowning." This is not a full mind read, although it does have aspects of one. If you see a person's brow contracted and mouth turned downward, that by definition could be a frown. But it could also be a wince, grimace, or a natural state of muscle tension. Additionally, a frown is associated with a state of being "down," so if the listener had a contracted brow and downturned mouth but was feeling in a fairly positive or neutral state—or even thought she was in a positive or neutral state—then she would likely disagree with the sentence. Each of these scenarios could become sources of disagreement from the listener. Interpretations stated as facts can often be sources of disagreement.

Removed mind read: "Some people would think you are sad about this." This is a mind read—of "sad"—but it is given from the perspective of "some people." This makes the mind read more likely to be accepted by the listener as pacing his or her model of the world.

Removed interpretation: "Some people would think that you are frowning." This is an interpretation—interpreting "frown" from seeing a contracted brow and downturned mouth—from the perspective of "some people." Again, the listener is more likely to accept this as pacing his or her experience than to accept a standard interpretation.

Observation: "I can see your mouth turned somewhat downward." This is a strict observation. It is measurable. This type of statement has the highest potential for being perceived as true and for creating agreement from your listener. People are generally unaccustomed to speaking in these terms; however, with some practice you may find it to be one of the most useful verbal patterns available to you.

The "removed" perspectives can take various forms. *Some people, many people, not many people, anyone, an observant person, an unlearned person, a novice in the field, a perfectionist person,* and so on are examples of other phrases that can be used in these situations.

Conclusions

Conclusion presented as fact: "We need to make a decision about this contract." This is a conclusion on the part of speaker, but it is presented as if it were a globally recognized truth. This type of construction has a high likelihood of sparking disagreement or debate. It creates a close-minded atmosphere, which implies that other options aren't being considered. Those people interested in looking at all options will object to such a statement, even if they are in agreement with the conclusion. They'll feel it's premature to close down debate on the issue. This type of construction is the root source of "devil's advocates." Conclusions presented as facts should be used only in special circumstances once rapport and trust are fully established.

Conclusion presented as opinion: "In my opinion we need to make a decision about this contract." This is a conclusion on the part of the speaker, but in this case the speaker presents it as such. It avoids the problem of presenting the opinion as a strict fact. This statement may also initiate debate; however, it still gives you more leeway with the listener. Because it is presented as an opinion, it helps the listener feel secure that you are not prematurely discounting other options and that you are open to hearing other opinions. The listener is less compelled to disagree at this point and is more likely to allow you to continue your discussion. This type of statement has a good chance of creating agreement from your listener.

Removed conclusion: "Some would say that we need to make a decision about this contract." This is the safest and surest way to express a conclusion and have the statement be accepted. It has the highest likelihood of incurring agreement by the listener. The subject choice for the removed perspective should be a reasonable choice—for example, "An *anxious* person would say that ..." could lead to a disagreement, whereas "*Part of me* wants to say that ..." might be a better choice.

Judgments

Judgment: "This is a good company." Judgments make categorizations according to "good" or "bad." In this case, the speaker has decided what "good" is and has determined that the company falls within that category. There is a high chance that listeners will disagree with a judgment. Either the listeners will have a different idea about what "good" is or they will have different ideas about how well this company fits into that category. In either case, disagreement occurs. Judgments should generally be avoided due to their high potential for creating disagreement or debate. Trying to impose your judgments on others is generally considered abusive.

Preference: "I like this company." This is the truer expression of a judgment. Rather than determining the "good" or "bad" aspect of the company, this sentence simply states a personal preference. We're all entitled to our preferences, and we generally know what those preferences are; and so preference statements generally are accepted quite easily and spark little or no disagreement. They do, however, sometimes spur debate. The listener may decide this is a good time to debate the quality of the company and "convince" the speaker to think otherwise. So these types of statements also carry the potential of creating debate and causing the conversation to digress from where you hope it will go.

Removed judgment 1: "Some would say that this is a good company." This statement has the highest likelihood of being accepted by the listener. This is an excellent way to maintain trust and rapport even while presenting a potentially controversial viewpoint. If you're going to present a controversial viewpoint, it is often effective to present it in this removed format, introduce the objection yourself, then immediately countersell it. We'll cover this excellent process in more detail in a later section.

Removed judgment 2: "We have a reputation of being a good company." This is simply another version of a removed judgment.

Moral Judgments

Moral judgment: "This is the right thing to do." Morality pertains to aspects of "right" or "wrong." Moral judgments are similar to judgments in many respects. A moral judgment has a high potential to spur debate or disagreement and should generally be avoided. Trying to impose your morality on others is generally considered abusive. On the other hand, if your listener does accept this statement, it can be a powerful leverage point. By appealing to high moral standards, leaders for centuries have pressured others to follow them, which is a process that can be abusive. Be wary of those who would dare to tell you what is right and wrong.

Personal moral judgment: "I feel this is the right thing to do." Again, this is your opinion, so it would have a reasonable chance of being accepted as a true statement. However, it still creates an opportunity to debate the issue and encourages the listener to "convince" you otherwise—thus diverting the focus of your conversation.

Personal observation: "I feel morally in alignment with this." This statement is more specifically truthful than a personal value judgment and somewhat more likely to create full agreement. Again, it is strictly outside the realm of others' experience to say what you feel and don't feel, and attempts to do so are generally considered abusive. An observation like this is often more effective at avoiding debate than a personal value judgment, especially because it is a rather uncommon form of expression.

Removed value judgment: "Some would argue that this is the right thing to do." This is the most highly accepted structure for value statements. It has the highest likelihood of being accepted by the listener without debate or interruption.

Opinions

Opinion presented as fact: "Red is the best color for what we're trying to accomplish." This is an opinion on the part of the speaker and has a high likelihood of spurring debate or objections. The criteria for "best" are not stated, and the listener is likely to have a different understanding of what "best" would be. Opinions presented as facts should generally be avoided, except in special circumstances when strong rapport already exists.

Opinion presented as opinion: "I feel red is the best color for what we're trying to accomplish." This is an opinion stated as an opinion. Because we all have opinions and we generally know what they are, this approach is likely to pace the listener's experience. But, again, it still provides an opening to debate the issue, which could derail your conversation.

Removed opinion: "Some would argue that red is the best color for what we're trying to accomplish." This has the highest likelihood of being accepted by your listeners and keeping them from debating or derailing the conversation.

Each time you begin to speak with people, you will have occasion to use observations, conclusions, judgments, moral judgments, and opinions. This is the beginning of the process of introducing others to your model of the world, and it's a necessary part of the persuasion and influence process. The manner in which you present these statements will make a tremendous difference in how effective you are at creating a receptive listener.

The level of rapport you have with your listeners will have a significant effect on the liberties you can take in your pacing and leading. If you have a hostile listener, then I recommend that you do lots and lots of pacing and only rarely and carefully venture into observations, conclusions, judgments, values, and opinions—using predominantly the most acceptable versions. This will usually open the way for effective communication in the future, although it may take multiple interactions. If you already have a highly receptive listener, then you may wish to go quickly into some of the more debatable realms.

The more agreement you create with your listener, the broader your common base of understanding and the more effective you will be at the later process of having your ideas understood and accepted.

Verbal Influence

I've already made mention several times of verbal persuasion and influence. However, I haven't yet filled out my definition of just what those processes are, nor what kinds of situations they can be useful for. Many people still hold on to the idea that persuasion is win-lose oriented, that influence is about getting someone else to agree with you regardless of what would be best for the other person. However, this is a faulty paradigm that eventually sabotages the processes of those who have the misfortune of using it.

Persuasion is *not* the process of getting someone to agree with you—it is the process of encouraging someone to understand your model of the world.

Influence is *not* the process of getting people to do what you want—it is the process of giving people more choices in behavior and getting them to see, from your model of the world, the advantages to the behaviors you are suggesting.

Persuasion and influence do *not* require others to take any action whatsoever—they support others in understanding that other choices are available and give them ideas about how those choices may be better. They support others in succeeding with whatever choice they make.

When you're thorough in your process of determining win-win, then you will take into account other perspectives, other points of views, and other models of the world, as well as your own. You take into account the values, beliefs, and desires of the person or people you are dealing with, as well as your own. With this more comprehensive understanding, you will often find yourself in the position of having excellent solutions. When you maintain unquestionable win-win, then it follows that people will *want* to partake in the process if they understand it the same way you do. Persuasion and influence are the means by which you help others see the overall win-win benefits of the things you are proposing and by which you encourage and support them to take action.

Using the skills of influence and persuasion potentially positions you to take on the role of leader. As you increase the scope of your influence, you will naturally begin functioning in a leadership role. This can be an excellent and useful role.

Unfortunately, many people still hold on to ineffective paradigms about leadership, too. Many equate leadership with responsibility and work or equate it with making decisions on behalf of others. Some equate leadership with having power over others. Some view leadership as a means of driving people toward a given choice, thus taking away their freedom of choice. Again, that is win-lose thinking.

When people still operate from ineffective paradigms about persuasion, influence, and leadership, they often decide they don't want any part of those processes. It's a decision I happen to agree with—it's inappropriate to play any role in the ineffective paradigms I've just mentioned; they are win-lose. However, by embracing effective paradigms about these healthy, supportive processes, you find that you can become more of the person you want to be, and others around you do too.

The leaders of today express a different paradigm, one that supports win-win. Leadership is a supportive process. It is about getting people's attention and showing them a better way. The greater the number of people who give you their attention, the greater the magnitude of your leadership. The better the proposed way, the greater the quality of your leadership. People benefit from having these kinds of leaders in their environment.

The process of pacing and leading begins with simply regarding the other person's model of the world. It continues with introducing that person to parts of your model of the world. It eventually continues with persuasion, influence, and leadership.

Let's look at an example that recently happened in my life: A friend of mine was filled with anxiety; in fact, she had been visibly upset for a week. The cause of her anxiety was the behavior of her ex-boyfriend, who she thought had been a jerk ever since he ended the relationship.

From listening, I realized that she was not taking responsibility for the situation, and so she felt powerless and victimized about their breakup. She had distorted the events of the past weeks to support her generalizations about what a jerk this man had been. She was incongruent about her negative feelings toward him.

By leading, I helped her see things from the viewpoint of responsibility. I brought her attention to *her* role in the process of the breakup and helped her reexamine how she contributed to that situation. We reexamined those behaviors on the part of the boyfriend that upset her so much, and we accessed and explored her internal source of incongruency.

As a result, she came to see that she was instrumental in creating the situation in which the breakup occurred; she realized the decision was a good one. She re-accessed the loving feelings she had for this man and resolved her internal conflict. She achieved a centered, self-assured feeling that gave her an increased self-confidence and certainty. For the next week, she continued to remark about how centered and calm she felt as a result of our conversation.

This is the kind of situation most of us experience on a regular basis. The quality of our life is determined by how we handle situations like these, both for ourselves and with others. The persuasion and influence process is about getting people's attention and showing them a better way.

VERBAL PERSUASION AND INFLUENCE PROCESS

The process of verbal persuasion and influence is relatively straightforward, and we've already covered several parts of it. We'll be continuing to develop the remaining parts of it throughout the entire section on verbal skills. Here's the overall process:

1. Have regard for the other person's model of the world.
2. Listen to the other person. Get an idea of who he or she is, what he or she wants, what he or she is concerned about, and so on. Listen for any pertinent limitations expressed in their language patterns.
3. Foster and maintain rapport.
4. Reach common ground. Use verbal patterns to create maximum agreement with your listener.
5. Calibrate for an emotional state of receptivity. Think in terms of the flow and what direction it is going.
6. Lead your listener to your ideas.
7. Calibrate for continued agreement or areas of concern. Calibrate to determine the continual flow.
8. Address concerns and potential concerns. Continue to have profound respect for the other person and his or her points of view.
9. Calibrate for resolution of concerns, continued agreement.
10. Continue to maintain rapport at all times. If rapport is lost, reestablish it before moving forward. Move backward in the process if needed to reestablish rapport.
11. Refuse to accept anything less than unquestionable win-win.
12. (Optional) For inspiring action, help determine courses of win-win actions that help fulfill the other person's values and criteria.

This process works; it is a way of interacting with and persuading people that allows you to maintain your respect for others and your own integrity. When you use this process, you are very effective in your dealings with people. People will respect you and feel good about their interchanges with you. You will function as a leader, and people will willingly look to you for guidance. They will seek you out, and they will be rewarded because of it. You will help others understand the outcomes they truly want, help them succeed, and inspire them to work together to create outcomes that work well for everyone involved. People will feel good about having you on their team. This process can be a significant foundation of your success.

We'll continue to refer to this verbal persuasion and influence process throughout other parts of this book. So far, we have covered all but Items 4, 6, and 8, each of which has to do with verbal skills. We've begun Items 4 and 6 and will continue to explore them in the next section. Items 6 and 8 will be interwoven with the material in the rest of the verbal skills sections and chapters, and each of the items will be reinforced as we go along. So let's continue.

Use of Language Patterns

Thus far, we've identified some specific types of verbal skills. We've discussed the process of reaching common ground. We've discussed the process of pacing, in which you not only say things that are true, but also say things that will pace the listeners' experience and be perceived as true from their perspective. We've demonstrated how observations, conclusions, judgments, moral judgments, and opinions can be transformed into statements that are more easily received by others, and how that process can begin to help your listener start to explore your model of the world. We've begun to examine the process of influence and persuasion and shared something about what leading is all about. Now we're going to explore how to enhance these skills.

Learning how to rephrase your statements so that they pace your listener's experience is the first step in creating strong verbal communications. This will be the cornerstone for each of the subsequent verbal skills. By the time you're done with the verbal skills chapters, you will have been exposed to this process many times, and you may find it quite easy to incorporate into your own communication right away.

Let's look at an example that highlights some extensions of the verbal skills we've already covered. It involves only a portion of the persuasion and influence process, so for the purposes of this example, assume the following: Extensive listening has already occurred, both alternatives would be win-win, and calibration is continuing on a regular basis. In this example, comments about each important segment are inserted in parentheses:

Situation: You're a manager and you want to hire a new clerical person to support your staff. You need approval from your senior manager, and you're seeking to persuade him to give you that approval. He has the authority to make the decision but is typically opposed to hiring new people due to the costs involved and the time spent on training; however, he is in agreement with company directives about increasing sales and getting higher productivity.

> *Weak Approach* (with explanatory comments): I wanted to talk to you today because we need to hire a new person (*"we need to hire a new person" is a conclusion stated as a fact*). This new person will save time (*another conclusion*) for all the other eight people in the office, thus making them more effective (*opinion and conclusion*). Currently, most of us spend several hours a day doing clerical work that could be done by someone who makes less money (*a conclusion that could initiate a debate; for example, "Why are you spending so much time doing this? You shouldn't have that much clerical work to do… "*). A better thing (*a judgment stated as a fact*) to do is hire a new person. We can do it with just a minimum of interviewing (*conclusion could initiate a debate*), and we can increase our productivity by at least 15 percent (*opinion and conclusion without supportive data, could initiate a debate*). That will more than pay for the new person in direct-cost savings right away (*opinion and conclusion could initiate an accounting debate, thus diverting the conversation off the subject*). Can I have your approval? (*This last sentence forces a yes or no decision and locks the manager into a "no" if that's his first emotional choice. Limits the ability to persuade later.*)

Potential problems: This is a logical, methodical approach. If you're a down-to-earth kind of person, just wanting someone to give you the bottom line, then this approach might appeal to you. Many people incorrectly think that this directness is the best method of persuading people. Unfortunately, it is rarely effective. It might work for Spock, but it rarely works in the real world. It fails to create a space of emotional agreement.

There are some structural difficulties that contribute to the ineffectiveness of this statement. Most significantly, it is filled with opinions and conclusions stated as facts.

Any sentence in that paragraph could be debated and would divert attention from the approval process. For example, if the senior manager thinks you aren't really spending several hours a day doing clerical work or, even worse, thinks you are but shouldn't be, then that could initiate a debate. Debating this point causes you to diverge from the path that would lead to a decision. A hard logical debate can always be defeated by another brand of logic. Contrary to our beliefs about logic, it can be used to justify virtually any side of an argument.

> *More effective approach* (with explanatory comments): I wanted to talk to you today to discuss something that you may not be aware of *(begins the approach pacing current experience; "may not be aware of" is by definition impossible to logically disagree with)*. Most of the people in my department have been coming to me with their concerns about the clerical work they're doing *(would be perceived as true)*. They feel as if *("feel as if" is truth; to say "they are spending…" would be an opinion, but "they feel as if they are spending…" is describing their feelings, which are by definition outside of the awareness of others)* they're spending too much time on it and that their productivity is suffering. I'm doing my best to deal with these issues as they come in *(would be perceived as true)*. I share with them *(paces actual activities which have occurred)* the fact that we shouldn't have to spend *(supports the probable opinion of the manager, thus diverting a potential debate and sidetrack)* that much time doing clerical activities, that there must be ways to minimize the time spent *(again prevents a diversion; all five of those sentences pace current experience)*.
>
> Unfortunately, I don't feel as if I'm very effective with them *(opinion stated as an opinion)*, because I myself have felt the same challenges *(would be perceived as true, you know what you "feel")*. I'm spending far more time than I think is useful doing my own clerical activities *(conclusion presented as an opinion; "than I think" makes the statement into a fact, avoiding a debate)*. I know that we need to be very concerned about increasing costs *(paces his belief system, encourages common ground)*, but I also know that we need to be very attentive to ways of saving money as well *(paces his belief system, encourages common ground)* and increasing revenues *(all*

three pace the manager's belief system and are likely to be agreeable to him). In my opinion *(anything said after "in my opinion" should be perceived as true and will minimize an immediate need to debate the conclusion),* we will be far better off *(judgment and conclusion presented as opinion)* hiring a lower-paid clerical person to relieve us of some of this paperwork burden.

It's not always the best way to go *(paces his possible immediate rejection of the idea),* especially with the time it takes to hire someone *(we'll cover counterselling of objections in a later section),* but in this case, I'd really like you to consider it *("I'd really like you to" gives him the opportunity to refuse, thus preventing the "pushing into a corner" reaction).* I've thought about this a lot *(paces your actual activity),* and I didn't really enjoy the idea of trying to sell you on it *(also paces your actual activity),* but in this case, I feel *("I feel" makes this a truthful sentence, perhaps deferring the debate)* it is in our best interests *(conclusion and judgment presented as opinion).* But before I ask for your approval *(subtle shift in phrasing; "ask you to approve it" would indicate an action, "your approval" uses the nominalization "approval" to presuppose the existence of an approval),* do you understand where I'm coming from? *(this question sets a positive direction and keeps the manager uncommitted and open to further persuasion)*

Strengths—Each sentence is a true statement and presents your opinions as your opinions, not facts. It also presents the expected objections, then addresses your countersell to them. Notice that this approach is much more verbose. It's not as direct, but it is far more likely to generate into a productive discussion and a higher level of effectiveness.

I'll be continuing to present analyses like these for the next several sections, so things will start making more sense as you read on.

Talking More

This section is presented only for those people who are not already comfortable talking extensively. If you are one of those people who can talk and talk to anyone you meet, then please skip to the bottom of page 185 where I have some special messages for you.

The previous example illustrates that the stronger approaches are more verbose. That happens. The speech John F. Kennedy made announcing this country's entry into the space race could have been two sentences long. But it wasn't. The skills needed for persuasion and influence will require you to speak more often and for longer periods of time. You will learn how to be an active participant in directing your discussions. Although you can be very influential in the listening process (especially by asking questions), your more effective persuasion power comes when you are speaking.

This isn't always what people want to do. In fact, the more ineffective you are, the more likely it is that this process won't appeal to you when it is suggested. However, being willing to speak freely (using the persuasion and influence process) is important enough that we need to address it right up front.

There are three major reasons why people sometimes are reluctant to be verbose, and we're going to look at each of them before we go on (there's actually a fourth that we'll look at later in this chapter). These three reasons are:

1. You think talking too much is a waste of time.
2. You don't know what to say, or you're not comfortable talking.
3. You are constantly interrupted.

Let's look at each of these individually. If you think talking is a waste of time, then you're probably right. If you think that way, then the way you are talking is probably wasting time! Truly effective communicators realize the power of speaking because when they speak, they get powerful results. But not everyone does.

When you learn the verbal skills and the behavior models presented in this book, you will value the power of speech much more. You will find that a fifteen-minute conversation can save you a week's worth of work and an aspirin bottle's worth of frustrations. You will find that a series of five-minute conversations will help you get raises and promotions that years of good work and good results won't necessarily get you. You will find that you feel better on a regular basis, and you will reduce the tension and stress level in your everyday life. Talking more can do a lot for you, but only when you do it effectively.

The second challenge to talking more revolves around skill level. If you're not comfortable talking, or you find you don't know what to say, then that's an indication of skill level. Consider yourself lucky—a lot of people in the world are in the same situation that you are, but they haven't yet found a book like this to help guide them. This book may not be the cure for all your life's woes, but it does a very good job of giving you guidelines about what to say and when to say it. Most people spend their whole lives never having been given this opportunity.

Your first jump in skill level will come simply from planning your approaches. As we've shown, just saying what you want is not effective. You have to use the verbal persuasion and influence process. Just the process of pacing current experience opens you up to bringing up, then counterselling, possible objections and to presenting more of your opinions. By the time you do all three of these things, you'll find that you've already said a lot more. When you have the recipe for good communication, then it's simply a matter of following the instructions. The mystery is gone, replaced with sound procedures that work.

If you're not comfortable talking, there's probably a reason for that too—you're not being effective when you do, so it feels like a failure each time you try. Anyone who continues to do something with poor results will soon lose any motivation to keep doing it. That's natural. As we've already discovered, interpersonal skills *can* be learned. Among those skills is learning how to talk more.

When you apply these skills, you will start to have successes. Each time you converse, you will have yet another example of how conversing helped you get something you wanted. In a very short time, you will feel very good about communicating, and you will feel very comfortable doing it.

Of course, some people are easier to talk to than others, but your overall level of comfort and success will increase. You will not only feel better as you're speaking, but you will also feel better knowing that you know what you're doing. It won't be dumb luck anymore; it will be your own skill shining through!

The third challenge to talking more is that you may find yourself interrupted when you talk too much or, worse yet, you may find yourself having to bully your way over others just to get your words out. These are common problems and can certainly limit your effectiveness. A large percentage of interruptions come from an objection to a statement. If there are no objections, then the listener will generally be content to keep listening. When you say things that are objectionable to your listeners, even if the listeners don't interrupt you, they will often prepare a counter-response in their head, and not hear what you're saying next. Talking more is not always effective; you can't just bully your way through a conversation. But it can be part of a highly effective process when you pace current experience and begin to share your model of the world. If you find yourself constantly being interrupted, then you are also finding that your conversations get off track and get muddied up. People "fight" what you have to say, and you fail to direct the conversations effectively.

Being interrupted is a function of two factors. First, it signifies some lack of rapport. If the person you are communicating with feels a very high level of trust and rapport, then you can say almost anything you want and will continue to have a contented listener. Second, it signifies a failure to use these effective verbal strategies. Next we'll look at strategies for counterselling objections before they occur; counterselling is an effective way to maintain control of a conversation without being interrupted. Several of the other patterns will also be directly applicable to this issue. In summary, if you are being interrupted, it signifies a certain communication skill level that can be improved (in some cases, it also signifies an inconsiderate person; however, that's far more rare than you might first imagine).

So if you are finding yourself feeling a bit stretched when you are instructed to talk more, realize that is a common response. But let me emphasize, it is well worth the challenge. Remember that change sometimes requires you to do things that are "not you." When you meet this challenge, and you incorporate these skills, you will make meaningful differences in your life.

There are several reasons that talking more is so important. The basic three are:

1. When you are able to talk longer without being interrupted, that is an indication of an increased ability to gain and maintain high levels of trust and rapport.
2. When you're talking, you have maximum control over what topics and information are considered and from what perspective they are initially considered.
3. When you're talking, you have increased potential to persuade and influence.

If you've spent most of your life speaking infrequently, then the idea of speaking a lot more may not be appealing. Let me assure you, however, that when you start using the verbal strategies in this book, your experience of speaking will change dramatically!

Rather than finding yourself debated with and argued with at every turn, you will find your listeners nodding in agreement. Rather than having them wait for you to stop so they can counter your argument, they will listen to what you are saying and consider it more thoughtfully. Of course, you will always get varying opinions, but these opinions will no longer be argumentative and discounting; instead, they will be constructive and supportive. You will find that the verbal persuasion and influence process helps you bring great things into your life, with the help of great people around you.

If you were already comfortable and skilled at talking at length, I hope you followed my advice and skipped the previous section! The following information is for all readers.

Now that I've expounded on the virtues of talking at length, I have one final thing left to say. Talking is always a two-way process, and extensive listening should be done concurrently. You must continue to calibrate your listeners, keep a sense of the flow of the conversation, and watch for nonverbal indicators throughout your speaking. The verbal skills we are discussing are important but are not the entire process. You must couple them with a constant attentiveness to determining the receptivity of your listener. Receptivity is the key. Verbal pacing is one way to get there, but performing the verbal skills "correctly" is not the goal—creating receptivity is!

Counterselling Objections Before They Occur

Persuasion is a very important part of being effective, and your only obstacle to being persuasive is objections. If nobody ever objected to what you said, you would be able to persuade people of anything. Dealing effectively with objections is a very important part of persuading and influencing. The skill of counterselling objections before they occur teaches you to create an atmosphere of agreement and trust and teaches you to divert objections before they become issues. This strengthens your arguments and increases the trust level of your listener. Additionally, you create the atmosphere of togetherness and teamwork and avoid the atmosphere of conflict and opposition. This is a very valuable strategy!

Let me say very clearly, however, that the kind of objections I'm talking about are different from the ones that relate to values conflicts. An objection based on a values conflict must be worked with until the conflict is cleared. The objections I'm talking about here are the objections that represent a failure to understand your model of the world. These objections can come from listeners seeming to be close-minded, opinionated, and unwilling to hear other perspectives, but more frequently they come from listeners genuinely trying to understand your ideas but not having the information needed to do so. When you have a model of the world that differs from your listener's (which is always the case), then many of the things you say will conflict with some aspect of their model of the world. That's an objection.

These objections are principally a matter of having an incomplete picture and noting that the picture doesn't yet make sense. These are the objections that must be cleared in order for any person to receive your information.

These kinds of objections can be dealt with effectively using verbal techniques. In several of the previous examples, I illustrated the verbal strategy of bringing up possible objections, then counterselling them.

Many people incorrectly think you should avoid mentioning possible objections so that you don't weaken your case. If your price is higher than the competition's, try to change the subject. If your proposal necessitates getting approval from corporate, brush that under the table. If the new house is too expensive, talk about the swimming pool instead. You hope that nobody will mention these things, right?

However, the strategy we are about to cover does just the opposite. It proposes that when you foresee possible objections, you must mention them —then countersell them.

What does this do? Why does it help? What makes it work? Mentioning possible objections, followed by a countersell, does at least the following important things:

1. Mentioning possible objections creates the perception that you're giving your listener a full picture of the issue: People feel safer when they feel you are presenting all the facts. They don't have to look for the holes; you're showing the holes to them. They don't have to find the problems; you're telling them what they are. They don't have to be on their guard. They don't have to be defensive. They can relax. Mentioning possible objections increases your credibility substantially. It's a very respectful thing to do for a listener.

2. Mentioning possible objections frees the listener to just listen: When listeners have a concern that they feel won't be addressed, they will make a mental note of the concern and think about how to bring it up with you. Sometimes they won't even bring it up, but they still think about how to verbalize the concern. In either case, when they are thinking

about their concern, they're not listening to what you're saying at the moment. And when your listeners aren't listening, you're not being effective.

3. Mentioning possible objections allows you to control how an objection is handled: If you present the objection in a confident and reassured manner and then immediately countersell it, the listener gets a sense that you are in total control. You've shown that you know all about the issue at hand, and you have a solid response. If you fail to mention the objection and wait for the listener to bring it up, you are placed on the defensive. Even if you come back strong, your position is still weaker than it would have been if you had mentioned the issue in the first place. You've turned your presentation into a debate. Debates have winners and losers (win-lose), and you are looking for win-win!

4. Mentioning possible objections allows the listener to hear your countersell: If your countersell is a good point, then mentioning the objection is just a nice way to introduce a new selling point. Many listeners don't feel comfortable bringing up objections, even when they have them. When you mention their unspoken objections for them, you get to present countersells that your listeners otherwise would not have heard. You also "let them off the hook," because they no longer feel the need to object.

5. Mentioning possible objections creates a better understanding by the listener: If you can create a presentation that makes your listener feel like an expert on the topic, then you've created a sense of confidence on the part of your listener. Remember that people do things for emotional reasons; instilling confidence is a good thing to do for your listener.

   This becomes very important when your listener needs to share the final opinion or decision with others. When you're not there, you want this person to be able to answer others' objections in a thoughtful way. If you sell your manager on hiring a new person, and he has to explain it to his boss, you want to make sure he is equipped to explain and defend it. If his boss comes up with an objection that your manager can't defend, he looks bad and feels worse. If you get him prepared by providing him with the potential objections, he will be equipped to sell it to his boss. He'll feel very good about you and the decision, thus paving the way for more receptivity in the future.

6. Mentioning possible objections helps you maintain emotional states of receptivity in your listeners: Keeping your listeners receptive is critical in any communication process. You want to create a space where your listeners can relax and rest assured that their objections, questions, and concerns will be addressed, or can comfortably be discussed as needed. It avoids much of the anxiety and angst associated with fearing a potential conflict or disagreement and makes the entire process far more enjoyable.

So let's look at how to present objections, then countersell. Here are three paragraphs from a previous part of this chapter. Notice what I did:

How would you like to become incredibly elegant in your communication? What if you were never at a loss for words? How about being able to make your ideas incredibly appealing? What if you could do all those things after just reading this chapter?

Well don't get too excited, because achieving that kind of eloquence takes time. It takes more than fifteen minutes to develop, and most people never attain it in their entire lifetimes.

However, if you'd like to have skills like these, read on! This chapter contains excellent strategies for increasing your current level of eloquence. All of them can be carried out with a minimal amount of practice, and all of them will help you to be much more effective in your verbal communication.

Notice the pattern. The first paragraph made some outlandish claims, all in the form of questions. Because questions by nature are neither true nor false, there was no problem in saying something that stretched your ideas about what's possible and realistic. The second paragraph raised the obvious objections—eloquence takes time and some people never learn it. The third paragraph directed your attention to where I really wanted it be—to consider that the strategies I'm sharing will be of value to you.

I could just have started with the third paragraph, changing a few words, of course. I could have told you how valuable these strategies are and then told you that you could attain all kinds of wonderful things by using them. But would you have believed me? Would you have been receptive to that idea, or would you have been stuck on the objections? Wouldn't you have been thinking, "Boy, he sure made a lot of promises, but get real! There's no way you can just read a few things in a book, then be a great communicator. It just doesn't work that way"? Many people would have that response.

But if I just mention some possibilities, then verbalize your objection, you become more open to the countersell—which, in this case, is that these strategies are useful and can help you be more effective. That's much more realistic. I haven't actually promised that you'll always have the right thing to say, but I've left it as a possibility. Additionally, by mentioning the possibilities, I am demonstrating another powerful verbal process that we will cover later. It deals with "internal representations" and creating specific directions for the thoughts of your listeners.

A likely reaction to this approach might be "Well at least this guy's not promising me the world. He's pretty down to earth about things. He says these techniques are good and that they can help me. Maybe he's right. Boy, it sure would be nice to always have the right thing to say! It sure would come in handy when I'm in those meetings and…"

Counterselling objections before they occur amplifies your persuasion power. You gain the ability to keep control of conversations, and you build deeper foundations of trust and rapport with your listener. You can take the conversation where you want to, and your listener is happy to come along with you. It's an easy pattern to learn, and you will probably find that it is one of the verbal patterns you will use on a regular basis. It can be a cornerstone for all your verbal influence and persuasion skills.

Okay, so here's the pattern. It's a simple three-step approach:

1. Make a case for your outcome: Let people know just what you have in mind. Exaggerate if you wish.
2. Verbalize the obvious objections: Use words like *of course, obviously, unfortunately,* and so on. Make it seem as if the

objection is completely obvious and it would be silly to
try to hide it.
3. Immediately follow the objection with your countersell:
If you can do Steps 2 and 3 in the same sentence, begin
the countersell with a "but"; that's even better.

One more thing to remember. Continue using the verbal persuasion and influence process. This particular verbal strategy is one way of performing Step 9 (address concerns and potential concerns; continue to have profound respect for the other person and his or her points of view).

These techniques have the potential of making you much more effective. Of course, you can't expect to be great with them just since you've read this section. You need to become familiar with them so you can use them easily; but once you do, you may find that they were easier to learn than you might have thought.

You can't expect to master them right away. These skills can take some time to learn and especially to integrate into your own communication style. The nice thing is that you have a very specific, learnable pattern for doing it. It's an easy, three-step approach.

This may not have made total sense to you right away. It is sometimes a bit unclear at first. But given some time, and especially after you try it once or twice, you'll probably start to become very familiar with the pattern. You may even recognize it when someone is doing it with you!

Perhaps you noticed that the last three paragraphs were demonstrations of the pattern. If you did notice, congratulations; that shows great awareness. If you didn't notice, that's okay. It only demonstrates that this pattern is a very natural way of speaking and conversing. There is absolutely nothing artificial or contrived about this pattern. It's a respectful and courteous way of helping people understand and deal with their immediate concerns and objections.

Again, this strategy is useful only for the kinds of objections that stem from a failure to understand your model of the world. This is not a way to solve deeper objections that stem from value conflicts. Those types of objections must be handled in a much more thorough way and involve extensive use of both verbal and nonverbal listening skills. However, the ratio of model-of-the-world objections to value-conflict objections that you run across is likely to be about 100 to 1. When you're active and busy making things happen with others, you will find that you come across these surface objections over and over again. They can be resolved very quickly most of the time with this process.

When you learn these skills, you may, for the first time in your life, "know what you're doing" in your communication. This may be an unfamiliar feeling. But it's a necessary process for becoming highly effective. Think how unfortunate it would be if the president of the country didn't know what he was doing! Remember that you need to become consciously competent before you become unconsciously competent.

A Brief Conversation with a Fellow Employee

I once had the opportunity to attend a communication skills training session held at my place of work. It was designed to teach some of the basic skills of communicating, some of which were similar to those we have covered in this book. If you've ever had the opportunity to attend a skills training session in the workplace, you have probably experienced some very interesting dynamics. At first, many people resist this type of training vigorously. They feel threatened and coerced into "changing," and they are very uncomfortable with the process. Often they have fears of feeling exposed or of exploring something too personal in a room with their fellow employees. Depending on the company atmosphere, people respond with anything from mild excitement about the opportunity to downright hostility to the process. When hostility is present, sabotage can follow close behind.

In our case, most of the people were skeptical that this training session would be of value to them. They resisted it and tried to avoid attending by claiming they had too much work to do. Most of those who weren't able to avoid it attended the session with a closed mind and closed attitude. I felt a lot of compassion for the trainer!

With one exercise in particular, we covered some basic information about sensory-based observations and mind reads. We were asked to get together with a partner and do a simple exercise. The instructions were for Person 1 to say five or six sentences to Person 2. Person 2 was to listen to the words used and then ask yes or no questions of Person 1. Person 2 was to continue asking these questions until he received three "yes" responses in a row.

The challenge in this type of exercise is that people generally insert mind reads, conclusions, opinions, judgments, and a variety of other distortions into their questions. They fail to stay with sensory-based topics as part of their questions. For example, if Person 1 says, "I had a thrilling ride down the roller coaster," Person 2 often responds with things like, "Did you enjoy the ride down the roller coaster?" ("No, it was thrilling, but I didn't really enjoy it.") "Were you excited to go down the roller coaster?" ("No, I was thrilled, but that's different from being excited for me.") And so on. But with simple linguistic training (like that we've just gone through), it is very easy to be successful in this exercise. "Did you ride down a roller coaster?" ("Yes.") "Was it thrilling?" ("Yes.") "Do you remember having ridden down a roller coaster at some time?" ("Yes.") Because I was already highly trained in these skills, I was quite confident that it would be a fairly quick and mundane process. I was even a bit disappointed that I wouldn't be getting much from the exercise. But I was wrong.

I was teamed with a fellow worker who had worked at the company for some time, but we had never had the chance to get to know each other well. I was unsure of what kind of person she was, and I'm sure she was equally unsure about what kind of person I was. I could tell, though, that she was relatively uneasy in this class. She apparently had some objections to it and questioned its value. She was a resistant participant, although thoroughly professional and willing "to play along."

Before we began the exercise, I took a moment to say some things to her which paced her experience (always a great way to break the ice). I said things like, "Well, it looks as if we're about to do an exercise. I'm looking forward to it because I haven't really had the chance to meet you yet, and maybe this will be a chance for us to talk a little more than we might otherwise have spoken." I even anticipated a possible objection of hers, saying, "I know a lot of people aren't really thinking this is worth their time, but at least they're going through the process without any direct conflict. That tends to make it nicer for most of the others." She agreed and this began the process of helping us establish some rapport. Both of us were fairly comfortable at this point. Despite her resistance to the training, by this time she seemed mostly willing to do the exercise as instructed.

She began in the role of Person 1, and spoke several sentences to me. I listened attentively and picked up the needed information to complete my task. I methodically asked three straight questions, all of which were very simple and perfectly suited to pace her sentences. I got three immediate yes's and thought the exercise was over. But as I looked at this woman, she was now looking at me very differently. In her eyes, I saw a look that I had previously seen only in lovers' eyes. She seemed to want to say something, but couldn't quite bring herself to say it. I asked her what it was, and in the most compassionate and caring voice I had ever heard her use, she said, "I feel as if you just read my mind."

This is the power of pacing current experience!

CHAPTER 8

HANDLING DIFFICULT SITUATIONS

Earlier in this book, we talked about making fine distinctions, the difference that makes the difference. In communication, the difference that makes the difference is that of handling difficult situations.

When you find yourself discussing emotionally charged topics or when you are in the midst of emotionally charged situations, then you have an excellent opportunity to strengthen relationships and make lasting impressions. People become emotionally charged only when something affects them at deep emotional levels; when this happens, you have an opportunity to communicate directly at these deeper levels. In emotionally charged situations, your actions can potentially register with people in more profound ways.

This chapter describes how to take certain negative or "weak" situations and transform them into positive and "strong" situations. We'll look at three kinds of situations that often create conflict and describe how to transform them into positive and motivating experiences. You will learn how to give bad news gracefully and how to encourage your listener to move from a negative state of mind into a motivated state of mind. You will learn how to disagree gracefully, getting your points across more effectively and increasing the potential for creating a positive response from your listener. Finally, you will learn a simple method for giving constructive feed-back, in which your listener feels better about the interchange and has a higher motivation to respond to it. Each of these situations is a communicational challenge that you will learn how to turn into an opportunity. Rather than avoid them, you will learn how to use them constructively.

Thus far, we've covered an excellent process for com-munication (the verbal persuasion and influence process) and filled in some of the steps with certain important verbal skills. In a nutshell, these verbal skills are

1. Pace current experience using sensory-based observations.
2. Structure your language so that your opinions and ideas are more easily accepted by others.
3. Lead and set direction in your conversations.
4. Mention and countersell objections.
5. Talk more (unless you already talk too much, in which case, talk more effectively).

These will be the mainstays for each of the techniques you are about to learn.

Giving Bad News Gracefully

Imagine that you are a manager and that your employee Ted has done everything you've asked of him; you know he is expecting and hoping for a good raise. And you would really like to give him one because he deserves it. Added to that, he has waited longer than a lot of other employees, so he's very much overdue.

His annual review is due, and you request a nice raise for him. Unfortunately, it is denied. Budget cuts and potential layoffs have made it impossible to give raises. The head office has instituted a salary freeze, and you have no options. You've had to do some fancy dancing just to keep from reducing staff. Despite your adherence to the responsibility mind-set, this situation seems largely outside of your control.

How are you going to tell Ted? You don't want him to quit, but you realize that might be a better option for him.

You don't want him to lose his motivation, but you know that's understandable. What can you do?

You call him in for his review. You cover all the performance issues, and you're finally at the point where money will be discussed. We're about to look at the later stage in this process, so assume that you have already completed the appropriate parts of the persuasion and influence process: You've listened to Ted, you've elicited important information about his values and desires, and you have a good understanding of what would constitute a win for Ted. You've got a good idea about what his model of the world is like, and you've created a good level of rapport. You have been calibrating Ted for potentially mixed communication, and you continue to calibrate to get a sense of how he is receiving your communication. The review has gone well to this point, and the conversation is flowing in a supportive manner. You say: "I'm sorry Ted, but there's a corporate salary freeze. I can't give you a raise. Maybe next year the freeze will be off."

What do you think his reaction will be? Do you think he'll be inspired to work harder? Do you think he will be even more loyal to the company? Probably not. He'll probably be very angry and disappointed, even if he doesn't show it. He'll probably immediately start thinking about his options. Could he get a better job elsewhere? Where? What should he do? Boy, what a crummy deal!

So, is there anything else you could have said? Anything that could have made a difference for Ted? Anything that might have been more effective? Well, believe it or not, I have a few suggestions! What if you said this instead: "Ted, you have been the perfect worker. I'm so happy that you work here and that I get the chance to work with you. I really respect you, and I'd like to give you a very nice raise. Unfortunately, though, I have some bad news. It's news that I hate telling you, because I think it's really a bummer. But I have to tell you anyway.

"As you know, we're having a challenging year. It's really required us to make some big sacrifices. The company is faced with possible layoffs and cutbacks. But don't worry, you still have your job, and I'm not cutting your wage. It's just that I can't give you a raise yet. There's been a wage freeze instituted, and there's nothing I can do about it. I hate that, especially in your case, because you've been such a great person to have around here. If I could give just one raise, it would be to you. But I can't.

"I want you to know that I understand if you want to look for another job. I know this has got to be disappointing. It is to me, too. I do think, however, that you've still got a good future here. We're faced with tough times, but I feel confident that these times will turn good very soon. And I feel that you're one of the people who will help us make the turn. With people like you sticking to the company, I think we'll make it through very nicely. And I hope to be able to reward you when that happens. I'd really like you to stay.

"And even though it may be hard, I'd like to ask you to step it up another notch. All of us are going to need to do even more than we do now. But we'll get through it.

"I know this wasn't what you expected from this review. I imagine you're really disappointed. But I also know that you're the type of person who responds well to tough times. I know I can count on you. I already count on you for a lot. Thanks for being such a great worker. And a great person. So take some time to think about what I said today. Your review was great, and I'm very happy to have you here. I hope you choose to stay with us and to really dig in. We work very well together, and there's a lot more benefit to working here than just the money. But you know that.

"I wish I could have given you a big raise. But hopefully that will come in time. Thanks Ted."

I know, I know, that's a lot of talking to do! But once you get the pattern, you'll find it easy to talk that much. When you have a method and a process, then it's easy to just fill it in with the words. A process gives you reasons to say the words you say.

It's important that you be able to imagine how Ted will respond to this type of approach. Of course he'll still be disappointed, but can you imagine his being even more motivated? Don't you think he'll work even harder? Don't you think he'll walk out of that review feeling better about you as his manager? Even though you couldn't give him the raise, he knows that you like him, you appreciate him, you respect him, you level with him, and you want to give him a raise. How much more can anyone ask from a manager? And you've done all this without making the company out to be the bad guy.

I can tell you from experience, that is exactly how Ted will walk out of that review. Of course, this monologue is still just part of the overall process, and you continue to communicate with Ted as long as it's needed—but the heart of the process might look very much like what I just described. Let's look at the mechanics of how it's done. It's a rather simple extension of the mechanics already presented. We've already covered the following:

1. Pace current experience using sensory-based observations.
2. Structure your language so that your opinions and ideas are more easily accepted by others.
3. Lead and set direction in your conversations.
4. Mention and countersell objections.
5. Talk more (unless you already talk too much, in which case, talk more effectively).

Now let's examine each part of that strategy, and see how it applies to the example with Ted. First, *pace current experience*. That's generally a good place to start. In Ted's interchange, we picked it up after a review had already taken place, so much of the pacing would have already been done, but this part of the conversation still contained ample pacing. It began with, "I have some bad news," "As you know, we're having a challenging year," "The company is faced with possible layoffs and cutbacks," "you still have your job," and "there's been a wage freeze instituted."

Second, *structure your language so that your opinions and ideas are more easily accepted by others.* Here's where the artistry comes in. Which ideas and opinions do you share? Of all the millions of thoughts circulating in your mind, which ones do you pick? You already know how to construct a more easily received statement from just about any opinion or idea, but which ones do you pick?

This is where you must revert back to the notion that people do things for emotional reasons, not logical ones. You need to appeal to emotions. So when you've got some bad news to convey, appeal to the emotions that you are feeling and the emotions that you think the listener is feeling.

Look at some of the things I said: "I'm so happy that you work here... I think it's really a bummer... I hate that,... I know this has got to be disappointing. It is to me too... I feel confident that these times will turn good very soon. And I feel that you're one of the people... And I hope to... I'd really like you to stay. And even though it may be hard... I imagine you're really disappointed... I wish I could have given you a big raise."

Each of these phrases expresses an emotion, either mine or what I anticipate his will be. It's often called "talking from your gut." You say what you feel. Some people, especially in business, think you shouldn't talk about your feelings, that it's not professional—you know, the old "suck it up and be a man" syndrome. "Show no fear." That kind of nonsense. But humans are emotional, and if you want to communicate well with others, you will let them connect with you on an emotional level.

If you hate giving him bad news, tell him. If you'd like to give him a big raise, tell him. Let him know what's going on with you emotionally. And let him know that you're attuned to what he is feeling. If you think he is going to be disappointed, then tell him. If you think he might lose some of his motivation, tell him. Let him know that you understand. That's another way of pacing his experience. He may not have told you or shown you what his experience is, but you can usually make good guesses. Then phrase your guesses so that they can be universally accepted; that is, change "you feel disappointed," to "I imagine you might feel disappointed."

Give people permission to be human. So many people foolishly avoid giving other people permission to have "negative" reactions. They ignore the fact that people might get depressed, angry, disappointed, discouraged, and so on. They act as if people should always be optimistic and cheerful.

They try to be a good example themselves—in other words, they try to be an optimistic robot. They pretend to never feel down or angry or rejected, and if they feel a negative emotion coming on, they hide in an office, shut the door, and hope like heck nobody sees they're human! Whom do they think they're kidding?

I advocate a more humane way of communicating. You recognize that we're all human beings and that we all have emotions and feelings. You acknowledge the existence of our emotions and realize that they are a healthy way of dealing with the various conditions in life. Of course, your actions remain appropriate. You can't just yell and scream at people when you're angry. But you have a right to feel anger. You have a right to feel disappointment, frustration, reduced motivation, and so on. You act in appropriate ways, but you also acknowledge that your negative emotions are part of a normal, healthy life. You deal with people on an emotional level.

There were a few other things I did in that monologue to Ted. Perhaps you noticed a few of them. The third item in the list above is *lead and set direction in your conversations.* Most of the monologue was geared toward setting a potential direction for Ted. I'm not coercing him or negatively manipulating him in any way. Instead, I'm suggesting that he think of things in certain ways, and I'm hoping that I can entice him to see things from this perspective. I'm leading him to consider my model of the world and to consider responding in certain ways: "don't worry... I feel that you're one of the people who will help us make the turn... With... you sticking to the company... we'll make it through very nicely... I'd really like you to stay... I'd like to ask you to step it up another notch... do even more than [you] do now... I also know that you're the type of person who responds well to tough times... I know I can count on you... take some time to think about what I said today... I hope you choose to stay with us and to really dig in."

As part of an overall communication process, I would also be including other parts of the verbal persuasion and influence process, including calibration of congruent agreement with any actions Ted considers taking. Remember that this is just one verbal part of a much more involved process.

The fourth item in the list says *mention and countersell objections*. I absolutely did that, but in this case, it wasn't just objections. I responded to potential *reactions*. Reactions and objections are closely related. Ted might react by looking for a new job. He might react with diminished motivation. These are potential reactions, and I addressed them just like potential objections. I mentioned them and then gave him an idea of how I would rather he respond.

For added elegance, mention and countersell both potential objections and potential reactions.

Fifth, *talk more*. I'd say I did that rather well! But it wasn't just mindless babble; all the words had a purpose and supported the structure of what I was doing.

Next is something that I haven't explicitly mentioned yet: Tell the truth, and maintain your own high standards of integrity. What I shared with Ted was true for me. If I truly believe that things will get better and I truly plan to share the benefits with Ted when they do, then it is a perfectly appropriate thing to tell him so. Word for word, literal truthfulness is vital. If you don't believe something, then don't give it lip service.

It is very detrimental to speak words that have no meaning for you or words that do have meaning but you won't be able to deliver on. There are plenty of colloquialisms—such as "Things will work out," "In time, everything works out," "You'll get your chance," "Good things come to those who wait," and so on—but I suggest that you avoid them. They've lost their impact through overuse and misuse, and they're usually inappropriate for the situations anyway.

Really talk to your listeners. Tell them exactly what you see and what you'd like to create. A collection of meaningless adages is nothing compared to the words of a compassionate and inspiring communicator! Aim for the latter!

There's one more thing that I did in Ted's monologue that we have not covered yet. I started to stretch things a bit beyond just saying things that I thought Ted would perceive as true. I started to say some things that didn't strictly follow our guidelines for pacing current experience. Twice in that monologue, I started to extend things a bit:

1. "I know this wasn't what you expected from this review. I imagine you're really disappointed. But I also know that *you're the type of person that responds well to tough times.* I know I can count on you."
2. "There's a lot more benefit to working here than just the money. But *you know that.*"

Here's where you can start to set new and better directions for your listeners. Once you say a lot of things that pace their experience, and you've established trust and rapport, you can start to lead them toward newer, more far-reaching ideas. You get them to consider things that you know about and want them to consider. You get them to think about things that you are aware of and want them to think about. You even encourage them to believe things that you believe and hope they will believe. This is what leadership is all about.

With the case of Ted, I encouraged him to think of himself as someone who responded well to tough times. I thought of him that way, so it was true for me, but I wasn't sure if he thought of himself that way. But I bet he did after this conversation—at least more so than before! And in my opinion, Ted would get a nice win out of incorporating that belief into his life.

I also encouraged him to appreciate more in his job than just the money. I felt that at a deeper level, Ted was aware of the nonmonetary benefits of his job. However, I was not sure how conscious he was of that belief. But by planting that seed at an opportune time, I felt sure he would start to bring that understanding into his conscious awareness. Again, in my opinion, that was a healthy way for Ted to view his job, and it would result in yet another win for Ted.

These two thoughts could potentially have a significant impact on Ted. Make no mistake about it—they were my ideas, not Ted's, and I purposely interjected them into the conversation, hoping that Ted would eventually come to accept them to some degree. By making these kinds of insertions, I am fully aware that I am attempting to influence Ted's life in some way.

Every day, people try to influence others' lives in some way. However, when you do it, I ask that you be fully conscious of what you are doing, why you are doing it, and whether it's best for all concerned as far as you can tell. With these premises as a foundation for your actions, your great verbal skills work synergistically to achieve wonderful results in your life, and in the lives of those around you.

For Ted, this was one of the those conversations that was likely to help him shape his views of himself and his work life. It was likely to have a major impact on Ted—the conversation was both well-timed and emotionally charged. We already had great rapport and the flow of the conversation was really moving—that's great timing. Additionally, both of us were in the process of accessing some potentially deep, supportive, compassionate emotions. We were emotionally connected and Ted was highly receptive! The event was definitely emotionally charged.

To increase receptivity in your listener, use good timing and strong emotions.

Here's how that works. Here's what is likely to be going on in Ted's mind *(in parentheses)* as the monologue progresses (remember that you will be calibrating as you are speaking): "Ted, you have been the perfect worker. I'm so happy that you work here and that I get the chance to work with you. I really respect you, and I'd like to give you a very nice raise." *(Wow, he sure is saying some nice things about me. He seems to really believe them, too. It's not just a bunch of words.)*

"Unfortunately, though, I have some bad news. It's news that I hate telling you, because I think it's really a bummer. But I have to tell you anyway." *(Uh oh, bad news. I bet it's about my raise. Boy, he's upset about it. It must be pretty bad. Damn.)*

"As you know, we're having a challenging year. It's really required us to make some big sacrifices. The company is faced with possible layoffs and cutbacks." *(Yeah, I know that. I was worried about it, too. I wonder if any of those things could affect me! Surely he's not about to lay me off, is he?)*

"But don't worry, you still have your job, and I'm not cutting your wage." *(That's a relief! Lose my job or get a wage cut. That would be awful!)*

"It's just that I can't give you a raise yet. There's been a wage freeze instituted, and there's nothing I can do about it." *(Damn, that really sucks. I might just have to quit and find a better job.)*

"I hate that, especially in your case, because you've been such a great person to have around here. If I could give just one raise, it would be to you. But I can't." *(Well at least he appreciates me.)*

"I want you to know that I understand if you want to look for another job." *(Wow, I can't believe he said that. That's what I was thinking, but usually you don't hear that from a boss.)*

"I know this has got to be disappointing. It is to me too." *(Yeah, it's a real bummer. He's bummed too, I can tell.)*

"I do think, however, that you've still got a good future here. We're faced with tough times, but I feel confident that these times will turn good very soon. And I feel that you're one of the people who will help us make the turn. With people like you sticking to the company, I think we'll make it through very nicely." *(Well, it's starting to sound at least a little brighter. Maybe I should stay. But what's in it for me?)*

"And I hope to be able to reward you when that happens. I'd really like you to stay." *(Wow, maybe things will work out here.)*

"And even though it may be hard, I'd like to ask you to step it up another notch. All of us are going to need to do even more than we do now. But we'll get through it." *(Damn, more work. But I can do that. I think I can.)*

"I know this wasn't what you expected from this review. I imagine you're really disappointed. But I also know that you're the type of person who responds well to tough times. I know I can count on you. I already count on you for a lot." *(He thinks I'm the type of person to stick it out. Maybe he's right. Maybe I am that way. I wonder what he sees in me.)*

"Thanks for being such a great worker. And a great person. So take some time to think about what I said today. Your review was great, and I'm very happy to have you here.

I hope you choose to stay with us and to really dig in." *(It sure is nice to work for this guy. He really appreciates me.)*

"We work very well together, and there's a lot more benefit to working here than just the money. But you know that." *(Ooh, what do I know? There's more than just money? I guess I know that. What does he mean? Like the atmosphere? The people I work with? My boss? I guess he's right. I wonder what else he thinks I know. I'll have to think about this some more when I get some free time.)*

"I wish I could have given you a big raise. But hopefully that will come in time. Thanks Ted." *(Yeah, I wish so too. I really wanted that raise. I hope it does come. This guy seems pretty honest and straightforward. If he thinks it will come, I'll trust him.)*

Because I addressed Ted's model of the world as best as I knew how, he was freed up to spend his time responding to what he was feeling. He didn't have to wonder what was true and what was baloney. He knew what I was saying was true. So when I said some things that he wasn't sure about, like the fact that he responded well to tough times, he probably just accepted them as reasonable assumptions. After all, everything else I said was true, so I couldn't be too far off with those other things. If you had a friend who was always right, wouldn't you tend to trust her if she told you something that you weren't sure about?

Ironically, sharing bad news can be a great way to motivate people and to create a strong emotional bond. There's no sense in wasting an opportunity! If you have to share some bad news, do your listeners a favor and help them leave the situation in good spirits. Had I used the first approach, Ted could have been really down in the dumps after our talk. Instead, he was more motivated and relatively upbeat, and our relationship grew to be even stronger.

Graceful Disagreement

You've seen couples on television who are fighting and yelling at each other. Their small child comes up and asks, "Are you two fighting?" The reply: "No, we're just having a disagreement."

Even a child knows the difference between a disagreement and a fight. But the fact of the matter is that they're closely related. Most people take offense when someone disagrees with them, and many people respond with anger.

Because emotion is a key to being effective with people, you need to be aware of the emotional impact of what you say and do. Anytime you need to disagree with someone, you should be cognizant of what you're saying and doing. If you're not, you may find yourself with an angry listener (or screamer), and anger is rarely useful in communicational situations.

So how do you disagree with people while encouraging them to be receptive rather than angry? What strategy works in that case? Should you just say you agree with them, even though you don't?

There are ways to disagree that create anger and hostility. And there are other ways to disagree that create appreciation and respect. Let's aim for the latter!

The strategy for gracefully disagreeing is very similar to what we've already learned. It involves pacing the listener's experience, then stretching it a bit. The way I told Ted that he was the kind of person who responds well when things get tough is the way to gracefully disagree.

Here are the mechanics:

1. Pace the listener's experience sufficiently to maintain reasonable rapport.
2. Make your disagreement.
3. Give your listener a way out.

Suppose you're a manager of a sales team. Everyone's working to sell a new product, but results are very poor. The sales team is getting discouraged. They start talking among themselves and decide they'd like to cancel the product introduction. The company has canceled these kinds of introductions before, and the salespeople feel as if their time would be better spent selling more established products.

You disagree. You know that you've already invested too much in the new product, and you're going to keep it going no matter what the results are.

Here's a potential conversation:

> *You:* How are the sales figures for the new product?
>
> *Salesperson:* Not so good. It's really been a tough product to sell.
>
> *You:* What's been the challenge?
>
> *Salesperson:* It's been difficult educating our customers about our new product. It's been hard to reach people, and when we do, we have to spend a lot of time talking about the product. That makes it tough to contact very many people. And when we do reach people, they're just not real open to the idea. I think we need to cancel this product introduction. It's just too much work, and we're not getting anywhere. If we focus on our other products, we can bring in better results. (Notice how the direction of the previous question allowed the response to move in this direction. Sometimes that's appropriate, but you should know when you're doing it.)
>
> *You:* That's not an option. We need to do this; we've got too much invested already, so keep on it. You're responsible for the results, so get them. That's what you're paid for. If the results aren't there, then you're not doing your job. So get on it.

What kind of response do you think this conversation will get? Anger? Frustration? How motivated do you think that salesperson will be now? What kind of results do you think the team will get now?

This is a simple disagreement. The salesperson wants to cancel, and you don't. You have the final say, so your decision stands. This much is clear. But how can you disagree, uphold your decision, and help the salesperson be motivated and successful?

Let's replace that last line with another:

> *You:* I can see you're having some challenges with this. Sometimes introducing a new product can be a lot of work. It's probably not much fun either, especially if the results aren't there yet. It may even seem like an easy way out to just cancel the introduction. Unfortunately it's not.
>
> We've got a lot invested in this project, and if we cancel the introduction, we'll lose a lot more than you may realize. We have to keep it going. It's

simply not an option to cancel. We have to do the introduction, even if the results aren't there.

Look, you've worked here a long time. You know how to sell, and you know how to overcome obstacles. You also know how to turn things around. I've seen you do it. It's times like this when I really need your support. I need you to be the leader, to rally all of us to make this thing work. If you get discouraged, that spreads. Pretty soon, everyone else gets that way, too. I bet everyone's talking about canceling now. And you know how bad results get when everyone's discouraged.

You're the person I'm relying on. And you can do it. That's why you've got this job. That's why you've done so well here. So help get us out of this jam. Gather your ideas together, and let's figure out how to really make it work. I'm sure you've got some ideas up your sleeve about how to deal with the challenges. Let's get them on the table, and we'll tackle this head on. I really appreciate you, especially in times like this.

This approach works. It follows the steps as shown. First, it paces current experience. Second, it states the disagreement very plainly: "It's not an option to cancel the event." And third, it gives the salesperson a way out. The salesperson gets to save face. You told her that she's got great skills, you've asked her to be a leader, and you've given her a chance to respond with some new ideas.

In addition to stating your disagreement in a way that will be accepted, you have probably motivated this salesperson to work much more at selling the product. Such motivation in itself is often enough to solve the problem. Again, this conversation is a more verbose version of the earlier one, but we're not just trying to say the same thing. We're trying to create the emotions that are needed. Anger is not needed. Motivation and confidence are.

Giving people a way out is vital. When you don't do it, you create emotions that are rarely useful, such as shame, disgrace, insecurity, failure, anger, frustration, and so on. You back them into a corner. These emotions are destructive, and they will contribute to further failure.

When you give people a way out, you give them motivation. They realize they have a chance to get out of the mess they're in and to look like the hero. They have a chance to be proud, successful, confident, excited, happy, fulfilled, satisfied, and so on. That's a lot better than shame!

If you find a group of people in a bad place, and you want them to get out of it, there are at least two ways to approach the problem. If you threaten them and call them stupid, they usually get angry. But if you show them the door and give them permission to leave, you'd better get out of their way. And they'll thank you for showing them the door!

Sandwich Feedback

Imagine a colleague of yours giving a presentation. She's spent six months with her team designing a new blender. She's wanting to sell the new features to senior management so that she can continue to the next phase of engineering. She describes the new shape of the container, the special alloy blade, the sleek cosmetic look, the special daiquiri feature. In all, she thinks it's very well designed and ready to go. And she tells the managers that.

Most of the group seems very pleased, but one person is obviously discontent. After her presentation, she asks for questions and comments. He is first, and he says, "You didn't do anything to reduce the noise. That's important, so I think you still need to work on it some more."

Bam! Isn't that a harsh response? Even if he's right, and doing something about the noise will make a better blender, how will she feel about it? Won't that burst her bubble! How do you think she's going to feel going back to her fellow workers with this kind of response?

But what if he said things a bit differently? What if he said, "You've got some really great ideas here. I specifically like the new sleek design. Homeowners are more conscious of looks these days, so I think you're right on track with that. And the daiquiri function is fantastic. That will hit the a large part of the market segment straight on.

"There's one thing, however, that I'm wondering about which you didn't mention in your presentation: the issue of noise. If we can reduce the amount of noise that our blender creates, I think we'll have another major selling point. If you haven't significantly reduced the noise, then I'd like you to look into that further.

"But you've done a great job so far. I think we're going to have a super product. Thanks, and great presentation."

Isn't that a much more appealing way to give feedback? Wouldn't she feel better about hearing this? The result is the same, she still has to do more work on the noise issue, but in the first case she feels discouraged and in the second case she feels encouraged.

How would you like to affect the people you give feedback to? What emotions would you like to evoke in them?

This type of feedback is often referred to as "sandwich feedback." The process is simple to learn and use and makes a tremendous difference in how your feedback is received. Remember, the point in giving feedback should be for your listener to accept and consider it, not for you to look clever or smart. To do the former, you need to give your feedback in a way that makes it easy to accept. If you've ever been in a meeting where someone is out to make another person look bad, perhaps with cutting remarks, you know that's a fast way to create bad feelings and conflict. And it's also a very poor way to get someone to accept the feedback.

The generally accepted rules about feedback are that it should be pertinent, helpful, and specific. As long as you meet these criteria, then your feedback is supposedly good. Unfortunately, feedback that has only these criteria is often the source of resentment and resistance.

It's my assertion that feedback should also be presented in such a manner that it is easily received by your listener. Giving feedback is not about being right; it's about helping someone make an improvement. The best insights in the

world are useless unless somebody receives them and acts upon them.

Here are the mechanics for giving sandwich feedback:

1. Begin by mentioning aspects that you liked and/or agreed with. Pace current experience.
2. Mention the areas that you disagreed with or the areas in which you saw room for further improvement. Depending upon the situation, you can soften the feedback with modal operators of possibility.
3. Give your recipient a "way out"—a way to save face.
4. Finish with a larger perspective, positive observations, usually an overall statement of appreciation.

Let's look at the previous example. It's repeated here, with comments in parentheses: "You've got some really great ideas here." *(overall positive statement)* "I specifically like the new sleek design. Homeowners are more conscious these days to looks, so I think you're right on track with that." *(specific aspect he liked)* "And the daiquiri function is fantastic. That will hit a large part of the market segment straight on." *(specific aspect he liked)*

"There's one thing, however, that I'm wondering about that you didn't mention in your presentation: the issue of noise. If we can reduce the amount of noise that our blender creates, I think we'll have another major selling point. If you haven't significantly reduced the noise, then I'd like you to look into that further." *(aspect for improvement or further investigation)*

"I know we weren't specific up front about addressing the noise issue, but we really should have been." *(gives the recipient a way out, so she can save face)*

"But you've done a great job so far. I think we're going to have a super product. Thanks, and great presentation." *(overall positive comment and expression of appreciation)*

Notice the impact of this kind of feedback. It gives the presenter a respectable way out and some encouragement. If she didn't consider the noise issue, she still has a lot of items there she can be proud of. She can walk out of the room saying, "We've done a lot of good work, and we just need to fine-tune it a bit." When she goes back to her team, this can be her mind-set. This kind of process may even help her to enhance her self-esteem, fostering feelings of pride and motivation.

Recall the first, ineffective example of feedback in this situation: "You didn't do anything to reduce the noise. That's important, so I think you still need to work on it some more."

This approach makes several critical mistakes. First, it does not acknowledge the positive aspects of the work. That's a crushing blow to motivation and inspiration.

Second, it doesn't give the person a way out. It seems as if this were a pass-or-fail presentation, and she failed. It presents an attitude of "Go back and try it again. This time, do it right!" All growth stops at this point. The presenter is left in front of her senior managers, possibly feeling embarrassed and without her dignity. It's a very dehumanizing position to put someone in. In this situation, she is apt to respond with anger—which will obviously not contribute to the success of the new blender!

Third, it forces the situation to end on a bad note. Many professional presenters are taught that people remember best the first thing you say and the last thing you say. Of course, when you give sandwich feedback, people will certainly remember the middle part, because that forms their instructions for when they leave the room. But the emotional impact of what's said will come from the first and last parts of the feedback. With straight, negative feedback, all they hear is the negative. They respond to negativity.

Sandwich feedback is a respectful, humanistic approach. It acknowledges the listener's worth. Notice I didn't say it acknowledges the presentation, or other content, for its worth. That's a critical distinction. A lot of people will tell you that feedback should be directed at content, not at the person. They'll tell you that you can say a person's work is crummy, but you shouldn't say the person is crummy. They tell you that if you phrase feedback in this way, then the person won't take it personally.

Let's be realistic. All feedback is taken personally! As "professionals," we might try to pretend it's not taken personally, but of course it is. You should assume that any negative feedback will be felt negatively by the listener. People want to feel proud and successful. When they're not successful, they typically feel bad. It's not logical, but it's a fact of human nature. Structure your feedback so that the listener has the best opportunity to respond positively to it.

If you think this is "candy coating" the feedback, it is— in a way. But that doesn't mean your listener won't hear it. Remember, candy coating is a way to make some bad-tasting medicine go down okay. You still get the effects of the medicine, but you didn't have to choke down some awful-tasting pill. In effect, it makes it easier to take more pills in the future.

Your listeners will still get the benefits of the medicine. Believe me, they will hear the "room for improvement" part of the feedback. Guaranteed. The candy coating simply acknowledges the person and his or her work. It makes it a much more pleasant process and makes it such that another pill later in the day won't be such a bad thing after all.

Remember, when people are receiving feedback, they are in a vulnerable position. Their work is up for scrutiny and criticism, and they will take all feedback personally! Nobody else is being criticized at that time, and it's a one-way process (there's not even an opportunity to fire back). It's like being on trial. So be a merciful judge!

This is a very simple technique, so there's no need to go on with it much further. I'll give one more simple example, this time in a home, rather than business, context.

Imagine that you come home from work and your teenage daughter surprises you with a fish dinner already prepared for you. This is the first time she's ever cooked dinner for you, and you'd like to encourage her as much as you can. When you sit down and start eating, she eagerly asks you if you like it. Unfortunately, it's really bad. She overcooked the fish so that it came out very dry and tough.

When she asks if you like it, what do you say? Before you read this section, you might have said something like the following (I'll give you multiple choice!):

a. "It's really good." *(lying)*
b. "It's okay." *(hiding the truth)*
c. "Well, the fish is a little dry, but I like it." *(trying to tell the truth, but wimping out)*
d. "Well, I don't care much for the fish, but I'm glad you cooked tonight." *(honest, but not very effective)*
e. "You overcooked the fish. It's too dry. Don't you know that fish is different from beef? You don't need to cook it so long!" *(honest, but dehumanizing)*

But now you have new skills! New choices! So let's construct a sandwich feedback that will keep your daughter motivated to cook again some time and that will give her some insight into how to cook fish.

First, some positive comments. What do you like about the meal? Does it look good? Were the other parts of the meal good? Were you impressed with her confidence in the kitchen? What did you like? Let's imagine the following:

Positive comments: "Honey, you did such a good job. You prepared an entire meal by yourself. I didn't even know you could do that. And you seem so confident about it. Where did you get the recipes? I'm really impressed! And the way you laid it out, it looks like a gourmet meal in a great restaurant. And the carrots are awesome—I love carrots."

That may be a bit more than you need, but what the heck. Be generous with your praise. Now the room for improvement.

Room for Improvement: "I will say, though, that you probably cooked the fish a bit longer than you needed to. Fish is a tough dish to start out with. Most people—even chefs in restaurants—think it cooks like beef or chicken, but it doesn't. If you cook fish just a little bit, it will be moist and tender."

She probably knows the fish is dry. You told her you noticed it, you said it in a soft way (*probably* cooked it a *bit* longer...), then gave her a way out; it's an understandable thing, most people think of fish like beef or chicken, even chefs in restaurants! You then gave her some useful information, so the next time she cooks, she'll feel even more confident. And very importantly, you told her the truth. She will learn to trust you for that.

Now the close: some positive, overall comments of praise and appreciation. Why not take advantage of this wonderful opportunity your daughter has provided and really bond and connect with her? You can make this evening one of those special times that both of you recall for years to come. Come on, let's be emotional.

Positive overall comments: "But you know, honey, I couldn't have had a more perfect meal. I feel so special tonight. And I feel so proud of you. You've grown up to be a wonderful woman. There are so many kids out there who are having difficult times and getting into a lot of trouble. But you're my pride and joy. I know that in a few years you will be leaving for college, and all I'll have each night when I come home are my memories of you. Memories of nights like this. Thank you so much. I love you."

What more can I say?

CHAPTER 9

DEFENDING YOURSELF

UP UNTIL NOW, we have concentrated mostly on verbal skills that can be used in a proactive manner. I chose to begin with the proactive nature of communication to emphasize that you are in total control of your effectiveness. You can make things happen. You can *initiate* success in your life.

Unfortunately, there will be times in your life when you will be emotionally and verbally attacked. You need to know how to be reactive, too. Most of the time, these attacks aren't motivated by spite or meanness, but are the only way some people know to address their concerns, problems, and fears. Most people have never had the kind of verbal training contained in this book, and they are unaware of the implications of language. Without the skills you have developed, they probably just aren't very good at relating in healthy, supportive, empowering ways—in personal or workplace relationships.

The verbal abuse that this chapter addresses is different from verbal criticism. More than likely, there will be times in your life when people give you feedback and criticism— with the intent of asking you to address some behavior—in as straightforward and supportive a manner as they know how. That is not abuse; that is criticism. Whether they are able to do it in as graceful a manner as I've described in this book is beside the point.

However, verbal *abuse* is an insidious act; it consists of underhanded insults and disapprovals. It involves sideswipes and low blows. It fails to address issues directly, openly, and with the intention of being supportive. Verbal abuse rarely results in anything but antagonism, conflict, and personal affronts. But despite the ugliness of the process, you'll also find that this is the only way some very good people know how to deal with certain problems. We'll discuss that in more detail shortly.

You may have noticed that most of my examples are given in the context of a work environment. The workplace can be our most challenging environment. At work, we are under external pressure to get results. We are forced to cooperate with people whom we might not otherwise have anything to do with. Whether you like them or not, you are expected to work with, get along with, and achieve with your coworkers.

You can leave a social gathering if you don't like the people there. Work is different. In your spiritual life and your personal growth, you do what inspires you. Not necessarily so at work. In relationships and in family environments, you have close emotional bonds with the people involved. Again, not so at work. In your home, if you have guests whom you don't like or who do things you don't like, you can ask them to leave. Work is different. Work environments often dictate whom you work with, how you work, when you work, what you wear, what you work on, even how clean your desk must be. The other areas of your life are usually far less restrictive.

For these reasons and others, work environments often create a disproportionately high number of interpersonal challenges. It is at work especially that you are likely to face verbal attacks, which are sometimes the only way people know how to relate in such a difficult and confusing environment. Unfortunately, verbal attacks can be real problems if you don't know how to deal with them.

Verbal attacks are clear examples of win-lose scenarios. When someone directs an abusive statement at you, you face the prospect of getting into a losing situation. Although firing right back at the abuser might seem to be an effective approach, you won't want to create another win-lose situation, even though you can skillfully manage to be the winner. You might be tempted to punish abusers for their unkind deeds; however, acting on that temptation only serves to add fuel to the fire. Doing so can result in the fire flashing right back in your face!

Our plan is to take this win-lose situation and to create a win-win as a final result.

These next few sections will describe how you can identify the more challenging verbal attacks and respond to them. It begins by describing the semantic structure of indirect verbal abuse. You will learn how to recognize different levels of verbal attacks and how to deal with them at comparable levels. You will understand why some communication sounds okay but makes you feel bad anyway. You will learn how to respond to verbal abuse, knowing when to be graceful and when to be forceful. You will learn the key elements of power struggles and how to recognize power struggle situations. You will learn how to fend off encroaching attacks and how to prevent future encroachments. You will learn all these things within the context of showing respect for your attackers and demonstrating high levels of integrity and personal strength.

Verbal abuse is often directed at people who don't know how to deal with it well. If you have been the subject of verbal abuse or you simply feel that people have been getting the best of you, then this chapter can help. By incorporating the skills demonstrated here, you will become a difficult person to pick on, and you will avert future abuse. A few effective responses on your part can wipe away many future conflicts and frustrations.

It is helpful to realize that verbal abuse is a *symptom* of a *dis-ease*, not a disease on its own. If verbal abuse is present in your life, then learning how to respond to it will help (it will help a lot), but a better, long-term approach is to look for the root cause and address it.

In the last chapter, we studied how to communicate in difficult situations. We examined ways not just to minimize the detrimental effects, but also ways to create opportunities from them—to turn lemons into lemonade. In the case of verbal abuse, our goal is the same. As ironic as it may seem, when you become a target for verbal attacks, you have an opportunity to address a real problem, an opportunity to generate respect and admiration. Our goal is to take a belittling, confrontational situation and change it into an empowering, productive situation.

Verbal Presupposition-Based Abuse

As we've seen, presuppositions are a natural part of speaking and communicating. They provide deeper levels of meaning than words alone do, and they give us an indication of the structures and limitations in our models of the world. When you listen to someone, you can hear presuppositions that help you understand people at greater levels, and that help you identify the challenges facing that person. When listening to yourself, you can also do exactly those same things for yourself. When speaking, you can use presuppositions in purposeful ways so that your message has far more impact and meaning. In many ways, presuppositions form the basis of meaningful and lasting relations with others.

Unfortunately, these same structures can also be used in negative ways. Much of the piercing verbal abuse in the English language is carried out through use of presuppositions. A presupposition-based verbal attack is far more potent than a straightforward attack because presuppositions bypass our conscious filtering processes and register at deeper, unconscious levels. When someone says to someone else, "You're an idiot," you can be very certain that the recipient of the comment knows that he's just been insulted. You can also be certain that the speaker has just diminished his own credibility in the process. This kind of abuse is ineffective and doesn't require much of a response at all. However, presuppositional verbal abuse is different, and it absolutely requires effective responses.

Consider the abusive phrase "If you loved me, you would come home earlier after work." The presupposition is that you do not love the speaker. Even deeper, the meta-presupposition is that the speaker *knows* whether or not you feel love. It's probable that neither of those assumptions is accurate, but they can have significant impact when spoken. Unless you address the presuppositions, they will stand unchallenged and can be accepted as truth. Both the speaker and listeners will register them at unconscious levels and, worse yet, often come to believe them, too.

Let's look at a typically abusive interchange. The leader of a meeting asks you for a report. As you report, the leader proceeds to ask more and more detailed questions until at some point you don't have the answers. This is done a few times, then:

Abuser: If you were doing your job, you'd be better prepared.

You: I am prepared; I just don't have the specific answer you're looking for.

Abuser: A good manager knows what answers will be required.

You: Look, I had only a short time to prepare for this meeting, and I got the most pertinent facts available. You just happened to focus on a specific part I didn't have time to research.

At first reading, you may think that this was a fairly good defense. You may think that you did a good job of defending your position. You stood up for yourself, saying that you were prepared, especially considering the time you had available to prepare. Logically, you did fine. However, I regret to say you didn't do so well. You failed to defend yourself from some critical attacks. The attacks were subtle and came in the form of presuppositions. This is the kind of interchange where you would leave the meeting feeling beaten, but logically, consciously, not knowing how or why.

The first sentence, "If you were doing your job, you'd be better prepared," presupposed that you were not doing your job. That's a direct attack on your overall job performance, not just your performance at this mundane meeting. It's a much stronger attack on you than is just saying you're not prepared. The second, deeper presupposition is that the abuser is fully capable of knowing whether or not you're doing your job. This implies that you are inferior to this person—who is therefore fully qualified to judge your performance. In most situations, this is not only false, but also puts you in an ineffective position. You can't stand your ground effectively against a superior position, and that's what your abuser has just taken.

Your defense to this attack was "I am prepared; I just don't have the specific answer you're looking for." You got suckered! You fell for the "bait." The issue of whether you are prepared for a mundane meeting is much less serious than are the issues raised by the other two presuppositions. Sure, you can defend yourself against the bait as best you can, but then you leave the really destructive part of the statement undefended. And worse yet, you probably won't be able to defend even the weaker charges very well anyway. You walk away from the attack totally beaten; and unless you understand the power of presuppositions, you won't even know how and why.

Penetrating verbal abuse uses enticing bait.[1] Sometimes, this bait is something you're not well positioned to defend. Sometimes the bait is emotionally charged, such that you're almost compelled to defend it. This example used an effective bait. If you don't have the answer to a legitimate question, you aren't fully prepared. You may not like to think of it in that way, but it's a part of the definition of being prepared. The fact that nobody would be prepared for those questions doesn't really matter—you're still not fully prepared, and it's tough to argue with that.

The other presupposition, which is mostly hidden, is the implication that not being prepared is "wrong" or "bad." You could debate that at another time, though, because it is still not the main thrust of the abuse.

The second assault was, "A good manager knows what answers will be required." The presupposition was that you're not a good manager. Even deeper again is the presupposition that the abuser is fully qualified to determine what defines a good manager and whether or not you are one. Again, your overall performance is attacked, and the abuser is positioned as your superior. The bait (knowing which answers you need to have) is inconsequential. If you were to defend that bait, you would be allowing the more abusive parts of the assault to go undefended.

The true destructiveness of this type of abuse is amplified by a quirk in our human nature. We have a tendency in verbal interactions to assume an accusation is true if it goes undefended. When Paula Jones charged that President Clinton had sexually abused her, we would have believed her for certain if his only response had been "I'd rather not talk about that." Presuppositions can be subtle ways of making accusations and therefore can go unrecognized and undefended. While at the conscious level, we are often unaware of the attacks, at a deeper level, we are fully aware of the attack and of our failure to defend it. We leave the conversation with a sense of futility, frustration, or lowered self-esteem. We're not totally sure why, but we do feel it.

Consider the classic presupposition, "If you really loved me, you would ... [bait]." Whether that bait involves coming home from work earlier, taking out the trash, buying flowers, or greeting someone at the door, the bait is not the real issue. "If you really loved me..." presupposes that you don't love that person. When undefended, it leaves both parties with a sense of emptiness, a feeling that there is a lack of love—even when the love is there.

This is an aggravating symptom of many fundamental problems in relationships. Day after day, people expose themselves to verbal abuse, and they abuse others in order to cope. It results in a degeneration of the spirit of anyone involved in the process, whether attacker or receiver. With verbal abuse, whether it's intentional or unintentional, everyone loses. Unfortunately, it happens quite a bit.

So what can we do? How can we deal with these issues? How can we minimize the problems associated with verbal abuse?

Defending Against Abusive Presuppositions

The structure of abusive presuppositions may be quite clear by now. There are presuppositions and there is a bait. The destructive power of the abusive presuppositions rests in the assumption that you will address the bait and leave the presuppositions undefended. However, much better strategies are available to you.

To defuse an abusive presupposition, you do just the opposite—you leave the bait undefended and address the presupposition. Let's look at some possible responses to the previous attack.

> **Abusive attack:** "If you were doing your job, you'd be better prepared."

>> **Potential response #1:** "Are you trying to say that I'm not doing my job?" *(responding to the presupposition that you're not doing your job)*

>> **Potential response #2:** "I am doing my job, and I'm doing it very well." *(more assertive response to the presupposition that you're not doing your job)*

>> **Potential response #3:** "Are you implying that you're qualified to pass judgment on my performance? *(responding to the deeper meta-presupposition that the person is qualified to determine if you're doing your job)*

>> **Potential response #4:** "What makes you think that you're qualified to determine whether or not I'm doing my job? *(more assertive response to the deeper meta-presupposition that the person is qualified to determine if you're doing your job)*

>> **Potential response #5 (more aggressive):** "What makes you think that you're qualified to determine whether or not I'm doing my job? The purpose of this meeting is to share information, not for you to try to give me a performance appraisal. If you were doing your job, you'd stick to the matter at hand, rather than making such offhand and totally inappropriate remarks." *(responding more strongly to the deeper presupposition, then using the same pattern on the abuser, "if you were doing your job…," then giving some fairly enticing bait of your own)*

>> **Initial response (inserted here for comparison):** "I am prepared, I just don't have the specific answer you're looking for." *(notice how much weaker this response seems now that you have the others to compare it to)*

The second attack is very much like the first and can be handled in similar ways:

> **Abusive attack:** "A good manager knows what answers will be required."

> > **Potential response #1:** "Are you implying that I'm not a good manager?" *(responding to the presupposition that you're not a good manager)*

> > **Potential response #2:** "I am a good manager, and I would appreciate it if you would stop trying to imply that I'm not." *(more assertive response to the presupposition that you're not a good manager)*

> > **Potential response #3:** "Are you implying that you are qualified to pass judgment on my management capabilities?" *(responding to the deeper meta-presupposition that the abuser is qualified to determine if you're a good manager)*

> > **Potential response #4:** "What makes you think that you're qualified to determine who's a good manager and who isn't?" *(more assertive response to the deeper presupposition that the abuser is qualified to determine if you're a good manager)*

> > **Potential response #5 (more aggressive):** "What makes you think that you're qualified to determine who's a good manager and who isn't? The purpose of this meeting is to share information, not for you to expound upon your philosophies of good management. A good manager would know when it's time to get down to work and not make things more difficult by being insulting and condescending." *(responding more strongly to the deeper presupposition, then using the same pattern on the abuser, "a good manager would...," with the enticing bait of "insulting and condescending")*

> > **Initial response (again inserted for comparison):** "Look, I had only a short time to prepare for this meeting, and I got the most pertinent facts available. You just happened to focus on a specific part that I didn't have time to research." *(notice again how much weaker this response seems now that you have the others to compare it to)*

Notice once more that the impact of abusive attacks has far less to do with the actual words being used than with the *structure* of the words being used. It's usually not the content that matters as much as the process. Communication often hinges on hidden assumptions and messages. Many times, what isn't said is much more powerful than what is said. To be effective, you must consider all aspects of a message and consider especially the hidden assumptions and messages. Presuppositions are a major vehicle for hidden assumptions and messages.

In my examples of how to respond to abusive presuppositions, I showed both moderate responses and also more assertive responses. Different levels of assertion are appropriate at different times; however, you must keep assertion separate from vindictiveness or malice. Assertive responses are much more effective when they are coupled with win-win mentality and a desire to remedy a difficult situation.

Remember that behavior is adaptive in nature, and abusive behavior is an adapted response to a different source problem. It's simply the best response available to the person who has the problem. People who are abusive in their interactions need our support, not our malice.

So let's consider acting assertive in the cases of (1) infrequent abusers, and (2) habitual abusers. There are people in your life who are very important to you, and there are relationships with other people that are important to what you want in life. Whether these relationships are boss-employee, husband-wife, girlfriend-boyfriend, parent-child, social acquaintance–social acquaintance, personal friend–personal friend, or whatever, there are probably times when things go well and times when things don't go well. If you find that an important person in your life occasionally belts out some verbal abuse, but it's not his or her regular method of communicating, then it's useful to keep the overall framework in mind. When someone who does not usually resort to verbal abuse does so, then that person is probably dealing with an unusual problem and does not feel that his or her routine methods of communication will solve the problem. When the verbal abuse rests on presuppositions, then the person is probably not aware of being abusive.

Response to this type of abuse is straightforward; call attention to the presupposition-based abuse in a nonconfrontational way, then address your attention to finding the root source of the problem. For example, in a work situation:

Boss: If you really wanted to do a good job, I wouldn't have to waste my time fixing all your goof-ups.

You: Are you implying that I don't want to do a good job? *(non-assertive method of addressing the first-level presupposition of not wanting to do a good job)*

Boss: Well, if you wanted to do a good job, then these things wouldn't happen, would they?

You: Let me be clear right up front. I do want to do a good job *(addresses the presupposition)*, and frankly, you don't have the key to my brain to tell me whether I do or don't *(addresses the deeper meta-presupposition that the boss is qualified to determine if you want to do a good job)*. But that's not the issue here. You don't normally talk to me this way, so I know there's something going on here that we need to address. What's the real problem here, and how can I help? *(directs the conversation toward the source problem)*

Notice what happens here. The presupposition-based abuse is addressed, so you avoid the problem of having it become unconsciously accepted. You also steer the conversation to the root source of the problem. Thus you address the dis-ease, as well as its symptoms.

Steps for Handling Infrequent Verbal Abuse from Important People in Your Life

1. Address the first-level presuppositions in a non-assertive manner. This will sometimes solve the problem right away.
2. If the abuse continues, address the deeper level meta-presuppositions in a non-assertive manner.
3. Call attention to the unusual behavior (pacing experience).
4. Direct attention toward exploring the source problem.
5. Maintain an emotional openness and willingness to help and support.

This approach is relatively non-assertive (don't confuse effectiveness with assertiveness), yet it gets right to the heart of the matter. By addressing the abusive presuppositions, you address the potentially damaging abuse in a respectful, high-integrity way and stop it right in its tracks. The end result is that both of you will have a conscious and unconscious understanding that you are there to help.

Habitual and frequent abuse is a different situation. If you experience habitual and frequent abuse in your own life, then that indicates a deeper problem. Here is where it is helpful to think in terms of responsibility. Avoid the trap of feeling victimized, and take fuller responsibility for your life and your role in it. What could be happening to allow this abuse in your life? What could your role in the process be? What could you be doing to prevent it—which you aren't doing now?

If your house became infested with flying insects, you probably wouldn't blame the insects. You'd look for the openings that allowed the insects to get in, and you'd close them. That's the same process by which you stop verbal abuse from infesting your life. You look for the openings and close them. In many situations, abuse enters your life because you are playing the role of victim. When you take responsibility and adopt the responsibility mind-set, you close the opening and avert recurring problems.

When habitual abuse is constantly directed toward a specific individual, then responsibility is the key. However, when habitual abuse is constantly initiated by one individual (toward many recipients), then that is a different matter.

When someone exhibits frequent displays of verbal abuse, that suggests that the person is experiencing a recurring difficulty and exhibiting a habituated response intended to deal with the difficulty. The source problem may be one of low self-esteem or a strong desire to have control. Or the problem may be related to feelings of fear or pain. In any case, you can be sure that the abuser is having some difficulties. The verbal abuse is probably the only strategy the person has for dealing with the problem in any way whatsoever.

Unfortunately, someone else's problem can turn into your problem, and you need a reliable method of response. This is where assertiveness and perhaps aggressiveness are useful.

When I first began to play doubles tennis, I had the chance to play with an excellent doubles player. When a player serves, his or her partner stands near the net. The partner hopes to be able to "pick off" a return of service in order to be in a strong position to win the point. The partner often tries to pick off returns by moving across the court sideways to the expected place where the serve will be returned. It's called "poaching." An aggressive net player will poach often and can severely intimidate the person trying to return the serve. Once intimidated, the returner will start to miss returns or will hit poor shots. The returner can start losing every point, never even getting close to winning one. It can be very demoralizing. Once an aggressor intimidates a returner, it becomes virtually impossible for the returner to win a point. The docility of the returner increases, and the aggressiveness of the net player increases, too.

One of the returner's few counter-strategies to this poaching is to hit the return either at the net player or behind the player down the line. It's an aggressive tactic. When done at the right times, it tempers the aggressiveness of the net player, who doesn't want to lose points by moving away from where the shot might go.

In the first point I ever played in doubles, I was the returner. My partner made a specific point of giving me a strategy for that point. He said I should hit the return as hard as I could directly at the net player. It didn't matter if it would be a good shot or if it would hit the back of the fence, and it didn't matter if we won the point or not. In fact, he expected that we would lose it. The sole purpose was to hit it right at the net player, hard. If I could hit him with the ball, all the better.

I was a bit concerned about this lack of sportsmanship (even though tennis balls don't really hurt if they hit you), so I asked what the reasoning was behind the strategy. He said that a hard shot right at the net player at the beginning of the game establishes you as a returner. It tells the net player that you know what's being planned and that you have a response to it. If the net player gets too aggressive, you know how to handle it, so your opponent needs to be careful about how aggressive he or she gets.

The competitive aspect of tennis is analogous to the confrontational aspect of verbal abuse. If either of you is overmatched, then there's really no point in playing the game, so nobody bothers. But when the match-up is relatively equivalent, the motivation to win can be greatest.

I don't know how good your tennis game is, but your skills at dealing with verbal abuse will be exceptionally good when you apply the skills learned from this book and chapter. At some point, abusers will realize there's just no point in trying to compete against you. However, until that time, you need to have a strategy for dealing with the abuse. The process of firing right back, hard, is an effective, quick way to do that. The first time you find yourself being verbally abused, I recommend you fire that ball right back at the abuser, hard. Establish yourself as someone who knows what he or she is up to and as someone who has strong countering abilities. Bullies don't pick on tough guys; they pick on wimps.

After you fire back very hard, you will have tempered the aggression of the abuser, and you will be in a much better position to establish functional communication. Here's how that might play out:

> **Abusive attack:** If you were doing your job, you'd be better prepared.

> **Aggressive response:** (#5 from previous example): What makes you think that you're qualified to determine whether or not I'm doing my job? The purpose of this meeting is to share information, not for you to try to give me a performance appraisal. If you were doing your job, you'd stick to the matter at hand, rather than making such offhand and totally inappropriate remarks.

> **Abuser:** (now on the defensive): Hey, I wasn't trying to say you weren't doing your job; I was just trying to get the information that I need. I expected you to have that information, that's all.

Response: (reestablishing a functional, constructive interchange): "Well, maybe I misunderstood. It sounded like you were taking a potshot at me, and that just doesn't work. If you've got some kind of a problem with me, you need to address it with me in a responsible way. I just don't believe in handling important matters in inappropriate ways. Now if you don't have a problem with me, and I just misunderstood, then I apologize. And as far as the information goes, I'll check on it after the meeting's out. I'm happy to support you with anything like that. So that's all I have to say, and I'm ready to get on with the meeting. Does that work for you?

This type of interchange allows you to diffuse abusive attacks, then refocus the energy into a more useful, functional process. Third parties will notice this encounter and will unconsciously understand the entire process. They will have a sense that you were attacked and somehow know that you pushed right back—refusing to accept the attack. They will sense that you brought a potentially hostile situation to a rational, functional close. They may not consciously know what happened, but unconsciously they will take notice and somehow know that you're not a person to be messed with. Also, the abusers in the room will take special notice. "No poaching on this one, the ball's likely to come right back at me. I'd rather pick on someone more defenseless who isn't likely to embarrass me in the process."

This response has done something else, too. It has positioned you in the superior position. You become the person who seems qualified to judge whether or not the abuser is doing his or her job (by saying, "if you were doing your job, you'd stick to the matter at hand, rather than..."), and you become the person who determines how difficulties are addressed in the future (presupposing that you have control over these things). Additionally, you behaviorally presuppose that you have control over the meeting (by saying "So that's all I have to say, and I'm ready to get on with the meeting. Does that work for you?"). Then you tie all that up with the lasting impression that "I'm happy to support you with anything like that."

You leave the meeting with the upper hand. Everyone in the room will perceive that you not only defended yourself, but also ended up in a stronger position as a result. Do this just a few times and in front of enough people, and your strong responses will earn you respect and courtesy. Assertion and aggression are sometimes appropriate responses, and it's useful to have them in your repertoire.

As far as the habituated abuser goes, you've offered him or her a functional method of addressing concerns, and you've laid down the law about what's appropriate and inappropriate with respect to you. That's establishing functionality in your relationship, and that's about as much as you need to do. By closing off the opening for the verbal abuse, you encourage the abuser to seek solutions to his or her problems in other ways, potentially more effective and functional ways. By refusing to support dysfunctional patterns, you offer at least one instance where the abuser can begin to question his or her approach. If you're so inclined, you may choose to offer counsel in private or assist the abuser in seeking professional assistance.

We've covered a bit about the process of verbal abuse and the process of responding effectively to it. You'll find that the response is relatively easy once you learn to recognize the inherent presuppositions. Now let's call your attention to recognizing presupposition-based abuse in some specific examples. I'll list the abusive statements, then the presuppositions[2] (there are usually more than one, but I will list the most significant) and the bait:

1. "Your carelessness is jeopardizing the quality of this project. Already we're way behind schedule." Presupposition: you are careless, and the abuser is qualified to make that determination. Bait: we're behind schedule.

2. "Don't think you can come in here and determine what we're going to do. We're not going to do anything until you get some more facts." Presupposition: the abuser can decide what you're going to do as a group. Bait: get some more facts.

3. "We've got a lot of work to do, and we're going to have to work a lot of extra hours to get it all done." Presupposition:

the abuser has the authority to determine how many hours you will work. Bait: work extra hours.

4. "If you were a good student, you wouldn't have to study so much at night." Presupposition: you aren't a good student, and the abuser is qualified to determine that. Bait: study at night.

5. "Your problem is that you don't have enough maturity to be in a relationship." Presupposition: you have a problem, and the abuser is qualified to determine what it is. Bait: not mature enough.

6. "If you think you're going to buy that computer, you'd better start planning better." Presupposition: you may not get to buy that computer, and the abuser has the power to determine if you do. Bait: plan better.

7. "When you've got problems like this, don't even think about leaving at 5:00. You've got some long nights ahead of you." Presupposition: you've got problems, and the abuser can set your working hours. Bait: long nights.

8. "If you really want to fit in here, you'll start to pay more attention to your appearance. You'll cut your hair and dress like a respectable human being." Presupposition: you don't fit in, and the abuser is qualified to determine that you don't and why not. Bait: cut your hair and dress like a respectable human being.

As you can see, presupposition-based abuse can come in many forms. In a good percentage of instances, there will be two levels of presupposition. For example:

Statement: "If you really want to fit in here, you'll start to pay more attention to your appearance. You'll cut your hair and dress like a respectable human being."

The first-level presuppositions are

- You are not fitting in here.
- You may not really want to fit in here.
- You don't pay much attention to your appearance.
- Cutting your hair is considered paying attention to your appearance.
- You are not dressing like a respectable human being.
- Dressing like a respectable human being is considered paying attention to your appearance.

The meta-presuppositions are

- The abuser is qualified to determine if you are fitting in and if you really want to fit in.
- The abuser is qualified to determine if you are paying attention to your appearance.
- The abuser is knowledgeable about the requirements for appearance and is knowledgeable about how respectable human beings dress.
- The abuser has the power to force you to accept his or her views of how things are.

The meta-presuppositions are routinely the most devastating. They are also the most subtle. In this example, if the meta-presuppositions were to be accepted by you or any other listeners, they would imply a lot. They say that the abuser has authority and knowledge, and you don't. The abuser is almost saying "I see you're not fitting in, and I know how the process of fitting in works; and I'm going to tell you about it whether you like it or not. I have that authority, and you're going to listen to me, because you don't have a choice. So sit down and shut up, while I tell you how it is."

Addressing the bait is usually ineffective and should be avoided. Addressing the first-level presuppositions can be effective and should be done much of the time, non-assertively for infrequent abusers, more assertively for habituated abusers. Addressing the deeper meta-presuppositions makes the strongest and most effective counter-response; it can also be done either non-assertively, assertively, or aggressively. Aggression is appropriate only in rare instances with the most aggressive habituated abusers.

Remember, the deeper the presupposition, the more impact it can have and the more powerful your counter-response should be. Although it's great to have that power at your fingertips, it is not always required or appropriate to use it. As a general rule, you will be most effective when you transform the conflict into a more functional situation. Keep in mind that the goal is to turn lemons into lemonade—you don't need a two-ton hydraulic press to squeeze most lemons!

Power Struggles

You may remember a phrase used earlier in this book—"power struggles." The phrase is commonly used in organizations, but it describes a process that occurs in all contexts of life. Power struggles are commonly experienced, often talked about, but rarely understood. Verbal and non-verbal presuppositions make up a good part of the dynamics of power struggles. Verbal presuppositions, especially meta-presuppositions, imply power and authority and knowledge. In power struggles, the struggle is in coercing the "opponent" to accept your presuppositions.

Most of the time, this process is unconsciously driven and is not consciously understood even by parties involved in the struggle. They are driven by a desire for control and power, and they use the wording that is natural for them. They don't necessarily understand it in linguistic terms, but they are attuned to the results. They know when they have gained the upper hand or lost it. They fight to gain it, hate to lose it.

When faced with a power struggle, your goal is again to make the situation constructive. Respond directly and assertively to any direct confrontations and redirect attention to the underlying behaviors. By calling attention to the underlying, subtle intentions of the other person, you "expose" the abuser and make his or her intentions known. That strips away the power of the presupposition-based abuse. It's one thing to imply that you know it all, but it's another thing to tell everyone so.

Power struggles originate with people who have values that are not being fulfilled, but who have the energy to act. They try to fulfill their values in the only ways they know how, which are unfortunately sometimes aggressive and abusive. A "good fight" releases pent-up energy and relieves some symptomatic high-energy anxieties. In this way, the struggle can seem enjoyable, even exhilarating. To some degree, this aggressive, competitive process addresses the deeper needs of these people.

When you take away the competitive, confrontational nature of the power struggle, then abusers do not get relief in their usual way. If you don't provide an opening for them and you don't attack them back, then they have no place to direct their energies; and they will move on to more fertile ground or more prized trophies. Their relations with you will be more functional.

To distinguish yourself as someone who is strong and capable (although not willing to play) rather than weak and vulnerable, it is important that you hold your ground when needed. If your authority is being questioned or something that you feel very strongly about is being challenged, then you must hold your ground resolutely. The process is simple:

1. Counter any abusive presuppositions strongly.
2. Use the verbal patterns outlined in the previous chapters to make your points.

3. Give the abuser a way out.
4. Keep the power by talking more (through Steps 1, 2, and 3).
5. Close the encounter. End it. Walk out of the room if necessary. Use a convincing statement such as "That's all we're going to say about this right now. We're done. I'll discuss this stuff with you later, but not here, not now. So right now, we need to get back to doing what we came here for." And hold to that.

If you have found in the past that you have not held your ground well in verbal encounters, it is likely that you will increase your effectiveness by learning the strategies in this book.

I advise caution, however. Anyone who is naturally gifted with words and is highly motivated by the desire for power and control is likely to be too much to handle in a strictly verbal interaction. These people live their life fighting for power and often stop at nothing to wage their wars. They have far more energy to dedicate to a battle than you do and will be far more motivated to pursue it. If you can't overpower these people at will and bring functionality to the situation routinely, it is a lose-lose process to engage in the struggle over a long period of time. Use the five-step process listed above when needed, and end it quickly. Keep any significant conflicts within private quarters to minimize your losses. In corporate settings, if you outrank the other person, use your authority. If you are peers—and in other settings—use your strength of conviction.

A word about conviction seems appropriate here. When I was growing up, an older friend told me a story about bullies. Here was his advice: "If you're plagued by a bully, the best thing you can do is this: The next time you see him, walk right up to him, and punch him in the face as hard as you can, without provocation. He'll then proceed to beat you up. Then next time you see him, again walk right up to him and punch him in the face as hard as you can. Again, he'll proceed to beat you up. Do this at least three times, and do it until you notice that he starts to grimace when he sees you. Even if he beats you up each time, he won't look forward to that punch in the face. Pretty soon, he'll start to avoid you, and you will never have to worry about that bully again, nor his bully friends."

This advice is much easier to follow with verbal bullies. If you're plagued by a verbally gifted and talented bully, use your conviction. Each time you detect even a hint of abuse, put up a good fight. Eventually the bully will tire of the game and seek more docile victims. You may not win the fights against the most gifted abusers, but you will solve your bully problem. With the skills listed in this book, I guarantee you that you have the ability to put up a good fight! The bullies will grow to respect you, too.

Verbal abuse is a traumatic process. It leaves frustration and despair in its wake. Its power lies in its hidden nature and the fact that most people are unable to recognize the abuse and are therefore ill-equipped to respond to it. Fortunately, once you understand the behaviors and processes—specifically the structure of linguistic presuppositions—verbal abuse is simple to identify and respond to. The skills that we have already shared are enough firepower to eliminate all but the most powerful verbal abuses and to transform any conflict into constructive interactions.

Presuppositions are a natural part of language. Every sentence in the English language has some presuppositions in it. We have looked at them here in a relatively negative light, citing them as the source of verbal abuse. Yet presuppositions can also be used in a positive and powerful manner. As you become more aware of presuppositions and how they are being used, you will find that they are simply a tool of communication. That tool can be used in a variety of ways, and it gives you tremendous opportunity for increasing your persuasion skills. For practice, you may wish to notice the wide use of presuppositions in the text of this book and how they are used to inspire your continued success and effectiveness. Their effectiveness is as dramatic as any linguistic skill you may ever learn.

Behavioral Presuppositions

We began our discussion about listening by paying attention to behavior first. As we progressed, we made the transition into the realm of verbal skills. We've covered a wide variety of linguistic skills for gaining trust, inspiring others, persuading others, selling your ideas, and making your words as powerful as they can be. Additionally, we've covered presuppositions and their potential to be misused, as in the case of presupposition-based verbal abuse. These skills and strategies form a strong foundation of effective verbal abilities, and they will serve you well—probably for the rest of your life.

Now we return our discussion to the topic of behavior, coming full circle. We're going to be looking at a specific class of behaviors that can have great impact. For the remainder of this chapter, we will explore behavioral presuppositions.

I mentioned behavioral presuppositions earlier in this chapter, illustrating the fact that they are often accompanied by verbal presuppositions. The two are so closely related that it's difficult to speak about one without the other. Behavioral presuppositions convey the same level of depth as meta-presuppositions do, but they often have more impact and subtlety. That combination makes them powerful indeed. Let's look at an example.

Many years ago I worked in a company that had very important annual meetings. These meetings involved the general managers making presentations to the Board about the status of the company and future plans. For the first few years, the general manager was a man named Malcolm. Malcolm hated these meetings, and he let everyone know it. Each year, his anxiety would grow as the date of the meeting came near. He would go crazy drawing up graphs and charts and compiling all kinds of data, and he would do his best to justify new expenditures in light of these data. Malcolm knew his business very well, and he only made requests that he knew were absolutely needed. And each year, he would get hammered by the Board. He rarely got what he wanted, and when he did he got only half of it. Year after year he would expound upon how tough those meetings were and how much he hated them.

A few years later, Malcolm moved on and another general manager named Steven took over. Each year, Steven went to these meetings, and he got everything he wanted—

and then some! He felt no stress over them; in fact, he felt energized by the whole process. Steven asked for far more than Malcolm would ever have dreamed possible, and each year he got it all with ease. What was the difference? How could the very same meeting turn out so very differently? What were the key aspects Steven used to get what he wanted?

The answer lies in the use of behavioral presuppositions. Malcolm would always dress more formally for these meetings (behaviorally presupposing that this was out of the ordinary for him). He was anxious and nervous (behaviorally presupposing he was vulnerable to attack), and he would routinely justify his requests with large amounts of details and data (behaviorally presupposing that he needed to justify his requests). He presented information from a podium (presupposing a formal presentation and a distinction between himself and his audience). He began the presentations justifying the past year's results (behaviorally presupposing that they needed to be justified), and he ended by asking for new expenditures (behaviorally presupposing that he did not have the authority to decide on his own). When he got hammered, he would get defensive and belligerent, then storm out of the meetings (behaviorally presupposing he had been beaten). It was a very challenging process for him.

When Steven started conducting these meetings, he did things differently. He dressed the way he usually dressed (behaviorally presupposing this was just a normal part of his job). He was never nervous and always gave the appearance of utmost confidence (presupposing a high level of ability). Instead of using a podium, he sat in a chair next to one of the Board members (behaviorally presupposing he was one of them). Steven didn't even mention the past year's results, but instead focused solely on the plans that he had (presupposing that he didn't need to justify anything and that his vision for the future was the most important thing to talk about). He never asked for new expenditures, but simply informed the Board of the new expenditures that he had incorporated into his future plans (presupposing that he didn't need to ask permission, that he had all the authority he needed to do this already) and simply passed on the paperwork for signature as he was talking (presupposing it was no big deal).

Steven never got hammered. Steven got everything he wanted, and then some. His success stemmed from his behavioral—and the accompanying verbal—presuppositions.

There is an important concept that pertains to defending yourself against verbal abuse. Sometimes, the strongest defense is to change the game. Steven never stepped into the game the way Malcolm did, so the habituated patterns of attack were no longer part of the equation. They didn't apply to these new circumstances. By the time Steven got into the room, he had already averted several major confrontations simply by changing his method of participating. Attacking a frustrated, insecure loner as he's standing by himself behind a podium is very different from attacking a confident, team-oriented peer who is helping make things go better for the future. Although Steven's verbal skills were as good as they get, he never had to use them. The Board members felt Steven's strength and confidence. They felt it because he had it.

In review, here are some of the key concepts we have learned in this chapter:

1. Presuppositions form the basis of much of the destructive verbal abuse in our society.
2. Presuppositions are "hidden" from our awareness. The deeper the presupposition, the more powerful its effects can be.
3. There are at least three distinct types of presupposition: presuppositions, meta-presuppositions, and behavioral presuppositions.
4. Presupposition-based abuse is usually a symptom of another problem.
5. The goal in responding to presupposition-based abuse is to address the core problem and to transform the dysfunctional process into a functional process.
6. Defending against presupposition-based verbal abuse requires that you respond to the presupposition and avoid responding to the bait. The deeper the presupposition you are responding to, the more impact the response will have.
7. A critical aspect of power struggles is the process of trying to get others to accept presuppositions and respond accordingly.
8. When faced with individuals so highly skilled with verbal encounters and power-struggle situations that you can't deal

with them, it is lose-lose to battle with them on an ongoing basis. Cut your losses in front of groups by stopping the interaction quickly. Deal with these individuals in private when you can.

9. When faced with a verbal bully, fire back strongly in initial encounters and expose the underlying, inappropriate intentions.

10. The best defense is often to change the game using behavioral presuppositions. Behavioral presuppositions can have the most impact of all communication skills.

CHAPTER 10

SPECIAL WONDERS OF NLP— VERBAL SKILLS

MANY CHAPTERS AGO, I encouraged you to examine your goals in life. I asked you to consider the many aspects of your life and to look closely at what you wanted to create. I told you that I wanted to be your partner in the process and that I would give you some tools to help you get there.

In these next two chapters, we're going to look at how to enhance each of the tools you've been given so far and increase your ability to take charge both externally and internally. Externally, we'll enhance the processes of verbal communication. We'll cover not only saying what you want to say and getting your listener to hear what you have to say, but also communicating at a deeper level. We're going to be more concerned with what someone else is thinking in response to our words. We're going to adjust our wording to help guide others' thoughts. Sounds incredible? Seems outrageous? Makes a difference? Yes it does!

Internally, we're going to look not only at how to control our circumstances so we feel better, but also at how to feel better in any circumstances. We're going to go one step beyond the process of controlling our feelings and look toward ways of allowing ourselves true choice in feelings. Instead of controlling anger, we'll look at processes that help prevent us from ever getting unnecessarily angry in the first place. Thus we'll be faced with having to control our levels of satisfaction and happiness instead!

Before I get too outrageous with these ideas, I want you to realize that the processes we are about to learn are simply part of the basics of living and communicating. They are things that people do every day. Yet only a small minority do them well, and only a smaller minority realize what they are doing. These minority groups make up the successful, fulfilled, happy people of the world; and they're the kinds of people you probably love to be around. I'd like to help you become a member of this elite group.

Reframing

Reframes are essentially "different ways of looking at things." They transform the meaning of what is said or what is happening. One man's garbage is another man's treasure, and a reframe is a way to transform garbage into treasure. There are several ways to reframe an experience, and they're so easy to master that they become second nature after just a short while. Practice is the key. Let's start right away with some examples:

Objection #1: Your product is too darn expensive.

Reframe: It certainly is expensive. In fact, compared to our competitor's product, it's about 30 percent higher in price. In dollars, that's a lot; but when measured in your downtime, it adds up to only about ten hours of lost production. If it saves you just one hour of downtime per week, you will have paid for five units in the first year alone! Your downtime is far more expensive than any product you will ever buy. That's what we need to look at. *(reframes the issue of expense into the concept of being a money saver)*

Objection #2: I've never heard of your company before. I think I need to go with a brand name.

Reframe: I know you've never heard of our company before, and there are several reasons for that. Primarily, we don't market ourselves like the big guys. Just like Coca-Cola is the best-known cola in the world, and nobody's ever heard of the Safeway brand. But if you really tasted the two, you'd see that there isn't much difference, and Coca-Cola is 50 percent more expensive. You have to ask yourself, is that tiny difference worth 50 percent more money? For a commodity like we're selling, you might find some differences between ours and the name brand, like how pretty the box is, but you'll also find that 50 percent extra price tag. So if you can put up with some brochures that don't look like national magazines, and you'd like to save some money, you need to try our product. *(reframes a concern over an unknown brand into the advantage of being a less expensive equivalent)*

Objection #3: Your proposal doesn't fit into our current plans.

Reframe: Of course it doesn't fit into your current plans. You didn't know about it when you made your plans. If you had known about it, you would have given it serious consideration. You don't have to change all your plans, but you do need to be flexible enough to respond to the opportunities that come your way. The Swiss watch industry scoffed at digital watches when they had the chance to make them first. Now, Japan dominates that market because the Japanese saw the idea for what it was, something worth adapting to. Don't let your current plans lock you into something that's not as strong as you need. Take a look at my proposal again. I think you'll find it to be more interesting than you first realized. *(reframes an outcast idea into an overlooked opportunity)*

So how do reframes work? How can you do them? Well, once you know the objection, and you know the strength you want to sell, then it's just a matter of "flipping" it. These are the steps:

1. Affirm the objection; for example, "You're right, it sure is expensive. In fact,..."
2. Bring in your new perspective; for example, "It's expensive in dollars, but if you measure it in downtime, then it's only ten hours more than the competitor's."
3. Summarize the flip in as concise a manner as possible; for example, "Your real costs aren't in dollars; they're in downtime, so that's what we need to be looking at."

Ross Perot is one of the best reframers I've ever seen in politics. During the 1992 presidential race, one of his reframes struck me so strongly that I still enjoy it to this day. Although I don't recall the exact words, it went something like this:

Situation: A presidential debate, with President George Bush, looking very presidential; with Arkansas Governor Bill Clinton, looking very formidable; and with an uncommon sort of man, Mr. Perot, beginning on the defensive.

Facilitator: Mr. Perot, what do you have to say about Governor Clinton's experience as governor of Arkansas and how that prepares him for being President?

Ross Perot: It's irrelevant.

Facilitator: (Surprised) Excuse me. What did you say?

Ross Perot: I said it's irrelevant. (Long, uncomfortable pause) Arkansas has two million people, which is a drop in the bucket compared to the number of people in this great country of ours. I could go down the street and say I managed my corner store, but that certainly wouldn't prepare me to be CEO of Wal-Mart. It's a totally different ball game.

This was a beautiful example of reframing. Clinton was using his gubernatorial experience as a major selling point for his candidacy, and Perot minimized it in one fell swoop. Ross Perot's success in politics (as an Independent, he managed to get 19 percent of the popular vote, even after some major problems in his campaign) was very nicely supplemented by his frequent use of reframes.

The true gift of reframing is the ability to come up with a new perspective. Although it's generally something you just seem to pick up, here are some more specific ways in which you might get your ideas:

- *Chunk up:* If the objection is specific, it is sometimes useful to look at things from a broader perspective. If your customer is concerned about the radio in the car he's thinking about buying, you might chunk up to reliability. "That nice radio won't be very pleasant if your mechanic ends up listening to it more than you do."
- *Chunk down:* If the objection is general, it sometimes helps to get more specific. If you're trying to persuade someone that your product is better than the competitor's, you might pick a specific aspect. "Well, they may say their product is

better, but how thorough is their proposal? You have to look at every detail in a job like this. If they just slap a proposal together before you buy, what kind of service do you think you'll get once you've already paid them the money?

- *Context:* All objections depend upon a certain set of circumstances, the context. If you change the context, then the objection is often meaningless in the new context. There are several contexts that are useful to consider: people, places, things, activities, information. If you're selling a computer and it's slower than your competitor's, then you might sell in a context other than activities, such as people. "It doesn't matter how good your computer is if nobody ever uses it. That's the failure of businesses today. They buy hundreds of thousands of dollars of equipment and their people end up using them as typewriters and calculators. Your people will like our computers, and they will want to use them. You must satisfy your people first; then you'll get the results you want."

- *Content:* Sometimes all you have to do is redefine the meaning that your listener has assigned to a given observation. Look for a new way to evaluate that observation. Let's say your customer is annoyed because salespeople keep bothering her, and she can't get her work done. "Be glad you get this many calls. I once knew a manager who actually scheduled a certain amount of time per week for cold calls from random salespeople. It may have seemed like a waste of time, but every time he needed something in a hurry, he seemed to have a contact all ready. He saved tremendous amounts of time, and especially stress, by knowing what was out there already. You never know when the boss is going to ask you for just the thing that I want to show you now. You may be using some of your time now, but you're saving a lot of your time in the future. If you haven't been doing this, it's no wonder you feel like you don't have any time on your hands."

- *Apply to self:* Many times the objection can be reworked and used to object to the objection. This is a very effective reframe, but it can also come across as being overly clever or slick. To get excellent responses with this reframe, take care to use it with full respect for the person involved. Suppose some people are upset about something that's happened, which they believe will undermine what they're trying to accomplish. You might respond with, "I understand how you might think that, and I know this isn't the best thing that could have happened, but *that kind of thinking is what would undermine what we're trying to accomplish.* Right now, we need to pull together to make things right." You use the concern about undermining as a way of making your point. You can soften your wording with modal operators of possibility (words like *might, may, probably, could,* and so on) if desired.

As I stated previously, these are only a few of the ways in which you can create your own reframes. Soon, you will find that you are adept at creating reframes spontaneously and naturally. It's actually quite simple. You might even find one or two in this book somewhere.

FRAME

RE-FRAME

Future Pacing

When you communicate effectively with others, you will be part of a process of creating change. In a business setting, you may be responsible for increasing productivity or improving interpersonal relations. You may be instrumental in achieving goals and helping others to align themselves so that the goals are achieved. You may play an integral part in handling the problems people encounter. These circumstances are all examples of creating change.

In personal settings, you may be striving to improve your relationships and the effectiveness with which you and your partner support each other. You may be working to establish stronger friendships, better commitments, and improved emotional fulfillment. These circumstances are also examples of creating change. Whether the change reflects what you are doing or what those around you are doing, it is an ever present aspect of life.

When you go through a process of change with others, you are changing their ideas, insights, motivations, inspirations, and much more. You are encouraging others to do something and helping to make that process motivating and enjoyable.

Most of the time you will be asking others to change their perceptions. You will be asking people to look at and consider your model of the world. You are suggesting directions for their thoughts. And those activities can be supported with the process of *future pacing*.

Future pacing can help people reinforce their understanding of goals and outcomes. It can help them set direction in their ideas, and it can help bring the real world to mind. It's a process by which people can move from the intellectual abstraction of an idea to an understanding of real-world applications. It can help them explore initial objections and potential difficulties and resolve them prior to making a change. It can help them understand the broader implications of their potential actions and get a better sense of how well they are positioned within the win-win framework.

When you assist people in coming to a new understanding, you will also need to show them a process for putting that understanding into action. Your assistance is only partially complete until you also help them prepare for taking action. Future pacing helps reinforce and develop the change process.

So what is future pacing? How do you do it? When do you do it?

Future pacing is nothing more than having your listener think about the future.[1] If your listener is an upset customer, and your goal is to have a good customer relationship, then your future pace might be to have that customer think of how good the relationship will be after the two of you resolve the problem.

In this book, you are learning all kinds of skills to create more effective and powerful communication. You've probably already realized how effective these skills can help you become (*first future pace, introducing a new idea*). When you have interactions with others in the next several days, you will likely be seeing and understanding aspects of communication that you weren't aware of before (*second future pace, pacing what will likely be your experience*). Right away, some of the techniques will probably come very easy to you (*third future pace, a suggestion and pacing probable experience*), but at times you may find yourself consumed just trying to remember the patterns and to recognize them (*fourth future pace, pacing a potentially difficult situation*). However, with just a bit of practice and some review of the material (*fifth future pace, giving you an idea about how to handle the difficulties*), you will gain more and more experience with the techniques (*sixth future pace, encouraging success*). Each time you have a successful interchange through using this material (*seventh future pace, encouraging you to see success in realistic terms*), you just may find yourself even more motivated to learn this material even better (*eighth future pace, encouraging a positive, motivated response to your future successes*). You may even find that you're getting better and better with less and less effort as time goes on (*ninth future pace, encouraging success*).

The future pacing that was done in the previous paragraph is one of many examples in this book. Fundamentally, it just helps you imagine the future, but there are some additional aspects that deserve mentioning.

As I teach it, future pacing is best done through the following process:

1. Have a win-win outcome in mind for the future.
2. Begin with the present, and pace current experience.
3. Move to the relatively near future, and pace likely experience.
4. Address potential difficulties, objections, confusions, limitations, and hindrances.
5. Step through the processes involved with overcoming the challenges in Step 4.
6. Complete the process with a vision of the future that gives a fuller description of the win-win outcome and reflects the results of having overcome the challenges in Step 4.

Future pacing does more than just set a direction for your listener: It provides a pathway.

Many people think that speaking is about getting out the words they want to say. And for them it is. However, communicating is more than just speaking words: It's also about creating an environment that influences your listener to feel certain ways, encourages your listener to think certain things, and shows your listener a clear path toward taking action as a result. John F. Kennedy had such an idea in mind when he delivered his speech about the space race. He wanted the American people to feel pride in their country and feel excited enough to support his actions. He wanted people to envision his goal—to have a man on the moon by a certain date. He knew exactly what he was doing and was effective because of it. Would you have it any other way?

Your communication may be the foundation for developing great relationships, conducting excellent win-win negotiations, increasing career success, and many more things. And you can achieve these things much more consistently by also directing your listener's thoughts toward those futures you envision.

COMMON METHODS FOR FUTURE PACING

Let's look at several different verbal methods for constructing a future pace within the framework of the steps outlined previously and provide some simple examples.

1. *Ask questions* (rhetorical questions are usually best): "I know we're just in the beginning stages of this process, but what would it take to have a great working relationship for the next several years? Isn't that the ultimate goal that we're both working for? Wouldn't that make both our lives much easier and be a win-win?" *(future paces a long-term working relationship)*

2. *Describe the future:* "After we come to an agreement, we're going to have a lot of work to do, and we'll be working very closely together. There are a lot of details that we'll have to handle, and I want you to know that I will be perfectly willing to take care of them as they arise. You can feel perfectly secure knowing that these things will be handled." *(future paces an agreement)*

3. *Bring out the details:* "Next week when we deliver the equipment, we're going to need your help for the first hour or so. My technicians will need to know specifically what things they should be aware of, such as noise level, where they are allowed to enter and which areas they should avoid, what kinds of interactions you'd like them to have with your employees, and so on. These are the details that will make next week's installation a success." *(future paces a successful installation within a week)*

4. *Set a time frame:* "Since we've just started this process, it's premature to make your decision right now. Typically, managers in your position find that it takes about one week to fully consider the proposal and about another week to check with others about how it will work within the context of your other objectives. So, if you agree, I'd like to have a meeting in two weeks' time, when we can finalize any of the remaining issues that you haven't yet worked out." *(future paces agreement meeting in two weeks with most of the details already worked out)*

5. *Use if-then and when-then constructions and describe the benefits of the preferred choice:* "We don't yet know that we'll be coming to an agreement, but if we do, then you'll find that we are consummate professionals. Every detail, every item, will be handled with the ultimate in courtesy, thoroughness, and efficiency. You'll find that you are very glad to have entered into this agreement, and a year or two from now you may even wonder how you did without us!" *(future paces an agreement)*

6. *Use metaphors and personal stories:* "Being in your position can be quite a challenge sometimes. You get all kinds of consultants telling you what great things they can do for you. I know, because I've been there. I used to work in a position much like yours, and I've hired many consultants. Some were great, and some weren't very good at all. But when I found a great one, it made it worth all the time and effort I took to go through the others. I just found that you have to go with your gut instinct and make a decision to hire someone. That always worked out well for me." *(future paces hiring a consultant)*

7. *Presuppose the future pace:* "This is such a great opportunity for both of us. Since you asked for our proposal, I've been thrilled at the prospect of working with you. I can't wait to start working together on a daily basis and to get beyond this preliminary planning. I'm sure that I'll find you're even more enjoyable to work with as things really get going, and I'm really glad to get this opportunity." *(future paces working together, thus an acceptance of the proposal)*

As you can see, the methods that can be used to future pace are loaded with presuppositions, nominalizations, countersells, and many of the other patterns that we have covered so far. In fact, future pacing ties in with most of the techniques in this book.

Earlier in this book, we discussed detailed processes that can be used to help elicit information from others. In that context, we focused on listening for things that are important to others and on recognizing incongruencies. The goal of that chapter was to help us flush out the true needs and desires of others so that we could help them achieve their goals. This is the heart of creating real, in-depth, supportive win-win environments.

Future pacing is the process by which you check your work. When you future pace for another person, you are not only setting direction and suggesting ideas, but you are also calibrating for congruence. You are flushing out potential objections and problems, hoping to determine if there are any difficulties with what you're suggesting that need to be addressed. You are also looking for congruent excitement, motivation, satisfaction, and so on in regard to the ideas you're proposing. When you get these kinds of positive responses, you can be sure that the future you are describing is congruently a win for that person.

So as we conclude this section, it is useful to remember that the more techniques we cover, the more you will be able to get them to all work together *(future pace)*. As you continue to refine your skills *(future pace)*, you just may find that the techniques create a synergy *(future pace)*, in which each one becomes much more powerful when used in conjunction with the others *(future pace)*. In the end, you may find that your new verbal techniques end up having the power and effectiveness of years of on-the-job experience *(future pace)*.

Internal Representations

One of the most prevalent concepts used in NLP is that of the internal representation. When you are aware of how your words encourage others to generate experience and you purposely communicate to direct your listener to create the internal representations you choose, your communication abilities will improve tremendously. In fact, not only will your ability to communicate be improved, but you will also be seen as a more capable and positive person.

I've mentioned that you have the ability to direct and influence the thoughts of another person. I've hinted at how valuable that ability can be. And I've implied that you can make your win-win arrangements far more motivating and appealing. But I haven't given you the real meat of the process yet. How can you do this? How can you know what another person is thinking? How can you direct those thoughts?

The NLP model is reasonably simple. As we've discussed, each form of information we receive comes through our sense organs—visual information from the eyes, auditory information from the ears, touch or kinesthetic information from the body or skin, olfactory information from the nose, and gustatory information from the tongue. When we understand something, we represent it (re-present it) internally in these same ways. If you think of a pretty sunset, you typically represent that as a visual image. Think of the most beautiful sunset you've ever seen. What color is the sky? You probably have a color in mind. Green? No, probably not.

When you consider this model, you can start to see how miscommunication is possible. If I mention a sunset to you, I might be imagining a red sunset setting over the ocean with billowy clouds overhead. You, on the other hand may be imagining an orange sunset setting over tall blue mountains with a clear sky. A sentence later, when I mention the beautiful shimmering of the sun when it sets, I'll be thinking of the shimmer on the water. What would you be thinking of? It's hard to tell.

In order to form the image of that sun, you were forced to add information. What color is the sun as it sets? What is it setting on? What does the sky around it look like? Are there clouds? You didn't get the answers to these questions from me; but the answers are necessary to create a picture of a sunset. If one picture is worth a thousand words, and I just gave you the single word *sunset*, then where did the rest of the information come from so that you could create that picture?

Generally, that information seems to come predominantly from memories of our own experiences. Words remind you of what you already know, and they stimulate you to create new experiences.

Language—written and spoken—is a *model* of experience, not necessarily experience itself. It is indirect; it is symbolic. When you see the words on this page, you see the letters, but you are responding to the meanings associated with the letters, not the letters themselves. When I mentioned the sunset, you didn't see just an "s," "u," "n," and so on; you probably internally "saw" a picture of a sun setting on a horizon. The same thing occurs verbally. The sound of the word *sunset* is also different from the internal vision you may create when hearing it.

When people converse, they constantly manufacture their own internal representations. Some people are more aware of the process than others, but it seems to be a universal experience.[2] Understanding this, you can tremendously improve your ability to communicate.

Each time you converse, you have an impact on the internal representations your listener generates. If I ask you to imagine a blue tree, you will probably do that. You may not want to, but you will anyway. Just to process my sentence, you will make an internal representation, probably visual, of a blue tree.[3] Think of the sound that glass makes when it breaks—what do you internally "hear"? Think of the feeling of sunburn—what do you internally "feel"? Which part of your body feels the burn? What about the taste of chocolate, warm and partially melted, sticking to the roof of your mouth? Or the smell of cooked bacon, with the moist air reaching your nose, and the sensation of the juices teasing you in anticipation of the first taste?

If you just reexperienced any of those internal sensations, then consider that the only reason you experienced them was that I mentioned them. I "influenced" your internal representations. It was my choice whether to have you imagine the sound of glass breaking or of wind through the leaves of a tree. *My* choice; not yours! When you listen, you agree to allow other people to influence much of what goes on in your head. It's part of the process. When others agree to listen to what you have to say, they agree to allow you to influence much of what goes on in their head. This is an amazing insight that usually goes unrecognized and is rarely utilized with any awareness.

Most people are not aware of what they're doing. When they speak, they don't realize the impact of their words, so the internal representations they ask their listeners to generate are random. They're created without a purpose. But with practice, you can control this process.

Just for a moment, don't think of a blue tree. No matter what you do, don't think about it. Don't think about the branches or how long the branches are. Don't think about the leaves or about how many leaves are on the tree. Don't take a moment to look closely at an individual leaf, just to notice exactly how this leaf creates that special shade of blue. Don't imagine how much light could shine through the leaves, and don't even consider whether it would be a good tree to use for shade. Don't think about the roots or about how well planted that tree is in the ground. Don't even consider the specific color of blue on its bark, and especially don't wonder how many rings you might see in its trunk. No matter what, don't even think about it. Don't think about that blue tree at all for the next five minutes. Don't let it just pop into your head as you read on. Don't even pay a lot of attention to it each time you think about it. Don't do it, no matter how much you want to think of a blue tree.

So stop for a moment and allow me to ask you a question. What were you thinking about just then? How old is it? What color of blue is it? Is it like an oak tree, or a pine tree, or what? Most people think that the meaning of their words is the message that is semantically communicated. They think that if they tell someone not to do something, that their message is *very clear*. However, in this case, when I told you not to do something, my message was probably very *blue*. The semantic meanings of your words have very little to do with the actual communication they convey. Your communication is directly related to the internal representations that your listener creates. Your saying *not* to think of a blue tree drives your listeners to think of a blue tree just because you mention it.

Let's look at an example that will begin to show how useful this technique can be. As you read each of the following paragraphs, pay attention to what you are thinking about and how you are feeling:

> **Example 1**   *A description of someone "positive":* Gene is like nobody you will ever meet. There is no wickedness or evil to him at all. Of course, everybody has an ugly side, but with Gene, his ugliness never really shows itself. If he has any nasty thoughts or a streak of meanness, no one ever sees that side of him. I don't dislike being around Gene at all, because meanness and ugliness really make me sick; and with Gene, I don't have to put up with that kind of crap.

> **Example 2**   *A description of someone "negative":* Mario is a very special and unique person. Of course everyone has personal challenges to deal with, and Mario is no exception. Mario sometimes has a challenge allowing his love to shine through. The beauty of his soul and the warmth of

his heart don't always make their presence felt by those around him. He sometimes lets things get in the way of expressing the tenderness he feels. It's not that I love to be around Mario, because many times the things he does aren't in alignment with his own inner beauty. It's just that being in his presence makes me think about how fortunate I am to be in my present state of happiness.

After reading each of those examples, ask yourself some questions. How do you feel about that "positive" person Gene? What about the "negative" person Mario? Which paragraph did you feel better about reading? Did one paragraph make you feel better than another? And very importantly, how do you feel about the speaker of the first paragraph compared with the speaker of the second paragraph?

By mastering the concept of internal representations, you will find that no matter what the content of your message (no matter what specific things you have to say), you can communicate in an exquisitely positive (or negative) way. If you're speaking about a "negative" person like Mario, you can still promote a feeling of warmth and happiness in your listener. How useful is this when you need to handle a customer complaint? Or correct a mistake? Or give bad news? Just because you have something specific to say, it doesn't mean you have to direct your listener to re-present, or re-experience, that particular thing. You can get your semantic meaning across while simultaneously encouraging your listener to re-present completely different things! And all the while you will be saying what you need to say.

Tactical use of internal representations can give people the impression that you are a positive person. In effect, you can be a more positive person. At an unconscious level, people will associate you with the internal representations that you direct them to make. If you've ever been around a pessimist, you'll know what I'm talking about. Pessimists use most of their words in giving you the opportunity to imagine the worst, and that's no fun for you! They make you imagine ugly things, hear ugly sounds, and feel lousy feelings. They overwhelm you with the ugliness of the world and drive you to have negative feelings. Yuck!

Optimists, on the other hand, give you opportunity to imagine pleasant things, which is usually a lot more fun. You get to imagine beauty in the world, greatness in others, excellence and pride. You get to imagine lovely circumstances and get to feel heart-lifting emotions. Your energy becomes more positive, and your heart opens wide.

Whom would you rather be around? Whom would you trust more if all other things were equal? Whom would you want to do business and spend time with? The optimist, of course.

In the same way, you will be much more effective when you consistently direct people toward pleasant, uplifting, enjoyable internal representations. Even if they don't know what's going on, they will naturally be attracted to your interactions and conversation. They may not know why, but they will find you an enjoyable, pleasant, invigorating person to be with. You will enjoy a respect and courtesy that you will have fully earned.

Tactical Not's

In the previous section, we "looked" at a blue tree, even when I semantically asked you not to. We also used a positive slant to describe the negative attributes of a person, and we used a negative slant to describe the positive attributes of another person. In each example, the internal re-presentations were directed one way, while the semantic meaning of the words was directed in another way. This was done with the strategic use of the word *not*.

When reading the descriptions of Gene and Mario, you may have felt pleasant about semantically "negative" comments, or vice versa. This example may have given you some insight into the power of using the concept of internal representations with volition.

The response potential people have is related more directly to the internal representations they generate as a result of words than it is to the semantic meaning conveyed by words. This is an incredibly valuable insight to have!

CHRISTMAS WAS ALWAYS A STRESSFUL
TIME OF YEAR IN THE PINNOCHIO
HOUSEHOLD.

Tactical use of the words of negation can enhance the techniques presented in this book, especially those of future pacing, reframing, and handling objections. The use of *not* can be expanded to other words of negation, including *never, nothing, none,* and *no.*

Let's look at some examples. In each case, imagine that you want to communicate the semantic message listed (with its somewhat negative content), but you want to present it in such a way that the internal representations (thus the responses) of your listener will be more pleasant and easy to receive:

Future pacing example #1   *You want to semantically convey:* This project might fail, and you may have wasted your money. *You can say:* This project may not be as successful as either of us envisions, and there's a good chance that you may not feel it was the best investment you could have made.

Future pacing example #2   *You want to semantically convey:* The people in this organization are going to resist this decision and will probably sabotage it to the point that your career will be jeopardized. *You can say:* The people in this organization may not support this decision and may even respond in ways that limit its effectiveness to the point that your future success may not be guaranteed.

Reframing example *You want to semantically convey:* Buying that new house would be foolish and a huge mistake because of your financial position. *You can say:* Already your financial position isn't exactly sparkling, and buying that house would make it such that you wouldn't have any money left over for fixing it up and making it the dream house you want it be. When you combine that with the desires you have in other parts of your life, which also require money, then buying this house may not be the very best choice right now.

Handling objections example #1 *You want to semantically convey:* I know that most of you are very angry about this decision. *You can say:* I know that a good number of you are not totally happy about this decision. That's understandable.

Handling objections example #2 *You want to semantically convey:* We sent you some inferior product. It was a stupid mistake on our part. *You can say:* The product that we sent you was certainly not 100 percent perfect quality. There is nothing on our side that can possibly justify such an incident.

Flip-Flopping Internal Representations

In general, most of your communication will be directed toward encouraging your listeners to create pleasant, positive, easily received internal representations. You will be consciously planning the content of those internal representations. However, in some cases it will be more effective to encourage your listener to create unpleasant, negative representations. And in other cases, it will be more effective to sequence positive and negative internal representations in specific ways.[4] These strategies are in response to the thinking processes that various people have.

We have already discussed the process of generalizing, in which a relatively small subset of experience is used to draw conclusions about a larger subset of experience. If you've opened ten thousand doors in your life, and they all opened with the use of a doorknob, then you are likely to continue attempting to use doorknobs to open doors that you may never have opened before. This is a result of the process of generalization, and it is a useful process. You will have generalized the relationship between doors and door-knobs, and will act accordingly.

However, the process of generalization can also be limiting. If you generalize that you can't do something because you've failed a certain number of times, then you may be limiting yourself. As a result of your generalization, you may be missing some obvious ways to succeed at the task. This is an example of an unnecessary limitation. Thus, it is useful to question and challenge generalizations.

The process of questioning generalizations primarily involves seeking examples that run contrary to the rule. If you say that you can't do something because you failed at it a number of times, I might look for ways in which the generalization is invalid. If you say that the entire world is black, I might look for examples of how it isn't black. If you say that people are emotional, I might look for examples of behavior that is not emotional. This process is not about disagreeing, but is rather a healthy process of determining whether or not to accept another person's generalizations. It is often verbally expressed by the often heard "Yeah, but…" phrase.

Challenging generalizations is also not about being optimistic or pessimistic. It is nondiscriminatory. If you say that people are inherently selfish, I might look for examples of how that generalization is false. If you say that people are always beautiful on the inside, I might also look for examples of how that generalization is false. Even though I personally believe that everybody *is* inherently beautiful, my process would still cause me to question the generalization.

Some people challenge generalizations quite frequently. Others do so in moderation. Still others almost never do. Some people are outspoken with this process. Others do it primarily inside their heads. However, regardless of whether they do it frequently or infrequently, outspokenly or inwardly, most people question generalizations routinely, and it is worth addressing in your communication.

To pace and respond to others' challenges to what you have to say, the previously described process of counterselling objections can be adapted. Consider the following example:

You:	You can learn to be skilled at these language patterns and create incredible success in your life…
Listener's internal exception:	Yeah, but it might take too long.
You (continuing):	Of course, you won't necessarily master these right away… *(pacing the potential exception/objection)*
Listener's internal exception:	Yeah, but I might get some of them immediately.
You (continuing):	But you may find that you get good at them faster than you might have initially imagined, especially some of the ones you're already feeling comfortable with. *(pacing the potential exception/objection)*

The process of counterselling objections before they occur (more accurately, before they are verbalized) is a process that paces the behavior of questioning and challenging objections. Similarly, when directing the internal representations of your listener, it is useful to pace this kind of back-and-forth process as well. This is done by sequencing positive and negative internal representations, which I refer to as *flip-flopping* internal representations.

Flip-flopping internal representations involves sequencing three distinct internal representations in the following manner:

1. Present wording to generate neutral, positive, or exceptionally positive internal representations.
2. Address a potential objection by presenting wording to generate an exaggerated negative internal representation.
3. Transition from Step 2 to Step 4 with transition wording, calling attention to the distinct shift about to occur.
4. Address the potential objection to Step 2 (objection to the exaggerated wording) by presenting wording to generate a more realistic positive internal representation.
5. Go through this process as often as necessary until you have addressed the majority of the objections that you think may be a hindrance to your goal.

Here's an example:

> **Situation:** You are making a new proposal after failing on the first one. Because of your first failure, you suspect your listener is going to be highly resistant to hearing the new proposal.
>
> **How to introduce your proposal:** I'm enclosing a new pro-posal *(neutral internal representation)*. At first you might think it will be a dud like the last one, so you may be tempted to immediately throw it in the trash can *(wording to encourage an exaggerated negative internal representation)*, but I can assure you that would be a mistake *(transition wording)*. This pro-posal is different from the earlier one *(transition wording)*, and it's top-notch *(intended positive internal representation)*.
>
> **Analysis:** This wording is highly effective. Although at first it may seem as if you are directing the listener to have nega-tive internal representations with "dud" and "throw it in the trash can," something different happens instead. In this case, you are anticipating the internal representations that your listener will have anyway, mentioning them in an exagger-ated way, then directing their next internal representation to a positive representation.

Your goal in your communicating should be to influ-ence the *final* representations of the listener, using the tools and strategies at your disposal.

Responding to potential objections by flip-flopping inter-nal representations does several effective things. First, it paces the common process of questioning the generalizations. Talk-ing about objections often causes a break in rapport, especially when it is not handled well. But by pacing the internal ques-tioning process of your listeners, you can actually gain rapport, even with people who actively disagree with others.

Second, the process creates balance in your speaking. You avoid the perception of being a pollyanna by demon-strating your awareness of alternating possibilities.

Third, the process adds movement and flow to your speaking. The back-and-forth motion is easily followed and is comfortable to stay with.

Fourth, the process lets you address objections and ex-ceptions while bypassing potential conflict.

Fifth, the process allows you to verbalize the worst fears within the context of a positive presentation. This puts many people at ease while pacing fears, concerns, worries, and the like, which would normally be unspoken.

Sixth, the process addresses two alternative "types" of people: (1) those who respond most actively to desirability and move toward goals, and (2) those who respond most actively to undesirability and move away from problems.

Seventh, the process leaves the listener with a positive, more memorable internal representation. As professional speakers have noted for many years, people often remember the first thing and the last thing said in a speech, and this process gives positive internal representations in both those positions.

And finally eighth, the flowing nature of the process makes it very easy to perform. It's a very comfortable way of speaking.

Submodalities

One of the more fascinating concepts in NLP is that of representational systems and submodalities. We briefly covered representational systems in the section on internal representations. The concept states that information is perceived as sensory representations. We "think" in terms of pictures, sounds, feelings, smells, and tastes. These are the "modalities" of our representational system (with an additional modality special for internal words). Submodalities are the finer categories of distinctions within each of these modalities. For example, in the visual modality, the distinctions among the pictures would have do with aspects like brightness, color versus black and white, size of picture, distance of picture, location of picture, and so on. When you imagined a blue tree, did you imagine a bright picture or a dark one? Was it close or far away? Was is located in the center of your field of vision or in another position?

The internal representation model describes a process that seems to be fairly universal. It is further supported by the words we use in our speech. For example, consider phrases like "bright person," "larger than life," "dull person," "dimwitted," "distanced person," "off-centered person," "above the rest," and so on. The concept of submodalities would suggest that these types of phrases are not mere coincidences. In fact, NLP goes on to suggest that the way in which we draw conclusions about our internal representations is by coding our representations through the use of submodalities. For example, I might sort the people I know by location, placing the ones I admire in higher positions than the ones I don't particularly admire. When asked what I think about a specific person, I might subconsciously pull up his or her "picture," notice where it is located, and know immediately what I think of that person based on my previous coding.

Although that particular coding may be specific to me as an individual, some codings appear to be fairly universal. Visually, size and brightness have almost universal effects and tend to be more appealing to most people as they increase. Look at the packaging on the items in your grocery store. You won't find too many dull packages with small words! You'll find bright pictures and large, bold letters throughout the store.

As important as it is to create positive internal representations in the minds of your listeners, you can enhance these representations by making their internal representations "bigger and brighter" than ever before. Or you can dim someone's internal representations by making them "smaller and duller." Thus far, I've spoken primarily about visual submodalities, but there are similar submodalities in the other representational systems as well. NLP deals primarily with visual, auditory, and kinesthetic submodalities. There are submodalities for olfactory (smell) and gustatory (taste) information as well, but they are not as widely used.[5] The following is a partial list of submodalities that have impact when used in speaking (and writing) situations:

> *Visual:* brightness, size, three-dimensional or flat, color or black and white, self in or out of picture, still or moving, focus

> *Auditory:* volume, clarity, speed, tone, internal or external

> *Kinesthetic:* intensity, location, temperature, pressure, weight

Let's briefly review where we are. In theory, you can direct your listeners to have certain internal representations inside their heads. By listening to the words you say, they allow you to have a strong influence on what they think, imagine, and consider. By being conscious of the process of internal representations, you can control whether these internal representations are positive or negative. You can create both kinds depending upon your goals. Additionally, you can use submodalities to further enhance the quality of these representations, which will affect the listeners' response to them. By using some general assumptions, you can create internal representations in listeners that are almost universally more appealing (or unappealing). This is a significant power, coupled with a significant responsibility.

Let's look at some examples. First, we'll isolate each of the three major representational systems and "show" how to "brighten up" your wording.

> **Situation:** You are attempting to persuade your human relations director that an employee deserves a promotion.

> **Standard wording:** John is a very intelligent individual, who has succeeded well in this department. People really respect him. His accomplishments are definitely above the norm and are some of the best we've had in a long time.

> **Enhanced with visual submodalities:** John's an extremely *bright* individual, who *lights up* this department. He *shines* through as being so *brilliant* that people *see* him as being *larger than life*. His accomplishments stand far *above* those of his peers and *jump out* as being some of the *clearest* and most *dynamic* I've *seen* in a long time.

> **Enhanced with auditory submodalities:** John's an extremely *clear* thinker, who has really *pumped up the volume* here. He *resonates* precision and excellence and creates a beautiful *harmony* with everyone he works with. He's maintained a *tone* of creativity and expertise, and his work is *clearly* an *octave above the rest.*

> **Enhanced with kinesthetic submodalities:** John's an *intense* individual with a *hot* track record. He's perfectly *in touch* with this department and continues to keep things *moving*

and *shaking*. He *connects* so deeply with people that they tend to *feed* off his support and strength. He's *grappled* with some of the *toughest* situations, and his accomplishments *permeate* the organization, *generating* a *gut-level sense* of excellence.

Almost everyone will find that the enhanced versions appeal more strongly to them than does the original wording. One or two of them will probably appeal to you especially. Use of submodalities will help your listeners make the internal representations that you want them to make and make them more vividly, more clearly, more crisply. It's easier to "see what you're saying," to "hear what you're saying," and to "get a feel for what you're saying." These distinctions help your listener. And a person who finds your words "easy to understand" will generally be a receptive listener.

So how do you know when to speak with visual submodalities versus auditory and kinesthetic? Should you use all of them all the time? Or should you use just one modality at a time?

There are a variety of ideas about how to use this information to your best advantage. Rather than getting unnecessarily specific in this book, I'll provide some very general ideas for you to start with.

> **Visual processes**   When people exhibit visual behaviors, they exhibit the types of qualities that are inherent in visual processing. "A picture paints a thousand words," and visual processing handles tremendous amounts of information in very short times. Just like scenes on MTV, some people can move from subject to subject with "lightning speed," and they can grasp an entire concept in just a brief moment. With impressionist paintings, the details are not important. That's also the case with many visual processes. The details are too cumbersome to deal with because there are so many, and there are so many new insights and ideas that keep coming to mind. Visual processes are fast and changing, and they routinely deal with many things simultaneously. They are excellent to use for creativity, and are categorized as having a high level of energy. In a day when computers rule, fast processing and the ability to handle volumes of data appeal to many. On the flip side, visual

processes are less likely to be thorough, and can be scattered. Their strengths lie in the aspect of creativity and the ability to handle massive amounts of information.

Auditory processes   When people emphasize auditory behaviors, they emphasize the types of qualities that are inherent in sound. Auditory processes deal with only one or a few things at a time, and just as a sentence can mean many different things depending on how you stress the words, auditory processes are very useful for flushing out raw data and distinguishing what is important. Every good speaker knows that effective speech is more than just the words you use, it's how you emphasize and deliver the words. Auditory processes are categorized as having a moderate level of energy. On the flip side, auditory processes can seem one-dimensional and slow to people who prefer visual processing. Their strengths lie in their ability to entertain, build relationships, and flush out the "important" things.

Kinesthetic processes   When people manifest kinesthetic behaviors, they manifest the types of qualities that are inherent in feeling and sensing. Kinesthetic behaviors cover the range of behaviors that include emotions as well as the sensations of the body (the olfactory and gustatory representational systems are often included as a subset of the kinesthetic system). Kinesthetic processes are capable of dealing with information that is extremely important and can reach the "core" of our beings. They include the processing of emotions, such as incredible love and joy to intense despair. Kinesthetic processes are typically slow and steady. They are "beyond words" and work on the "unseen level,"—usually on only one topic at a time. Even though some people think of them as having low levels of energy, they are often responsible for high-energy states, such as passion. Kinesthetic processes have some perceived limitations; however, many people prize kinesthetic behaviors most of all. In a world where intellect is often prized and emotions are often discounted, kinesthetic behaviors are not always fully appreciated. They can seem slow and tedious; however, they are steady and more "in touch" with our most unchanging aspects. Kinesthetic processes are represented by fewer words in the English language than visual or auditory processes, so they are often more difficult to describe and explain. Couple that with a slower processing, and you have a recipe that is certain to frustrate those preferring visual processing. Their consistency and slow mode of change make them excellent for decision making and for helping people maintain a "grounded" state when things might otherwise go crazy. Their strengths lie in their ability to handle the things that are most important to us and the ability to connect in the deepest of ways. Although they are less appreciated in the intellectual arena, they are highly prized in the lovemaking arena.

Auditory digital processes   Although I haven't mentioned the auditory digital representational system before, it is an important aspect of human behaviors. The auditory digital system addresses a special process of language. Auditory digital processes are characterized by logic and speech. Just as legal agreements are extremely precise in their wording, auditory digital processes are also very detailed and precise. Details are critical to auditory digital processes, but only those details relevant to the topic at hand. The order in which the details are presented is also important. Digression is very disruptive to auditory digital processes. Auditory digital processes are precise, logical, and difficult to change. They are excellent processes for technical fields and are categorized as having a moderate level of energy. On the flip side, they can seem slow and cumbersome to people preferring visual processes; they lack emotion, and often fail to distinguish the "important" things. Their strengths lie in their ability to be very precise, thorough, and organized at handling the details. Logic and order prevail in auditory digital processes.

SPECIAL CASES

The preceding descriptions of visual, auditory, kinesthetic, and auditory digital processes addressed the major representation systems people use. Additionally, some circumstances provoke people to use specific systems, regardless of their general preferences for any of these systems. Some of the important ones are:

The future   Frequently people process the future in a visual way. People "look" toward the future, but they rarely "hear" toward the future or "feel" toward the future. When you are encouraging internal representations that deal with the future, you will generally help people to think about the future by using visual words. "As we look toward the future," "the way I see it," "it looks as if it's going to be...," and so on.

Planning   Detailed planning is generally an auditory digital process. It requires an attention to detail and sequence that is difficult in the other representational systems. Whenever it is necessary to deal with a detailed plan or to make an internal representation of a plan, you will be best off using auditory digital wording (covered in the next section).

Logic   Logic is generally an auditory digital process. Again, it relies on order and sequence. Whenever logic is the criterion, auditory digital wording is very useful.

Decision making   Contrary to popular belief, good decision making is not a logical process; it is a kinesthetic process. Most great decision makers will describe a "gut sense" they rely upon. This "gut feel" is so prevalent among good decision makers that I'm convinced it's universal. Logic is often used as part of the process in reaching that gut feeling; but in the end, we base our decisions on the feeling, not the intellect! Whenever you are appealing to people to make a decision, begin by giving them the information and conclude by appealing to kinesthetic processing. A powerful technique is to future pace (at first visually) a positive kinesthetic internal representation into a future situation after the decision is made.[6]

I could go into much greater detail on these topics, however, this is enough to get you started. The best way to use this information is to simply experiment with it. If what you do is working, then keep doing it. If it isn't working, then try something else. The information presented here gives you plenty to work with.

SENSORY DESCRIPTIVE WORDS

When you choose to be mindful of representational systems and submodalities in making your word choices, you will find that you start to have at least four "dialects" in your vocabulary. You will have a visual dialect, an auditory dialect, a

kinesthetic dialect, and an auditory digital dialect. It may surprise you to know that many of the words in our language are
descriptive of specific representational systems.

If you are going to ask your listener to perform a visual
task, such as the creative task of "looking" at how your proposal fits into the "whole picture," then you will benefit from
using visual words. If you are going to ask for an auditory
task, such as enjoying the "harmony" of your proposal, then
auditory words are useful. For a kinesthetic task, such as
making a "gut decision," kinesthetic words are useful. For
an auditory digital task, such as evaluating the logic, auditory digital words are useful.

Selective use of sensory descriptive words can help
people make more vivid internal representations, thus providing clearer communication that makes stronger impacts.
Listeners appreciate the assistance, and your communication becomes vastly improved.

Besides using sensory descriptive words yourself, you will
also routinely hear others using them as well. When you
become skilled at hearing these words, you will notice that
your associates sometimes communicate using certain types
of words more than others. For example, your boss may be
prone to using visual words much more than kinesthetic
words. This can give you clues about how to relate most
effectively with him or her, and how to enhance your ability
to reach common ground.

There are many levels of expertise involved with using
sensory descriptive words to their fullest benefit; however, it
is unlikely that the process of reading a book will give you
enough skill to use these words with the highest level of precision. Accordingly, I suggest you experiment with using all
dialects in your communication with others. This ensures
that you address any preferred systems others may have and
increases the likelihood that you will give your listeners a
fuller sensory experience of what you have to say.

Following is a partial list of sensory descriptive words for
each of the four major categories:

> **Visual words and word phrases**   angle, appear, as I see it,
> black and white, bright, brilliant, catch a glimpse of, center,

clear, contrast, cross the line, dawn, dim view of, dynamic, examine, exhibit, flashed on, focus, foggy, foresee, frame it up, glance, hazy, highlight, hindsight, illuminate, illustrate, image, imagine, in light of, in view of, insights, larger than life, lit up, look, looks like, make a scene, notice, observe, off-center, outlook, perspective, picture, reveal, scattered, scrutinize, see, see to it, shimmer, shine, short-sighted, show, shrink, sight, sketchy, sparkling, stands out, survey, transparent, up front, view, vision, visionary, vivid, watch

Auditory words and word phrases announce, articulate, attune, audible, be all ears, boisterous, call on, clear thinker, communicate, converse, deaf, discuss, dissonant, divulge, earful, earshot, emphasize (tonal) volume, enunciate, express yourself, harmony, hear, hidden message, hold your tongue, hush, inflection, listen, loud, loud and clear, make music, manner of speaking, mention, noise, octave above the rest, oral, outspoken, overtones, power of speech, proclaim, pump up the volume, remark, resonate, rhythmical, ring, rings a bell, roar, screech, shrill, silence, sound, sounding board, speak, squeal, state your purpose, stutter, talk, tattletale, tell, tempo, tone, tuned out, unheard of, unhearing, vocal, voice, within earshot

Kinesthetic words and word phrases bearable, budge, build a relationship, callous, coarse, cold, come through, come to grips with, concrete, connect, cover, cumbersome, deal with, dig up, draining, drive, feel, feeling, firm, flow, grasp, grip, grounded, gut-level, handle, hard, heated, heavy burden, hold on, hot, impression, in touch with, intense, light hearted, lighten the load, pound out, pressure, pull some strings, push through, rough, rough it out, rub, scrape, set, shallow, sharp as a tack, shift, silky, slam, slap in the face, smooth it over, softy, solid, sore, stir, stress, support, tension, throw out, touch, touch base, unsettled, vibrates, warm, whipped

Auditory digital words and word phrases analyze, cognate, cognizant, conceive, consider, consideration, criteria, data, decide, describe in detail, detail, determine, distinct, distinguish, experience, experiment, inquire into, know, learn, logic, make sense of, memorize, methodical, mindful, order, orderly, perceive, plan, precise, precision, procedures, process, question, rationalize, sense, sequence, speak, study, talk, tell, think, thorough, thoughtful, understand, utter, word for word

Did you realize that so many of the things we say are categorized by our senses? Language represents our experience of reality, and our experience of reality comes directly from our senses and indirectly from our interpretations of what comes from our senses. Because language expresses these experiences, it is only natural that our words would be very closely linked to our physical processes of sensing and our cognitive process of thinking.

When you use these sensory descriptive words with a purpose, you can direct your listener to have specific internal experiences. You can either say "Imagine a day that is 90 degrees Fahrenheit," or you can say "Imagine a hot, sultry day, in which you can smell the humidity as you breathe the hot, moist air and feel its heaviness in the depths of your lungs. Your skin feels sticky all over, and the pores down the back of your neck are drenched with moisture and sweat..." For most people, the latter will more completely conjure up an internal representation of a hot day. Novelists are experts at helping the reader develop vivid internal representations. We enjoy that. It makes good reading. You can do the same with your speaking and writing, whatever the context may be.

We live at a time when people are blasted with huge amounts of information on a regular basis. You're going to be competing with many others in trying to create vivid, moving, exciting, enticing experiences for others to remember. You need to use every skill you can to bring your ideas to life.

Guidelines for Using Sensory Descriptive Words

1. Use them when you really want something to stand out.
2. Avoid categorizing people into "types." Everyone is fully capable of using all the representational systems.
3. If you are aware of the representational system that your listener will be primarily using or preferring in the context of your conversation, use more of the words appropriate for that system—that is, kinesthetic for decision making and visual for future pacing.

4. Remember that when you are speaking to groups of people, it's best to use words from all representation systems, not just your favorite ones!

5. It's often most effective to use words from all the representational systems with any given listener—it can give the listener a fuller "sensory" experience of your communication. In addition, many phrases are easily "translated" by the listener into the system that is more comfortable, so feel free to use all categories.

Awareness and mindful use of sensory descriptive words and phrases enhances the many other verbal techniques in this book, making them even more elegant. Throughout your conversations with others, and even your continued reading of this book, you may start to notice these words more frequently. I'm not saying that they're going to start exploding off the page, bursting upon your attention, but I am saying that you may see a few twinkles and sparkles that grab you. When certain words take hold, get a sense of how well they harmonize with the flow of the writing. Eventually, you'll simply settle down to the natural rhythm of their use.

Overview of Verbal Skills

At this point, you may have noticed that the specific techniques are all blending into each other. A reframe looks a lot like handling an objection, a future pace incorporates sensory descriptive words, a nominalization relates closely with an internal representation, and so on. Earlier in this book, I was distinguishing each specific technique more, hoping to isolate each one so that you could see the pattern. As we have progressed, however, you have acquired so many tools that you can now start using them in combination—as you feel most comfortable, as you find them to be most effective. The common, underlying basis for all the verbal techniques should be the intent to create the kinds of sensory experiences (internal representations) and emotions that enhance an environment of win-win, understanding, and rapport, while encouraging energy states pertinent for the action at hand.

Each verbal technique we've covered so far directs your listener's internal representations toward these goals.

As you become accustomed to using these techniques, you will eventually gain an unconscious competence. At that point, you will no longer need to be consciously aware of what specific technique you are using; you will simply be speaking in ways that are naturally effective. Until that time, you will be using some level of conscious understanding as you use the techniques. And of course, the more you use them, the sooner unconscious competence will be yours.

When you converse, you will want to look not only at the content of your goal, but also at the sequence for getting there. You will want to "move" the listener from where he or she is at the start of the process to where you want him or her to be at the conclusion of the process. As in the case of flip-flopping internal representations, sometimes that path is not a straight one.

Sometimes you'll want the listeners' internal representations to be vivid and compelling. That will drive you to use techniques like sensory descriptive words and tactical *not*'s. Other times, you will prefer to let the internal representations stay relatively ordinary, but you will want to create a lot of them. That will drive you to use presuppositions and nominalizations—they can be used in abundance with very few words. Still other times, you will seek to exchange an internal representation that your listeners already have for another one that is better suited for the situation at hand. That will drive you to use reframes and to countersell objections.

The question of which techniques to use is more a question of how you want to direct your listeners' internal representations. Communication is a process by which you encourage listeners to make change. As a great communicator, it is your job to help guide them along a nice, inviting pathway. By knowing this process, you will be astonished and delighted with the results!

CHAPTER 11

SPECIAL WONDERS OF NLP—
PERSONAL STATE CONTROL

CHAPTER 10 DIRECTED our attention to using some special features of NLP to influence the thinking processes and emotional states of others. This chapter is going to focus on influencing your own thinking processes and emotional states. We're going to look at how some of the special features of NLP can be applied internally for your personal betterment and well-being.

The quality of your life revolves around your emotional states. How many people do you know who spend their time and money acquiring material possessions just so they can be happy? But it's the happiness that's important, not the possessions. Occasionally you will hear stories of people who "had it all" who commit suicide or overdose on narcotics. These are people who failed to achieve positive emotional states. Have you ever known someone who "gave up everything" in order to be happy? Or in love? Or at peace with himself or herself? These people know the value of emotional states.

It's very important to understand that your emotional states are within your control. Other people can affect your environment, as can you, but nobody else has a remote control that determines your emotions. You, however, do have that remote control, and it's just a matter of knowing how to use it.

Let's consider anger, an important emotion, often considered to be negative. How do you think you get angry? Does someone make you be angry? Do situations force anger upon you? Does it come from the universe? These are interesting questions.

Before I give you my answers, let's digress for a moment. We know that some people just make us angry. You can probably think of a few right now. If they're really good at it, they don't even have to be talking to you or doing anything to you, and you can still be angry.

We know that certain situations make us angry. Perhaps injustice in the world does it to you. Or disrespectful behavior toward others. Or lewd, vulgar behavior.

We know that certain outside situations can make us angry. Sometimes you might just walk into a room and feel tension so thick you could cut it with a knife. You start to pick up that tension and hostility almost right away.

Sometimes the outside world doesn't have anything to do with it. If you hit your finger with a hammer, you might yell and express your anger. If you want to play an aggressive game of tennis, you might generate some anger to help you. You might sit in a room thinking about an aspect of your life and just get angry—all by yourself.

We all know the emotion of anger, but do we really know how we bring it into being? Or even what it is? Wouldn't it be nice if being human required us to read the *Introductory Manual on Being a Human Being!* If you happen to see a copy, please send it my way.

So how do you get angry? Most people get angry by accessing "anchors," many of which are triggered by the internal representations we generate. An anchor is the NLP term for a rote emotional response to a given stimulus. Remember Pavlov and his bell? Each time he rang the bell, the dog began to salivate. The stimulus (the bell) caused the response (salivation). Pavlov became famous for that experiment. In NLP, when a stimulus-response relationship is created, the stimulus is called an anchor.

NLP teaches us to use this interesting stimulus-response relationship to do some useful things—particularly to encourage certain emotions in ourselves and others. Even outside of NLP, people naturally use anchors to create the moods they get into.

Through a combination of self-applied anchoring and control of our own physical bearing and facial expressions, we become adept at creating the emotional states we live our lives in.

Let's look at this thing we call anger once again (that thing we're always trying to "control"). Some people make us angry, right? Yes they do. They have become an anchor for us, a stimulus. We've been angry around them enough times that sometimes just looking at their face or hearing their voice can enrage us. It's a self-induced anchor gone awry.

Certain situations make us angry, right? Of course they do. Part of that is hard-wired into our nervous system; it's called the fight-or-flight response. However, we create that anger. How do we create it? Essentially, we adjust our physical aspects and create internal representations that are anchored to anger, and then we induce ourselves into a state of anger. It's not the situation that makes us angry, but the things we visualize inside our head, the things we say to ourselves, the sensations we re-create for ourselves, and the physical aspects we put ourselves into that combine to give us that emotional state of anger.

Certain outside situations make us angry. Certainly they do. We walk into a room filled with hostility, and we start to feel anger. But how do we do that? Essentially, we are entering into a state of rapport with the angry people. We subconsciously adopt their physical bearing, facial expressions, and vocal patterns, and voilà, we have anger.

The point is, we are the ones who create the anger, not the outside world. Things that happen in the outside world may be the reason we find ourselves in an environment suited for anger, but we ourselves do the work involved in getting angry. And because we put ourselves in an angry state in the first place, we can do something different!

In the next few sections, we're going to look at ways to create true emotional choice in your life—not at ways to control anger, but rather at ways to choose to have different emotional responses instead. And we'll look at ways to appreciate the emotions of anger—or sadness, guilt (remember that emotion which I said we should eliminate?), fear, anxiety, desperation, and others.

We're going to learn ways to reduce the frequency of unpleasant and non-useful emotions and ways to enhance your ability to benefit from the appropriate use of emotions. We're going to learn some things that must certainly have been included in that elusive *Introductory Manual on Being a Human Being.*

Emotional Choice

In a later section on anchoring, I'm going to share with you a technique that can help you gain a high level of control over your entire emotional life. It is a process that can help you eliminate the feelings of being controlled by your emotions and instead give you the feeling of having true emotional freedom. You can have the ability to *choose* which emotions you experience under most of the circumstances in your life.

Once you acquire emotional freedom, you will begin to find yourself with choices you may never have had before. For example, there may be times when you find yourself starting to feel a negative emotion—sadness, for example. Your external awareness may alert you to that fact, and you will have the choice of feeling sad or feeling a more positive emotion, such as happiness. However, do you always want to be happy?

I happen to believe that millions of years of evolution can't be all wrong, and that our so-called "negative" emotions aren't always the bad boys we make them out to be. In fact, they serve very important purposes and deserve our full respect. The problem lies not in negative emotions but in a lack of emotional choice. When people feel they have no choice about their emotions, then it often seems as if the negative emotions take over, holding them hostage for inordinate amounts of time. When you have emotional choice, you can refresh your ideas about these emotions and perhaps come to value them.

Let's look at some of the more common negative emotions and consider for a moment what *positive* purposes they may serve:

Anger   A high-energy emotion; can be used to help us respond and take action; can get us over hurdles and obstacles that might otherwise be too difficult to surpass. It is often associated with situations we don't like, and it provides us with the energy to take action in response to them.

Sadness   A low-energy emotion that encourages deep reflection. It is sometimes necessary if we are to cope with and manage difficult emotional situations, such as the death of a loved one.

Fear   A high-energy emotion. Fear heightens the senses and intensifies awareness, which can be useful for alerting us to potential problems; it helps us gain information we might otherwise not have obtained. It gives us the energy to respond quickly and escape if needed.

Guilt   An emotion tied to evaluations of right and wrong. If we don't have any other means of evaluating actions as they relate to values, guilt can limit our choices in the actions we take. Once we have the information presented in this book, we should be able to replace guilt with more productive methods of evaluation.

Hurt   Similar to sadness; a low-energy emotion encouraging deep reflection. It lets us know that what we are experiencing is not okay with us.

Disappointment   Occurs when expectations have been created and not fulfilled; a low-energy emotion encouraging reevaluation of expectations and the means to achieve them.

Anxiety   A high-energy emotion that focuses attention on an event yet to happen but whose consequences concern us. Anxiety keeps awareness high and can be transformed into excitement to give us the energy to prepare for the event.

Although many people will tell you that you should seek to avoid negative emotions, I believe that all emotions serve a purpose. People are emotional first, rational second, and I believe that emotions can be used with that in mind. When you have the ability to prevent negative emotions from spinning you out of control, then you are free to think in terms of how to use them productively.

When I begin to feel a negative emotion, my external awareness (which we'll be discussing in the next section) usually alerts me to that fact. My first step is to evaluate the negative emotion in terms of the context of my life. For example, if I'm feeling sadness, I'll ask myself if I need to take some time for deep reflection. If the answer is yes, and the situation at hand warrants it, then I will let myself feel sad. I make it my *choice*.

During this time, my external awareness will periodically call my attention to the sadness, and I will evaluate whether I've had what I consider to be the appropriate amount of reflective time. If so, I will choose a new state. For me, the appropriate amount of time is the time it takes for me to get the message and determine how to respond to it. Most of the so-called negative emotions call our attention to things in our lives that are not okay with us. By calling attention to what is not okay and giving us a state by which we are able to evaluate the situation, these negative emotional states can help us make sense of things and find solutions to our difficulties. If during the course of my reflective time, the outside world changes, I am fully free to adjust my emotional states to respond to these new circumstances. I don't have to sulk in the midst of a party if I don't want to! I have choice.

I have found this model of emotional choice works beautifully. Because I've learned and used the techniques described throughout this book, I have an awareness of my emotions and I'm able to make choices about how I feel at virtually any given point in time.

Interestingly enough, I find that most of the time, my emotions are appropriate for what I am going through in my life. Once I broke the habitual patterns of allowing negative emotions to linger (and learned how to make my life happen the way I want it to), I found that negative emotions were usually justified and useful. My body knows how to keep me emotionally healthy. I've learned to trust my emotional intelligence for its wise decisions. Once your slavery is over, you will see that negative emotions have a useful purpose and should be respected for their assistance in helping you resolve your difficulties. As I said before, millions of years of evolution can't be all wrong!

Association and Dissociation

Before we begin the next series of questions, I want you to take a moment to consider how you feel. Right now, just notice your emotional state.

Now, let me ask you a question. How do you feel about yourself? Are you proud of the person you've turned out to be? Are you impressed with the things you've done? Whatever the answers, these are not the most important questions I want you to answer.

How do you feel about how you feel about yourself? Do you feel guilty for not feeling better about yourself? Are you hard on yourself and feel as if you should lighten up? Whatever the answers, these are also not the most important questions I want you to answer.

If you were the one writing this book, would you know what advice to give yourself regarding how you feel about how you feel about yourself? Would you know how to respond, as a writer, to the varying needs that you as a person have about your feelings about yourself? In this situation, do you know what advice you might give or what you might want to say to the person reading this book? Whether you do or not, these are still not the most important questions that I want you to answer.

The most important question is one of perspective. Are you aware of your ability to shift perspectives? You've probably just experienced at least four different perspectives. They are:

Perspective 1. How you feel right now.
Perspective 2. How you feel *about* yourself.

Perspective 3. How you feel about how you feel about yourself.

Perspective 4. How you would feel if you were the author of this book thinking about how you would feel about how you feel about yourself.

Humans have the ability to shift perspective. We can experience the world through our senses. Or we can remove ourselves from our senses and experience the world even less directly. We can think *about* our life, rather than thinking in our life. We can think about what we think about our life, and we can think about what we think about that. We can shift perceptual positions many times over.

Yet, we can do even more. We can think about how we would be if we were actually a person of the opposite sex. Or if we were God, judging ourselves. Or if we were transformed into a child again. Or if we became an animal in nature. Or if we had actually been dreaming all along, and we were really someone else in some other place. We can imagine almost limitless scenarios, and we can fantasize about worlds that may never be or that actually are but aren't known.

This is the wonderful aspect of humanity that allows us to relate to others as if we understand them. It allows us to consider our actions and determine what might happen as a result. It allows us to plan, and it gives us something to look forward to. Without this ability, we wouldn't be able to ask the question, "What's our purpose in life?"—much less come up with an answer. This ability to shift perspectives is an integral part of managing our emotional states.

Some spiritual disciplines refer to an outside awareness, an awareness of what's happening while it's happening. This awareness allows you to monitor what you are doing, as you are doing it. If you happened to be acting irrationally, this awareness would rationally see that you were acting irrationally.

If you don't use it already, you can develop this awareness quite readily, and it is a very useful thing to have when you want to take emotional control of your life. In basic form, this awareness is nothing more than the point of view of someone else witnessing what you are doing, seeing, hearing, feeling, thinking as you do it. It is a dissociated perspective.

In NLP, the terms *association* and *dissociation* are used to broadly classify the different perspectives humans can create. Association describes the process of placing full attention on your sensory experiences (or even the sensory experience of another point of view). It's about "living in the moment," "getting caught up in things," "getting pulled in," and "getting carried away." These are the expressions we use to characterize a fully associated state. When we're purely associated, we don't have an external awareness that we're associated nor do we have an external awareness of what we're feeling, doing, or thinking. Purely emotional states are experienced when people are fully associated and "act out of" anger, fear, jealousy, love, pride, or any other strong emotion. Associated states are not logical, nor do they involve actions that have been thought out.

Dissociation describes the process of having an external awareness of yourself (or any other point of view). When you think "*about* yourself," "stop and take a look at things," "step back for a moment," "pull yourself out," "remove yourself from the situation," then you're experiencing a dissociated process. When you're purely dissociated, you have an external awareness about what you are feeling, thinking, or doing. Dissociated states can be logical, planned, orderly, and methodical. They can be rational states and result in actions and behaviors that probably "make sense" to you.

As a finer distinction, however, we're always associated in the point of view we're looking from, even when we're associated into a dissociated state.

Associated states typify our most intense experiences. Getting "lost in love" can be an intensely positive experience. Thinking about love is rarely so intense. Rage can be explosive. Understanding our rage can be done calmly through conversation. To get the fullest experience, association is the way to go. People often seek to live life in the moment, to enjoy it to the fullest at all times. This association can be exhilarating; however, when we are in an associated state, we fail to plan or prepare. In associated states, people take action, often without evaluating the circumstances thoroughly.

Dissociated states typify our most rational experiences. Planning, understanding, thinking about, considering, analyzing, and preparing are usually dissociated states. These are our more conservative states, preventing us from "losing control." Just having the idea that we could lose control typifies a dissociated process. It presupposes that one thing is controlling another; in this case your dissociated awareness is controlling the actions that your associated self might take. Dissociated states allow us to understand the concept that our actions have consequences and help us to curtail emotional responses that may lead to detrimental effects. Dissociated states account for the people who avoid taking action, but would rather continue to compile data and information so they can fully "understand" the issue.

Associating can also be approximated through imagination. When we go to a movie, we typically take on the perspective of one or more of the characters. We feel emotions almost as if we were really in the movie ourselves. Expert directors create compelling scenes that encourage your emotional involvement with the movie. When you get "sucked into" a movie, that is an associated process, even though the events are not actually happening in your life. Still, you lose your awareness of where you are, what you are doing, and how you are feeling. You're more attuned to the emotion in the film than you are to how your back feels sitting in that seat!

Association typically results in a more intense, more "full" experience at any given moment. It allows you to "get caught up in the moment" and to "be here now." The concepts of time and planning do not exist within associated states, and people in associated states can seem to be undependable. Someone in an associated state who is supposed to meet you at 6:00 might not show until 7:00, might just forget about the appointment altogether, or might have too much going on to show up or call. When people are in associated states, they typically resist making decisions because decisions limit their options to do what feels good at the time. It is an experience of action. When you are associated, it is easy to get lost in your emotions and fail to maintain emotional choice and an outside perspective. Thus you can feel jealousy or fear as deeply as love and freedom, and you may not have a full awareness of the consequences of your actions. Associated states are usually more emotional than they are intellectual.

Dissociation typically results in a more objective experience at any given moment. It allows you to see things from an overall viewpoint and to evaluate circumstances. An awareness of time is available in dissociated states, and thus planning becomes possible. People in dissociated states can seem to be dependable. Someone in a dissociated state who is supposed to meet you at 6:00 might not show until 6:05, but would have been fully aware of being about five minutes late. When people are in dissociated states, they often prefer to make decisions, predominantly in an intellectual way. It is an experience of contemplation and intellectualization. When you are dissociated, it is easy to lose touch with your emotions and easy to handle difficult experiences in resourceful ways. You are likely to have a full awareness of the consequences of your actions, predominantly in an intellectual way. Dissociated states are usually more intellectual than they are emotional and can result in more contemplation than action.

You can begin to gain emotional control in your life by mastering the ability to associate and dissociate yourself at will. Emotions diminish in intensity when you dissociate. Consider the common television portrayal of psychologists and their clients:

Psychologist: How are you feeling today?
    Client: I'm very angry. I'm incredibly angry!
Psychologist: How do you feel *about* your anger? *(takes the client into a dissociated state)*
    Client: I'm disappointed about it. *(a much lower energy state, and the emotion of anger immediately transforms)*

People have known about dissociation for a long time; however, it just hasn't been explicitly taught to us. How do you control anger? Many people will say you just "step out of it" or "pull back from the situation" or something to that effect. What they're saying is that you should dissociate from your experience.

Dissociation can be taught more explicitly than through those kinds of metaphors. When you're associated, you're fully attuned to your sensory input. You are seeing the world through your own eyes and hearing it through your own ears. You speak with active wording ("I feel hurt"), rather than indirect passive wording ("It's understandable that some level of hurt would be felt").

When you're dissociated, you have a different perspective. You can see the situation, with yourself in it. Visually, you might be imagining the situation from a shifted vantage point. Imagine looking at yourself right now from up above. What do you look like from that vantage point? Do you see the top of your head? What is that person down there thinking about? Now come back into your body and continue to read. When you saw yourself from above, did you have an awareness of seeing the letters on this page? Probably not.

Dissociation is about shifting yourself mentally. This is done extremely well with visualization. Seeing yourself from up above looking down is an imaginative process. You can imagine that you're in any perspective. You can look down from above (often representing a position of greater knowledge and moral authority); you can look from a different perspective, such as from a corner of the room (often representing an equivalent level of authority but with more ability to see the "whole picture"). In a dissociated perspective, your visualization is fabricated (you're not really on the ceiling), so you can adjust its submodalities too. You can further reduce the level of emotional involvement by going further out (increasing distance), by reducing the size of the picture (reducing its importance), by dimming the brightness, or by making it black and white. Let's play with this for just a moment:

1. Recall an intense argument you had with someone, an argument in which you felt intense anger.
2. Think about the argument as you were having it, and look through your own eyes at the face of that other person, who is speaking. Listen with your own ears to the words, and listen intently to exactly how that person is saying them. Feel

again exactly what you felt at that time. Take a few moments to get into the experience.

3. Now stop, and notice what you felt. Did you start to feel angry again?
4. Now imagine that experience again, but see yourself from about ten feet away. From that distance, watch the events and hear the sounds.
5. How does that affect you? Are you feeling more controlled and more aware?
6. Now imagine that same experience, but this time, imagine it in a very small picture very far away. See it in black and white, but dim it so it's almost just light gray. Reduce the sound so that you can barely hear what's being said. Put that picture far down below you so that you're looking down from above.
7. How does that affect you? Are you fully disengaged from the process?
8. Now associate back into the full-color, loud, bright, full-size event, again seeing and hearing through your own eyes and ears. Do you notice a change?
9. Dissociate once again, putting that picture far down below, and then allow it to fade off into the distance so that it's gone completely.

Most people will feel significantly different as they imagine themselves in each perspective. This is simply a process of conscious association and dissociation. You can do it with any event in your life at any time. All you have to have is enough of a dissociation to remember to do it!

Dissociation is a natural human process for lessening and evaluating emotions. On the other hand, association can do just the opposite. Here's another example:

1. Recall an experience when you felt a detached level of sexual attraction for someone.
2. See that experience from about ten feet away, and see the two of you interacting. Notice how you feel about it from this position.
3. Now step into your body, and see this person through your own eyes. Listen to the sounds through your ears now, and feel the sensations that you're experiencing as you're in this situation.

4. Now move closer to this person. Move so close that you can feel the warmth of his or her breath around your neck. So close that you can smell the warmth of his or her body, and feel the warmth and moisture of this body interacting with your own. Listen to the resonance of the other person's breath, and notice that you can feel his or her heart beating and that it's starting to beat faster.

5. From very, very close, look at this person. Perhaps you notice the moisture on the lips, the moisture in the mouth. Perhaps you notice the slight tremble, followed by a deep, resonant breath. Look closely into the eyes, one first, then the other. Notice the fine details that you can see only by being this close, as you continue to feel the breath flow over your body.

6. How do you feel now?

7. Now step back out of the situation, and see it again from about ten feet away. Feel different now?

The process of association and dissociation is as easy as that. You can associate or dissociate with events you imagine, or you can associate or dissociate with events that are happening at any given moment. If you desire your emotions to be stronger, more involved, then associate more fully, and intensify the submodalities so that you heighten your experience. If you want your emotions to be diminished, more detached, then dissociate more fully, and adjust the submodalities so that your level of experience is more to your liking. This process is often initiated visually, but can be done with all the senses. The following submodalities seem to have almost universal effect:

Key Submodalities for Adjusting
Levels of Association/Dissociation

- *Visual:* distance, brightness, color versus black and white, size of image, position (vantage point)
- *Auditory:* distance, loudness, sound quality, position (vantage point)
- *Kinesthetic:* temperature, moisture, intensity, location in body
- *Olfactory:* intensity, source location
- *Gustatory:* intensity

- *Auditory digital* (internal dialogue): speed, volume, location, pitch of voice, active or passive wording

By varying these attributes in your process, which is easy to do at will, you will most likely be able to vary the level of emotional involvement you have in the process. This is a very important aspect of emotional freedom!

Another very important aspect of emotional freedom involves being able to make choices about how associated or dissociated you are. It involves having a dissociated, outside awareness. This outside awareness serves as an evaluative monitor, making constant determinations about whether things are going the way you'd like them to be. When things are going fine, this awareness is simply a passive observer. It may even act as a helpful guide, letting you know that it's fully okay to get carried away now, allowing you to enjoy the process that much more.

When things are not necessarily going fine, or may need more evaluation, this awareness brings the situation to your attention. It summons you to momentarily dissociate to help evaluate the situation.

This awareness lets you know when things are starting to go awry and helps you adjust your actions before you get too involved. It triggers you to use the techniques in this book, and it triggers you *before* you get swept away and can't think straight. It gives you the opportunity to evaluate what's happening from a removed perspective and to make adjustments with respect to the larger perspective. This perspective allows you realize when you are in rapport or out of it, making progress in your communication or getting blocked, interacting constructively or being abused verbally, or whether you are involved in any of the other situations this book was meant to address. With this awareness, you have a greater understanding of what's going on and what you may want to do about it.

There's a good chance this description sounds familiar to you, because most everyone has had these kinds of experiences. Association and dissociation seem to be universal human experiences—as does this type of outside monitor. Sometimes this monitor is personified as a parent or an authority figure, but the process is the same. By being aware that an ouside awareness is natural, you can maintain your rightful place as your own monitor; and by practicing it with conscious intention, you can develop a habitual pattern of having it available to you. In NLP, this outside awareness is often referred to and personified as meta-position, meaning a perceptual position "outside of" the events.

Now that you've had the chance to read about and understand association and dissociation in a conscious way, you can begin to have routine conscious awareness of what you are doing. The more you practice, the more automatic it becomes. I suggest that you start by practicing associating and dissociating several times a day. Practice intensifying your feelings about a situation, then practice reducing them. Practice making contact with your external awareness and looking at situations from its perspective. Do this on routine events in your life, and soon it will become an integrated part of your emotional well-being. The following sections include methodical techniques that, in addition to giving you the benefits they were designed for, provide an opportunity to practice association and dissociation and awareness from different perspectives.

Visual Swish Pattern

The emotional states you experience on a regular basis are within your control. You have the ability to feel any way you want to any time you want to. In addition, your behavior is also within your control. Your behavior is inexorably linked to your emotional states. Some people seem to have better self-discipline and self-control than others; however, self-discipline is not the intellectual, logical process many people think it is. It is more accurately a process of acting in accordance with a strong internal feeling. Most everyone realizes that there is a strong propensity to act in accordance with how we feel. People are emotional first, rational second.

In the previous section, we started to look at ways to adjust how you feel. By associating into a situation, you can feel more intense emotions, and by dissociating you can reduce your emotional response. In addition, we looked at a few examples of how we can start to elicit emotions that we choose. For example, when we did the exercise about remembering someone we were sexually attracted to, you were probably able to muster up some level of sexual excitement in yourself. We could have chosen another emotion and also mustered some level of intensity.

If you continue to notice the chains of events that result in experience, you will start to see that the behavior in your life depends in a large part on the internal representations you create for yourself. Internal representations create emotional states; emotional states create behavior. When people try to make changes in their behavior, they often fail to make changes at the causal level. They try to change just their behavior, not realizing that the behavior is being caused by something else that must also be changed. If you boil a pot of water on a stove, you can cool down the water by putting ice in it. But if you don't turn off the burner, you're going to get hot water again relatively soon.

The next process we will explore is the NLP swish pattern. It is predominantly a visualization process and is best done by those who have conscious awareness of their visualization abilities. The process is principally used to directly change behaviors, especially habits. Many habits are behaviors that begin unconsciously. If you have a habit of putting your hand to your mouth before you speak, you probably find yourself with your hand up there before you even realize it. Similarly, if you have a habit of criticizing your spouse when you first get home, you probably do it without any prior planning. It just seems to happen.

Well, it doesn't actually just happen. You probably have an internal process for making it happen. How else could you do it so perfectly without even trying? The event is typically initiated by a "trigger," which often takes the form of an internal representation. It's this trigger that we'd like to identify and work with. The trigger is the internal representation that lets you know it's time to act out that behavior.

Here's the process:[1]

Visual Swish Pattern

1. Think of a habit or behavior that occurs routinely in your life—one that you would like to change.

2. Identify the trigger for the behavior you want to change. Ask yourself how you know when it's time to act out this behavior. What is your clue or your reminder? What happens just before you remember to perform this behavior?

3. Close your eyes and create an internal visualization that represents that trigger (preferred) or that behavior. This is Picture O (for old). Once you create that picture, set it aside for a moment.

4. Close your eyes and create an internal visualization that represents the new, desired behavior. This is Picture N (for new).

5. Adjust the submodalities of Picture N to make it maximally appealing. Adjust the brightness, the size, the placement, the distance, and anything else that makes this picture exciting and full of motivating energy. When you do this properly, you will feel more energy as you do it.

6. For Picture N, dissociate from the picture, keeping a perspective from outside the picture.

7. With Pictures O and N in mind, you are ready to begin the swish. Read the following instructions all the way through first, before you do the process on your own.

8. Bring out Picture O, and associate into the picture. Step into it as if you were fully there.

9. In the lower left-hand corner of your field of vision, insert a small, darkened picture of Picture N. Think of it as a tiny piece of film.

10. In an instant, simultaneously make Picture O shrink and recede far, far away, and make Picture N expand immediately to fill your field of vision. Make the sound of "Swisssshhh" as you do it (it's more fun that way). Do this in an instant—speed is important! If your head doesn't jolt back when you do it, then you didn't do it fast enough!

11. Open your eyes, and draw your attention to something other than the exercise you just did. In NLP, this is called a *break of state*, and it's an important part of the process. Stand up and change your physical state if needed.

12. Repeat Steps 8 through 11 at least five times, noticing that after just a few times it will start to happen all by itself.

One of the first times I did this process, I was in an NLP training course. I chose to address a habitual pattern of being nervous around attractive women. This nervousness drove my behavior such that I would avoid speaking with them. After we did the swish pattern, there was a break in the activities. Being in a hotel at the time, I left the training room and walked through the lobby, where I saw an incredibly beautiful, elegant woman at the front desk. Before I even had a chance to think about it, I found myself striking up a conversation with her, which I enjoyed thoroughly. The amazing thing to me was that I did this without even thinking about it. I felt compelled to approach her.

This process is a wonderful step toward taking internal control over your emotional states. If you have issues about controlling anger, you might want to look at the situations you get angry in. Use the process for each situation, and see what results you get in your life. The same thing goes for habitual patterns of other negative emotions, such as jealousy, greed, fear, depression, sadness, hate, boredom, powerlessness, negativity, pessimism, and so on. The first situations you may choose to try it on are times when you procrastinate instead of doing something that you know will help you! Do it now.

Manifestation

Our discussion leads us to the topic of manifestation. *Manifestation* is the process by which you create outcomes in your life without consciously going after them. It is the result of unconscious behavior; the methods by which the results are achieved are often outside conscious awareness. I often have the experience of just thinking about something and then, relatively soon afterward, finding that the something happens.

A few years back, I decided that I wanted to live in a house on a certain beach I liked. Additionally, I had a number of specific criteria about what kind of house this had to be. I was living on the Hawaiian island of Oahu, and this particular beach had only about twenty houses on it. Oahu has about one million inhabitants, with a large majority of them hoping and praying to find the same kind of house that I wanted. Of the twenty or so houses there, I'm sure that only a few of them would have fulfilled my desires, perhaps only one.

Two days before I was supposed to move from my old house, I had still not even started to look for a new place to live. I knew the right opportunity would just "come to me," and I placed my trust in that process. I was holding a garage sale to get rid of some of my things, and one of the people who stopped by got into a conversation with my girlfriend. He just so happened to know of a house that suited my needs perfectly. Two days later, I moved into the home that turned out to be a dream home for me.

If these kinds of things didn't happen so routinely in my life, I would say that they were coincidences. However, they do happen routinely, and I firmly believe it's due to my ability to consciously use my powers of manifestation.

Manifestation seems to be primarily about just a few things:

1. Having a clear outcome.
2. Being congruent about wanting that outcome.
3. Believing that you will get that outcome.
4. Instructing your unconscious mind to go get it for you.

We've addressed the first three items in detail in different parts of this book; however, we have not yet addressed Item 4. To do so, we need to speak briefly about time lines.

In NLP, it is believed that our representations about time, like everything else, are made through our submodalities. The primary submodalities that seem to be involved are those of distance and space—involving expressions like something being "far out" into the future, "way behind," "right ahead of us," "right on top of us," and so on. These expressions are probably more than just figurative ideas, and seem to be more closely related to actual submodalities of distance and location of our internal representations.

If you ask most people to point in the direction of their future, they will understand the question and point in a direction (often in front of them or to their right). If you ask them to point in the direction of their past, they will also point in a direction (often behind them or to their left). When these two directions are combined to form a metaphorical line, then that's a time line.

If you represent your personal time line to yourself as a series of internal representations organized along a line (I choose to represent it as flat pictures stacked closely side by side so tightly that they form a continuous stream of "events" in my life), then you have the ability to "pull out" certain events in your future and determine what they are.

As a quick example, imagine your time line, and go out two years into the future and pull out an event in your life. Notice what that event is and what your life is like at that time. When you do this, you will likely get an idea about what direction you are actually, unconsciously taking in your life.

Manifestation is in part a process of telling your unconscious what you want to have happen in your life. Unconsciously, you will go about achieving a given future; however, you have the potential to consciously determine what that future will be. The extensive time line processes in NLP can help you create unconscious manifestation processes. For now, let's explore something you can do right now that can have immediate effects in your life.

The process that I'm going to describe is a simple process that I use in everyday life, usually on a moment's notice. It takes only an instant. It requires you to become aware of your internal representations and to alert yourself to those internal representations you happen to make that are not in accordance with what you want in your life.

When you are thinking to yourself, or listening to others, you will notice that your internal representations aren't always representative of how you'd like the world to be. If you speak to someone at work who says that morale is going to get worse in the next two weeks, you are likely to make an internal representation of that. You might imagine a certain area of work where people are standing around complaining, or you might imagine sitting in your office feeling lousy. However you would form your internal representation, you are likely to form one that represents the worsened morale. Just as when you made an internal representation of the blue tree, your thinking and listening process will steer you to the suggested internal representation.

When you are aware of what you're doing inside your head, you can evaluate whether or not you want to make this kind of internal representation. Odds are, you would rather see a future where morale got better and people enjoyed their work. This conjures up a different internal representation and a different set of words to describe it.

Manifestation is enhanced by allowing yourself to replace the negative internal representations with positive internal representations. If you are encouraged to spontaneously create a negative internal representation, then you can immediately re-create a positive internal representation and replace the negative one—instantly. Using a quick version of the visual swish pattern is an excellent way to make the replacement. Place that new internal representation into your time line at the appropriate place in the future, and continue on with the conversation.

You can initiate this replacement process in either a visual manner or with auditory digital behavior (internal dialogue). When someone says "Everything's getting ugly here," you can verbally rephrase it inside your head or in the conversation by saying, "Yeah, things aren't going beautifully here right now."

Some personal growth techniques encourage you to respond to a negative suggestion by saying "Cancel, cancel." Although that can be great first step, an extension of that process is to then replace the phrase or internal representation with the preferred expression.

I use these internal processes routinely, and I can tell you that they are virtually immediate in my head. I never even lose a step in the conversation. The benefit is that my brain is constantly being flooded with images and ideas about how I want things in my life to be. These images are constantly being placed on my time line in the places when I want them to happen. Over and over, my unconscious mind gets instructions from me about just where I want my life to go. I believe that directly results in the number of amazing manifestations that happen seemingly without my effort.

Manifestation is an unconscious process of interacting in the world in alignment with certain goals and outcomes. When these goals and outcomes are created with conscious awareness, then you will see the effects of manifestation. You will see your thoughts turn into manifest form in the real world.

Manifestation is simply another affirmation that your life is the result of your actions and inaction (which is again the responsibility mind-set). Manifestation demonstrates that internal thought can be transformed into external form.

Simple Tips for Increasing Your Conscious Manifestation

- Continually notice what you are saying to yourself and visualizing for yourself.
- When you hear or say something that creates negative internal representations (internal representations that depict things you would rather not experience in your life), quickly rephrase or reframe them either internally or aloud.
- When you become aware of an internal visualization that depicts something you would rather not experience in your life, quickly swish it or replace it with one that you would like to experience.
- Make a habit of putting positive visualizations into the appropriate section of your time line. Allow your time line to make the adjustments that need to be made to incorporate that visualization.
- Supplement "cancel, cancel" with a rephrasing of the desired outcome, using tactical *not's* as appropriate.
- Know your outcome, and be consistent with your outcomes. When your unconscious keeps getting the same message, manifestation is far easier and more predictable.
- Understand that even manifestations of negative events follow this principle, and investigate what internal representations you were creating that contributed to the manifestation of any negative events you find in your life.
- Have fun with this. It's easy, fast, and enjoyable. You will feel better when your mind is continuously flooded with positive, nice, enjoyable, invigorating stimuli!

Anchoring

I used to work for a man couldn't help but answer the phone when it rang. He was a very busy man and often had five or six people waiting outside and inside his office for him. People would line up and wait their turn. Some would wait for over an hour.

One day, I turned the corner to go into his office and saw a long line of people waiting to talk to him. In the middle of one of his conversations, his phone rang. His attention darted toward the phone, and he was obviously trying to just let it ring. But he just couldn't stop himself. After a momentary struggle, he interrupted his conversation and answered the phone. He took care of that phone call, then returned to the people in his office.

Of course, I chose not to wait in line. I just walked back over to my office and called him on the telephone. Just like Pavlov's faithful dog, my boss was anchored to the ringing of a bell!

We've already spoken a bit about anchors. We know that they are conditioned responses to a specific stimuli. We know that they can be major contributors to our emotional states. We know that they have been understood for many years. Yet many people don't know exactly how to apply their knowledge of anchors in useful ways.

In almost every NLP training session, you will be taught about anchoring. You will be taught that you can anchor other people and that you can anchor yourself. These are two distinctly different approaches for distinctly different outcomes.

I have seen many people try to apply anchoring in their own lives. Many will favor one approach over the other, either preferring to anchor others or to use anchoring processes on themselves. When anchoring others in real-world situations, you covertly anchor one of that person's emotional states to a stimulus and then later use that stimulus to help direct the person's future emotions to the desired state at an opportune time. These stimuli can be used without the person's knowledge and can affect his or her emotional states without permission. In my experience, those who spend their attention and energy trying to anchor others early in their NLP training generally fail to be effective. If you're not fully clear about your intentions and your processes, your attempts to anchor others can be perceived as negative manipulation. The novelty of the process tempts novices to use it as trickery and gamesmanship. Novices find that, rather than helping inspire win-win, supportive communications, their attempts to anchor others often do just the opposite.

Those who choose to focus on self-directed anchoring processes have much different results. In self-directed anchoring, you use the stimulus response process in specific ways to change your natural, emotional responses to real-world circumstances. If you get impatient each time your child asks you a question, you might seek to "reprogram" yourself so that you have more emotional choice in that situation. When novices direct their attentions toward self first, they often find that their personal changes have significant effect on the environment in which they live. The world seems to change as a result of their personal, internal changes. In all your communication and persuasion processes, one thing will always ring true—you will get the most consistent and significant results in the external world when you first make the necessary adjustments in your *inner* world. With this in mind, we focus our discussion on the process of self-anchoring.

The anchoring process described in this section can help you gain emotional choice and freedom. It can help you develop a method by which you take full charge, and full responsibility, for your own emotional states and well-being. This process helps give you the skills to respond resourcefully to situations in your life.

The anchoring processes we are about to cover involve the purposeful use of stimulus and emotional states to bring about added emotional choice. When successful, you will have more emotional choice in your life in situations that were previously limiting. If you get nervous each time your spouse stays out past 9:00 at night, you can choose to have a different emotional response instead, perhaps one that allows peace of mind.

This is not a process of *controlling* your emotions; it is a process of having emotional *choice.* You give yourself the ability to respond to the stimuli in your world in resourceful, useful ways.

Let me share a personal experience. Many years ago, I was working in an industrial environment. One day, at about 9:30 a.m., my boss's secretary found me in the field and told me that my boss wanted to see me. A few minutes later, I was in my boss's office getting chewed out for something (I don't remember what it was; I just remember the experience). It was very rare that I got chewed out, and this came as a total surprise. As it was happening, I could feel rage starting to swell up inside me. It was all I could do to prevent myself from lashing out. I sat there in a highly controlled fashion, not saying a word until I was finally able to leave. I could barely contain myself and felt as if I would explode at any moment.

Once out of there, I returned to my office and began to rant and moan and complain. Anger, rage, sarcasm, criticism, and all-around ugly stuff was spewing out of me virtually uncontrollably. For the rest of the day, I vented my anger on those who would listen.

That night, before I went to bed, I used the collapsing-of-anchors process that we're going to cover next. I chose to collapse this angry feeling with some more desirable feelings. I chose happiness, laughter, and fun. It was a simple little process, and I didn't really know if it would help, but what the heck, right?

As good luck would have it (and it really was good luck for me), the next day at about 9:30 a.m., my boss's secretary found me in about the same place I had been the day before and again told me that my boss wanted to see me. A few minutes later, I found myself in my boss's office getting chewed out again in virtually the same way! Again, it was all I could do to control my emotions, and I got out of there as soon as I could. I went back to my office and spent the rest of the day talking about this situation, too.

However, there was a difference that second day. That second time, the reason I had to get out of my boss's office right away was not because I was so angry that I was about to explode. It was because I was having so much fun that I was about to laugh in his face! The rest of my day was filled with laughter and joking and cutting up with the guys about the whole affair.

That day taught me the incredible power of this simple technique. It also taught me to be more choosy with the emotions I chose to collapse!

From that day forward, I spent many nights collapsing anchors. Each day, I would come home and write down any event that made me feel differently from the way I wanted to feel. I listed times when I was nervous, angry, impatient, stressed, inconsiderate, upset, or fearful—or any time I felt

anything that didn't represent a healthy, well-balanced attitude. I kept this list going, and each time I did the collapsing-of-anchors process on a particular emotional state, I would cross it off the list.

At first, my list was long, sometimes growing to two pages in length. I was only comfortable doing two or three collapses a night. It seemed as if I would never finish the list. But after a few weeks of steady progress, I noticed that my list was getting shorter. After a few more weeks, my list got down to just an occasional item, and I carried out the process only sporadically when the occasion called for it. After a few months, my list was gone forever.

I moved from a point where each day in my life included ten to twenty events where I was feeling things I didn't want to feel to a point where my emotions were out of line only in rare occurrences. To me, collapsing of anchors is the part of NLP that showed me how to most significantly improve the quality of my life! I'd like to share this process with you.

The collapsing-of-anchors process that I use requires you to first know how to set anchors. There are four fundamental aspects to keep in mind when setting an effective anchor:

1. *The intensity of the emotional state:* One anchor can last a lifetime if tied to a strong enough emotional state.[2]
2. *Timing of stimulus:* The best timing for a given stimulus is to apply it when the intensity of the state is at its maximum.
3. *Uniqueness of stimulus:* If a stimulus is not unique, then it has already been related to a variety of other emotional states as well as to the one you're working with. This creates an ineffective anchor as well as a trigger that is out of context. For best results, use stimuli that are unique or uncommon and appropriate to context.
4. *Replication of stimulus:* An anchor is useful for our purposes only if the response can be replicated, which means that the stimulus must also be replicated. If you anchor yourself to feeling very happy every time you stand on your head, you may not be able to use that effectively in the workplace. For our purposes, the stimulus you'll be using is likely to be the touch of a finger to your knee or hand. These are relatively unique and easy to replicate; however, it will be important to replicate the touches accurately, always using the same finger and the same pressure.

By adhering to these four aspects of anchoring, you will likely be able to set an effective anchor. Here are the steps to follow for setting an anchor on yourself. The setting of anchors is an integral part of the collapsing of anchors process yet to be described:

Setting an Anchor

1. Have in mind a place for a unique, physical stimulus. It is common to use a finger to touch either the back of your hand or the top of your knee in a specific area. Use a two- or three-second touch with medium pressure. Make sure you know how to find that same place again, and avoid using patterns in clothing (which can move) to determine the location.

2. Elicit a desired emotional state, such as joy or excitement. Many people can simply create their states relatively straightforwardly. If you want to make it easier, simply re-call a time when you felt this emotional state. Associate into the state, seeing it again through your own eyes, hearing it through your own ears, and feeling what you felt once again. Re-create that experience, and intensify the feeling to help you re-create that same emotional state. It often helps to close your eyes.

3. Once you've re-created the emotional state, apply the stimulus (the touch to the knee) for two to three seconds. Apply at or near the peak of the experience.

4. Release the stimulus, and open your eyes. In some processes, it will be appropriate to "break state" by changing your focus of attention and/or changing your physiognomy. For a thorough break of state, get up and move around a bit, and think about something unrelated to the anchoring process.

5. When you are just beginning, it is helpful to test your anchors to make sure they were effective. To test an anchor, get into a centered state of mind, then apply the stimulus again. If you begin to automatically access the anchored emotional state, then the anchor is effective.

These types of anchors are generally short-lived and are designed to be used in anchoring processes, such as the collapsing-of-anchors process. If you anchor some emotion to a touch on the back of your hand, you are unlikely to create an anchor so strong that you will still have access to it after even a few days. However, the anchors should last for at least the duration of the process, after which time they won't be needed anyway.

This is the type of anchor that you will be using for the collapsing-of-anchors process. In NLP, there are several versions of collapsing of anchors, and there are a few different names for them with some subtle differences. The process we are about to cover is the one that I prefer, which has worked very nicely for me and many others. It is slightly different from what you might learn in an NLP training course.

Collapsing-of-Anchors Process

1. Find a quiet place where you can concentrate undisturbed for at least fifteen minutes.
2. Identify the experience, situation, or state that is not to your liking and in which you would like to have different emotional responses; for example, each time you have a discussion with Joe, you feel insecure about yourself. We'll refer to this as State U (unresourceful state).
3. Identify three other emotional states that might be useful within that same context such as feeling confidence, pride, or power. For best effects, choose states that are relatively high energy. We'll refer to these as States R1, R2, and R3 (resourceful states 1, 2, and 3).
4. Identify the four places where you are going to apply stimuli (one for each anchored state), and momentarily place your hand there to ensure that you can comfortably touch all four at the same time.
5. Anchor State U, using your first stimulus. Associate into the state only long enough to get a reasonable anchor, and avoid getting too involved in the state.
6. Move to a break state, but for no longer than you need to make sure you can access State R1. If you have any lingering effects from Step 5, get up, change your body position and make sure you get a stronger break state.
7. Anchor State R1, using your second stimulus. Afterwards, break state moderately.
8. Anchor State R2, using your third stimulus. Afterwards, break state moderately.

9. Anchor State R3, using your fourth stimulus. Afterwards, break state moderately.

10. For each of States R1, R2, and R3, confirm that the states were sufficiently strong, and re-anchor to the same stimulus if desired.

11. Break state completely, achieving a flat emotional state. Completely shake off any lingering emotional states.

12. Collapse the anchors. Apply the first stimulus, and then just as it's causing you to feel State U (one or two seconds at the most), apply the stimuli for States R1, R2, and R3 in succession.

13. As you are holding all four of the stimuli, release the stimuli for State U and imagine the following: You are in a situation in which the external events are similar to those that caused State U. With these new resources, imagine how this new situation will be different. Adjust the situation to make it to your liking. This is a future pace.

14. Give yourself a few moments to integrate the changes. The collapse of anchors often creates a state of momentary confusion; just stay with it. Release the remaining anchors when you are comfortable with your future pace.

15. Afterwards, you can choose to test your work (which will be necessary only the first few times you do it). For the test, make sure you create a full break state, then fire the State U stimulus. At this point, you should automatically feel the resourceful emotions.

16. Notice what happens in your life the next time a situation that previously would have caused you to be in State U comes up. If it's to your liking, you're done. If you still want to make adjustments (as I did when I almost laughed in my boss's face), then simply do the process again.

This collapsing-of-anchors process is my favorite process in this entire book. I attribute a large portion of my emotional well-being to my persistence with using it. The first several times I did it, I wasn't really comfortable with it, nor did I know if it was succeeding. But my persistence paid off, because soon it was a very easy, natural process to perform (I've done it waiting in lines, sitting in my car, during breaks at work, and many other places). I began to see tremendous rewards within a few weeks and immeasurable rewards after a couple months. Even to this day, it is my Old Faithful NLP technique, which I still pull out on occasion.

This entire chapter is dedicated to processes that give you further emotional choice and freedom. By realizing that your emotional states are within your control and by having techniques such as these to help you, you can start to experience the truth about the responsibility mind-set as it applies to your emotional well-being. You have the power and ability to make your emotional life, and your related behaviors, exactly the way you want them to be. The days of thinking you're a slave to someone else's behaviors or to your own emotions are over! There is no such thing as an emotional victim, and there is no such thing as someone else making you feel a certain way. You empower yourself with this awareness and now can use your powers with ever increasing choice.

CHAPTER 12

CONCLUSION

CONGRATULATIONS! By getting this far you've done something that many people will never do. You've read an entire book dedicated to helping you improve something about yourself and your life. That is an accomplishment you can be proud of.

This book has concentrated on four primary topics. First, it offered some very powerful mind-sets for effectiveness. When adopting these, you will enable yourself to learn and develop new skills and strategies. By successfully holding these mind-sets while you read this book, you likely got much more out of it than you would have otherwise. Second, the book described in-depth processes for being a highly effective listener. It highlighted things that you may not have known existed. Third, it presented some elegant verbal skills for practical use in the everyday situations of your life. And finally, it gave you some methods for gaining control over your emotional states.

You were also presented with several overall frameworks. We covered the three-step summary of NLP, which allowed you to understand the importance of goals, calibration, and responses. We covered the Three Steps of Effective Communication, highlighting the importance of getting to congruency with yourself first, then with the other person, before moving toward goals. And we covered the persuasion and influence process, which describes in detail a model for high-integrity influencing. These are the frames upon which all the other skills can be supported.

By putting it all together, you now know what to do, how to do it, and how it fits into the overall scheme of things.

There are many other skills and strategies that I could have shared in this book. In fact, as I wrote, the book kept getting longer and longer as I kept finding more and more I wanted to offer. However, there comes a point when a single book is complete and finished, at which point it's time to move on and do something with the information. That time is now.

The Final Word

Reading this book puts you at a distinct advantage. Even if you were aware of many of these skills and strategies before you began, having them affirmed and articulated is of tremendous value. If they are new to you, then you can integrate the ones you find useful into your repertoire.

Earlier I told you something: I said that if you decided to read this book because someone told you to, then you were in for a real treat. I said that if you were reading it so you could intellectually "understand" the information presented, then you should get ready for something more. I said that if you were reading it so you could use your new learning to "impress" others with your cleverness, then you were going to be surprised. I said that these reasons may have gotten you started, but that once you saw what was contained in this book, you would see it as a real gift. I hope that message was confirmed.

Now that you've read the book, your challenge is to do more than just understand it or try to impress others with your knowledge. I encourage you to actively use, master, and extend these skills and strategies. As a reader, you are free to just read the information and do nothing with it at all. That would be a waste.

The true gain in a process such as this is in your implementation. You'll find that some things work very well, some work moderately well, and some don't seem to work at all. But regardless of how well they work initially, you gain something more by using and working with the techniques. You enter into the process of NLP, in which you have a goal, you calibrate your environment, then you adjust your behaviors accordingly. It is within the iterative processes of calibrating and adjusting that you get your greatest gains. The skills outlined here are just the beginning of what you may do with them.

There is an old expression, "Give a man a fish, feed him for a day. Teach a man to fish, feed him for a lifetime." It is my hope that you not only learned this information, but that you also learned how to develop and expand it. This is the spirit I wish to convey.

This spirit is perhaps the greatest benefit of all. You develop your own insights and draw your own conclusions. You develop the habit of noticing what works and what doesn't. You instill in yourself the process of setting a goal, determining if you're getting it, and then adjusting your strategies and behaviors. These habits will serve you better than many of the specific techniques you may choose to use. These habits are the ultimate gift.

Use them well, and strive to become the person you know you really are.

AN OVERVIEW OF THE NLP FIELD

TRADITIONAL NLP TRAININGS are delineated into Practitioner, Master Practitioner, and NLP Trainer segments and involve a variety of NLP therapy and hypnosis techniques. NLP was originally directed toward the therapeutic community and continues to be used in therapeutic contexts. Traditional NLP trainings are often marketed as being able to "transform" the lives of participants. This claim stems from the two-fold approach giving participants personal experience of many of the therapeutic techniques during the course of the training and from teaching them NLP techniques for their later use.

The content of the trainings is primarily carried out through a combination of lectures, demonstrations, and experiential exercises. Participants are taught how to elicit specific outcomes from clients, how to critically observe and interpret information from clients, and how to use techniques to create change in clients. The NLP information is taught with a high level of precision, and great emphasis is placed on intricate details. Many participants become certified in the field and incorporate NLP therapy into some aspect of their current work.

Not all participants go the NLP trainings to be "transformed" or to become an NLP therapist. Many go because they have learned that NLP technology is highly valuable for communication, sales, and excellence in general. However, many trainings continue to be oriented toward a therapeutic model, thus participants sometimes have difficulty learning how to apply NLP information in practical ways in their everyday lives.

Anthony Robbins, one of the most successful motivational speakers and trainers in the world, addresses this difficulty. His presentation of NLP moves the focus away from teaching participants to be therapists (making impact on clients' lives) and directs it toward teaching participants to make maximum impact on their own lives. He presents key portions of NLP and teaches them in a nontraditional way, placing significant emphasis on motivation. Anthony Robbins' success is a testament to the value of the information and to the value of learning it from this nontraditional perspective.

As NLP has evolved, it has begun to encompass more than just the traditional NLP Practitioner, Master Practitioner, and Trainer delineations. Various trainers, including cofounder Richard Bandler, have created new variations and extensions of the material, often with different, creative names, but still purported to be under the NLP umbrella. This decentralization of NLP has blurred the boundaries between what truly constitutes NLP and what constitutes others' original work. This blurring is compounded by the fact that NLP source material is rarely referenced, thus many of the significant contributors to the field often go unrecognized by most participants.

In an effort to maintain the integrity of their work and to create proprietary ownership, many NLP developers choose to create their own terminology and to protect it with trademarks. As a result, you are likely to find a variety of terms in the NLP field, some of which constitute significant expansion of the field, and some of which more closely resemble a repackaging of established information.

There have been a variety of attempts to regulate and standardize NLP. Since NLP is not regulated by a governmental body or through any other pertinent government regulations, the potential for standardization and quality control rests in the hands of private organizations. Unfortunately, several certifying organizations have been established, each of which has different procedures and guidelines, and each of which tends to favor one or more institutes over others. Thus, attempts to standardize and unify the field have in many ways contributed to further fragmentation.

"Certification" trainings are offered to participants who wish to have their skills certified and approved by a specific NLP organization. The value of certification rests upon the credibility of the certifying organization, and there are a variety of standards upon which certifications are based.

For people wishing to attend NLP trainings, it can be difficult to make an educated decision about where to go. The NLP field is fragmented, competitive, diverse, and rather confusing. Certification guidelines can be rather loose, and the skill levels of the various trainers are quite varied. Add to that the wide variety of information taught in NLP courses, and you've got a wide selection of possible choices. In general, choosing an NLP training should take into account at least a few key elements:

1. Context of the training—Is the training primarily based on therapy, motivation, sales, or something else? Using NLP in work situations can be quite different from therapeutic situations, and mapping the information across contexts is not always easy.

2. Quality/Experience of the trainer(s)—Good trainers make a difference in any training situation, including NLP. However, length of service in the field is not always the best determinant of the quality of a trainer. Many organizations offer introductory seminars in which you can get a sense of the skill level and training ability of the trainer. Additionally, it is important to get a sense of how well the trainer's experience relates to the training context. If the context of the training is purported to be business, it is useful to know what level of actual business experience the trainer has had. It is all too common to find inconsistencies in this comparison.

3. Participant results—The bottom line in an NLP training is whether the participants gain useful outcomes as a result of

their experience. Many organizations can refer you to past participants. Success in their experiences can often be an indicator of the level of success you can expect to have.

4. Walk the talk—The training experience is generally improved when the trainer and the organization demonstrate NLP principles and exhibit their own success. Be wary of those who would claim to teach you things that they themselves have not yet been able to master.

5. Lack of biases—The fragmentation of the NLP field has caused some organizations to form "camps," in which they tout their own organization and criticize others. This is rarely useful for the participant. Excellent trainers with good success records will demonstrate professionalism and objectivity in this regard

NLP institutes are prevalent in North America and Europe, somewhat prevalent in Australia, and less prevalent in other parts of the world. NLP organizations come and go, so today's list of training centers is likely to be out of date in a matter of months. Current information about many North American institutes can be found in *Anchor Point* magazine (346 South 500 East, Suite 200, Salt Lake City, UT 84102), and increasingly on the Internet. Additionally, reputable NLP organizations will help you find the training that is right for you, even if it isn't necessarily the one they happen to offer themselves.

For information about additional books, seminars, avenues for further study, consulting, or to simply reach the author, contact:

John J. Emerick, Jr.
P.O. Box 2880
Kailua-Kona, HI 96745-2880
e-mail: jemerick@ilhawaii.net

NOTES

Chapter 2

1. This presupposition of NLP has its roots in the work of linguist Alfred Korzybski, who used the phrase as early as 1933 in *Science and Sanity: An Introduction to Non-Aristotelian Systems and General Semantics,* International Non-Aristotelian Library Publishing Company, 1958. The first edition was published in 1933.

Chapter 3

1. This story, or something very close to it, was related as part of a presentation by Wyatt Woodsmall, a respected NLP trainer.
2. This assignment, or something very close to it, was given to me by Jan Marszalek and John Marszalek, two respected NLP trainers in Dallas, Texas. I am unsure of the original source of the material.
3. *Dateline,* NBC, June, 1996.
4. Adapted from *NLP Comprehensive Trainer Training Manual,* 1992, Section V, page 6.

Chapter 4

1. Activities of the unconscious mind are distinguished from the activities associated with physiological survival, such as the beating of the heart and the process of breathing, which are maintained by a biological portion of the brain.
2. The less commonly used definition of manipulation is the one that has a positive connotation. It is the process of managing with skill and is akin to leading, influencing, and persuading.
3. NLP uses the term *strategy* in several different contexts. One of the more common usages refers to the sequencing of internal thinking processes that are detected with the help of eye-accessing clues. This specialized topic is not within the scope of this book and will not be addressed. For information about these specialized NLP strategies, I refer you to *Neuro Linguistic Programming: Volume 1, The Study of the Structure of Subjective Experience,* Richard Bandler, John Grinder, Robert Dilts, Judith Delozier, Meta Publications, 1980.

Chapter 5

1. The underlying emotional state of these physical cues is not necessarily universal; that is, not everyone who is smiling is happy. However, they are indicative of something. A person's smile will usually be representative of some subset of emotional states in that person, whatever those states may happen to be.
2. From Albert Mehrabian and Susan R. Ferris, University of California, Los Angeles, "Inference and Attitudes from Nonverbal Communication in Two Channels" in *The Journal of Consulting Psychology*, 1967, Volume 31(3), pp 248-252. This source also provides the 38 percent figure for tonal characteristics and 55 percent figure for body communication, which in their experiment was focused specifically on facial expressions.
3. On a formal level, the systematic study of the relationship between nonlinguistic body motions (such as blushes, shrugs, and eye movements) and communication is known as *kinesics*.
4. As with *all* generalizations, there are exceptions. Freudian slips are a kind of verbalization in which the words uttered seem to represent unconscious desires, information the individual does not consciously mean to convey. Examples of conscious body communication and tonal communication are more prevalent and include the process of acting. However, only a very few people are able to extend the process to include the subtleties detected by good sensory acuity; that is, very few people know how to instantly create a blush, dilate their pupils, swell their lower lip, or quiver their facial muscles.
5. Because lying brings about issues of judgment, right and wrong, good and bad, it is generally better to leave these issues out of the discussions about calibration and congruency. In this case, although it may seem as if this woman had been lying, it is more likely that she had been unaware of her anger. Being angry and being *aware* of being angry are two completely different processes. External awareness can be difficult to attain when a strong emotional state is involved, especially the states of fear and anger. It might be noted that most lying will provide some level of incongruity, albeit sometimes very subtle, while not all incongruity is indicative of lying.

Chapter 6

1. *The Structure of Magic*, Richard Bandler and John Grinder, Science and Behaviour Books, 1975, page 40; this original model relies partly on the work of Alfred Korzybski.
2. For those who wish to be rigorous in their studies, I refer you to some of the earlier source materials, especially Richard Bandler and John Grinder's *The Structure of Magic*, Volumes 1 and 2, and Alfred Korzybski's *Science and Sanity: An Introduction to Non-Aristotelian Systems and General Semantics*, fourth edition, International Non-Aristotelian Library Publishing Company, 1958.
3. The strict definition of nominalization is "a word or word group functioning as a noun." Basic grammar classes often define nominalizations

as "verbs turned into nouns," sometimes saying that "if you can't put your noun into a wheelbarrow, then it probably wasn't a noun in the first place." In NLP, the definition of nominalizations is somewhat more expanded, and includes a variety of intangible nouns, especially those related to feelings, emotions, and states of mind.

4. Some of the terminology used in this section has been simplified from traditional NLP terminology.

5. Adapted from *NLP Comprehensive Trainer Training Manual*, 1992, Section V, page 9; the story was told about John Grinder, one of the codevelopers of NLP.

6. This discussion will address criteria and equivalences as one group, which will be collectively referred to as criteria. As further clarification, equivalences are the external events that are interpreted to mean the same thing as another thing—in this case, to mean the same thing as a value. For example, "When someone loves you, that person will call you every day." Criteria are the internal processes that occur when a value is being fulfilled, the processes that help you to know that the value is being fulfilled—for example, "I know when someone loves me because I get this very special, unique fuzzy feeling all over my body." The elicitory questions outlined in this section will often yield information of both types.

Chapter 9

1. The term "bait" refers to the provoking portion of verbal abuse that serves to draw attention away from the damaging presuppositions. It is referred to in Suzette Haden Elgin's book, *The Gentle Art of Verbal Self-Defense*, Prentice Hall, 1980, page 28 of Dorset Press' 1980 edition, but is not a term used in traditional NLP.

2. As before, I am using the concept of presuppositions in a looser, more general way than it is sometimes taught in NLP. If we wanted to be linguistically rigid with how we analyzed these interchanges, we would be using a variety of technical terms and it could get quite complicated. However, linguistics was not necessarily created so that people could learn to defend themselves from verbal attacks, so I have taken some liberties to make it highly effective for verbal defense—and will continue to do so throughout the discussion.

Chapter 10

1. This process for future pacing is different from traditional NLP future pacing for therapeutic contexts. In this book, it has been adapted for application in everyday interactions.

2. A small percentage of people report that they are unaware of internal images. It is often assumed that this discrepancy with the NLP model is related more to a lack of awareness than to a lack of ability; that assumption, however, is difficult to verify. Regardless of the strict accuracy of the model, it has been my experience that communication with these people based on this model yields results similar to those for people who report conscious awareness of the visualization (or other internal sen-

sory) process; in other words, using this model increases communicational effectiveness regardless of whether the listener would subscribe to the model or not.

3. Due to the prompting of the word *blue,* you will likely make the representation as predominantly visual; however, you may just as easily experience a full range of internal sounds, feelings, smells, and tastes. Many people report having an "all around sense of" the item mentioned.

4. I have used the words *positive* and *negative* loosely in this chapter. To clarify, *positive* refers to things that are generally considered to be enjoyable, pleasant, nice, motivating, satisfying, comforting, and attractive. *Negative* refers to things that are generally considered not enjoyable— ugly, disheartening, dissatisfying, discomforting, and repulsive. As I'm using them here, neither word refers to aspects of good and bad, right and wrong, or moral and immoral. That would involve an aspect of judgment that I do not wish to make.

5. We'll also discuss auditory digital submodalities, which relate to internal words, in a later part of this section.

6. A mistake people often make lies in trying to categorize people as being either visual, auditory, kinesthetic, or auditory visual. People are people. We all have behaviors that fall into all the categories. Avoid trying to categorize people, and rather look at the specific behavior. As you continue to use this information, you'll continue to gain the experience specific to your purposes that will be most beneficial to you.

Chapter 11

1. Adapted from the model developed by Richard Bandler, as described in *Using Your Brain for a Change,* Real People Press, 1985.

2. Many phobias seem to be related to an emotional state so strong that a similar stimulus can create overwhelming fear for the rest of a person's life if not professionally treated—NLP has excellent techniques for dealing with and resolving phobias. Rather than running our lives on the basis of old anchors, our added awareness can help us create a much more empowered, fulfilling emotional life.

INDEX

A

Acknowledgment of others' right to their own ideas, 161

Anchor Point magazine, 316

Anchoring, 300–308
  process of, 301–2
  self-directed, 301

Anchors
  accessed to create moods, 279
  accessed to get angry, 278–79
  aspects to keep in mind for, 304–5
  break of state for, 305
  collapsing, 302–5
  setting, 304–6

Android assignment, 33–34

Anger
  anchors to arouse, 278–79
  avoiding arousing listener's, 207–10
  choosing emotional responses other than, 280
  people and situations involved in our, 278
  physiological and physical changes during, 81
  positive purposes of, 281
  situations arousing, 279
  tonal voice characteristics associated with, 83

Anxiety, positive purposes of, 281

Appreciation
  created by graceful disagreement, 207
  finishing feedback with statement of, 212, 216

"As If" Frame, 28

Association in NLP, 285–87
  process of, 289–90
  submodalities for adjusting level of, 290–92

Attacks, defending yourself from emotional and verbal, 217–42

Attention, gaining others', 26

Auditory dialect in your vocabulary, 271

Auditory digital dialect in your vocabulary, 272

Auditory digital processes, 270

Auditory digital wording, 271

Awareness
  bringing unconscious communication into conscious, 98, 100
  external, 282–84, 291, 318
  presupposition about, 122
  of what we want, 23–24, 77–78

B

Bad news, graceful expression of, 196–206

Bait in verbal abuse, 222–23, 224, 232–34, 319

Balance in life
  factors that affect, 44–46
  importance of, 43–44
  questions about, 44–46

Balance mind-set, 43–46

Bandler, Richard, 319, 321
  as cocreator of NLP, 18, 113–14, 314
  Milton Model discussed by, 163
  NLP expanded by, 314

Bannister, Roger Gilbert, 27, 113–14

Behavior
  adaptive, 162, 226
  conclusions based on patterns of, 87–88
  correlated with meaning, 91–94
  emotional basis of, 52
  nonverbal, 81–83, 86–88
  opposite to words, 102
  responsibility for others', 31–32
  separating belief from, 161
  source of, 161
  unconscious, 55–59
  varied according to feedback received, 24

Leadership
  ineffective paradigms about, 175
  of listeners, 203–4
  as support and assisting others in
    desirable change, 162, 175
  verbal pacing as using, 176
Learning, 55–78
  from anything, 46–47
  new behavior, 55–78
  process of, 21, 60
Learning process, 21, 60
Life changes as triggering weight
  changes, 58
Limitations. *See* False limitations
Listener, effective or good
  active role of, 138
  effects of being, 79
  importance of being, 14–15
  processes for becoming, 80
  purpose in listening of, 149–50
  recognizing presuppositions as part
    of being, 120
  skills required for, 94
Listening
  approaching objectivity in, 83–86
  concurrently with talking, 185–86
  creating meaning from, 49–50
  elicitory, 141–49
  as an interchange, 138
  maintaining respect, appreciation,
    and permission during, 150
  Meta Model in, 118
  as nonverbal communication, 80
  objective, 83–87
  to prepare you for influencing and
    persuading, 152
  roles of questions in, 138–39
  to yourself, 109–11
Listening process, overview of, 149–53
Listening skills
  directive and interactive, 142
  honed, 142
  nonverbal, 79–111
  verbal, 113–53
Logic
  as auditory digital process, 271
  defeating, 180
Lose-lose process in power struggles,
  237, 241–42
Love
  physiological and physical changes
    during, 82
  tonal voice characteristics
    associated with, 83

M

Manifestation, 295–99
  defined, 295

  enhancing, 298
  increasing your conscious, tips
    for, 299
  process of, 297–98
  using your power of, 296
Manipulation
  defined, 70, 317
  detecting, 71
  negative, as not working, 69–73
  negative, as symptom of a problem,
    71–72
Map in NLP
  defined, 19–20
  in this book, outcomes for, 20–21
Marszalek, Jan, 317
Marszalek, John, 317
Meaning
  correlation of behavior with,
    91–94
  created at unconscious levels, 124
  formed from nonverbal behavior,
    86–88
  formed from presuppositions,
    118–19
  of important words, clarifying, 151
  personal interpretations of, 124–26
  redefining listener's, 247
  of specific shifts in person doing
    communicating, 86
Mehraian, Albert, 318
Meta Model, 113–18
  determining additional meaning
    from linguistic structures
    through, 127
  diagram of, 137
  differences between surface
    structure and deep structure
    explored in, 114
  as an elicitory tool, 114
  learning patterns of, 137
  in listening, 118
  overuse of questions as problem
    in, 115
  parts of, 133–37. *See also*
    individual parts
  processes of human behavior
    stressed in, 117–18
Metaphors in future pacing, 253
Meta-presuppositions
  addressed nonassertively, 227
  defined, 122
  examples of, 121–22, 220–21
  examples of responding to, 224–25
  in verbal abuse, 234
Milton Model of NLP, 163
Mind
  conscious, 56
  unconscious, 56–59